QUANTUM COMPUTING

WITH

PYTHON

4 books in 1

PYTHON FOR BEGINNERS

PYTHON CRASH COURSE

PYTHON for DATA SCIENCE

QUANTUM PHYSICS for BEGINNERS

JASON TEST MARK BROKER

The new comprehensive guide to master applied artificial intelligence in Physics.

Learn Machine Learning and computer programming with a complete crash course

CONTENTS

QUANTUM PHYSICS FOR BEGINNERS

PYTHON

FOR

BEGINNERS

A crash course guide for machine learning and web programming.

Learn a computer language in easy steps with coding exercises.

JASON TEST

Design patterns are reusable model for solving known and common problems in software architecture.

They are best described as templates for working with a specific normal situation. An architect can have a template for designing certain types of door frames, which he fit into many of his project, and a software engineer or software architect must know the templates for solving common programming tasks.

An excellent presentation of the design pattern should include:

Name

Motivating problem

Decision

Effects

Equivalent Problems

If you thought it was a rather vague concept, you would be right. For example, we could say that the following "pattern" solves all your problems:

Gather and prepare the necessary data and other resources

Make the necessary calculations and do the necessary work

Make logs of what you do

Free all resources

???

Profit

This is an example of too abstract thinking. You cannot call it a template because it is not an excellent model to solve any problem, even though it is technically applicable to any of them (including cooking dinner).

On the other hand, you may have solutions that are too specific to be called a template. For example, you may wonder if QuickSort is a template to solve the sorting problem.

This is, of course, a common program problems, and QuickSort is a good solution for it. However, it can be applied to any sorting problem with virtually no change.

Once you have this in the library and you can call it, your only real job is to make somehow your object comparable, and you don't have to deal with its entity yourself to change it to fit your specific problem.

Equivalent problems lie somewhere between these concepts. These are different problems that are similar enough that you can apply the same model to them, but are different enough that this model is significantly customized to be applicable in each case.

Patterns that can be applied to these kinds of problems are what we can meaningfully call design patterns.

Why use design patterns?

You are probably familiar with some design patterns through code writing practice. Many good programmers end up gravitating towards them, not even being explicitly trained, or they simply take them from their seniors along the way.

The motivation to create, learn, and use design patterns has many meanings. This is a way to name complex abstract concepts to provide discussion and learning.

They make communication within the team faster because someone can simply use the template name instead of calling the board. They allow you to learn from the experiences of people who were before you, and not to reinvent the wheel, going through the whole crucible of gradually improving practices on your own (and constantly cringing from your old code).

Bad decisions that are usually made up because they seem logical at first glance are often called anti-patterns. For something to be rightly called an anti-pattern, it must be reinvented, and for the same problem, there must be a pattern that solves it better.

Despite the apparent usefulness in this practice, designing patterns are also useful for learning. They introduce you to many problems that you may not have considered and allow you to think about scenarios with which you may not have had hands-on experience.

They are mandatory for training for all, and they are an excellent learning resources for all aspiring architect and developing who may be at the beginning of their careers and who have no direct experience in dealing with the various problems that the industry provides.

Python Design Patterns

Traditionally, design models have been divided into three main categories: creative, structural, and behavioral. There are other categories, such as architectural patterns or concurrency patterns, but they are beyond the scope of this article.

There are also Python-specific design patterns that are created specifically around problems that the language structure itself provides, or that solve problems in unique ways that are only resolved due to the language structure.

Generating Patterns deal with creating classes or objects. They serve to abstract the specifics of classes, so that we are less dependent on their exact implementation, or that we do not have to deal with complex constructions whenever we need them, or that we provide some special properties of the instantiation. They are very useful for reducing dependency and controlling how the user interacts with our classes.

Structural patterns deal with assembling objects and classes into larger structures while keeping these structures flexible and efficient. They, as a rule, are really useful for improving the readability and maintainability of the code, ensuring the correct separation of functionality, encapsulation, and the presence of effective minimal interfaces between interdependent things.

Behavioral patterns deal with algorithms in general and the distribution of responsibility between interacting objects. For example, they are good practice when you may be tempted to implement a naive solution, such as busy waiting, or load your classes with unnecessary code for one specific purpose, which is not the core of their functionality.

Generative Patterns

Factory

Abstract factory

Builder

Prototype

Singleton

Object pool

Structural Patterns

Adapter

Bridge

Composite

Decorator

Facade

Flyweight

Proxy

Behavioral patterns

Chain of responsibility

Command

Iterator

Mediator

Memento

Observer

State

Strategy

Visitor

Python Specific Design Patterns

Global object pattern

Prebound method pattern

Sentinel object pattern

Type Annotation in Python

First, let's answer the question: why do we need annotations in Python? In short, the answer will be this: to increase the information content of the source code and to be able to analyze it using specialized tools. One of the most popular, in this sense, is the control of variable types. Even though Python is a language with dynamic typing, sometimes there is a need for type control. According to PEP 3107, there may be the following annotation use cases:

type checking:

expansion of the IDE functionality in terms of providing information about the expected types of arguments and the type of return value for functions:

overload of functions and work with generics:

interaction with other languages:

use in predicate logical functions:

mapping of requests in databases:

marshaling parameters in RPC (remote procedure call)

Using annotations in functions

In functions, we can annotate arguments and the return value.

It may look like this:

def repeater (s: str, n: int) -> str:
*return s * n*

An annotation for an argument is defined after the colon after its name:

argument_name: annotation

An annotation that determines the type of the value returned by the function is indicated after its name using the characters ->

def function_name () -> type

Annotations are not supported for lambda functions
Access to function annotations Access to the annotations
Used in the function can be obtained through the annotations
attribute, in which annotations are presented in the form of a
dictionary, where the keys are attributes, and the values are
annotations. The main value to returned by the function is
stored in the record with the return key.
Contents of repeater . annotations :

{'n': int, 'return': str, 's': str}

4 programming languages to learn, even if you are a humanist

The digital age dictates its own rules. Now, knowledge of programming languages is moving from the category of "too highly specialized skill" to must have for a successful career. We have compiled for you the four most useful programming languages that will help you become a truly effective specialist.

Vba

If you constantly work in Excel and spend time on the same routine operations every day, you should consider automating them. Macros - queries in the VBA language built into Excel will help you with this. Having mastered macros, you can not only save time, but also free up time for more interesting tasks (for example, to write new macros). By the way, to automate some operations, learning VBA is not necessary - just record a few actions using the macro recorder, and you can repeat them from time to time. But it's better to learn this language: macro recordings will give you only limited functionality.

Despite its attractiveness, macros have two drawbacks. Firstly, since a macro automatically does all the actions that you would do with your hands, it seriously loads RAM (for example, if you have 50,000 lines in a document, your poor computer may not withstand macro attacks). The second - VBA as a programming language is not very intuitive, and it can be difficult for a beginner to learn it from scratch.

SQL

In order to combine data from different databases, you can use the formulas VPR and INDEX (SEARCH). But what if you have ten different databases with 50 columns of 10,000 rows each? Chances are good to make a mistake and spend too much time. Therefore, it is better to use the Access program. Like VPR, it is designed to combine data from various databases, but it does it much faster. Access automates this function, as well as quickly filters information and allows you to work in a team. In addition to Access, there are other programs for working with databases (DBMS), in most of which you can work using a simple programming language - SQL (Structured Query Language). Knowledge of SQL is one of the basic requirements for business analysts along with knowledge of Excel, so we advise you to take a closer look if you want to work in this area.

R

R is a good alternative to VBA if you want to make data processing easier. How is he good? Firstly, unlike a fellow, it is really simple and understandable even for those who have never had anything to do with programming in their life. Secondly, R is designed to work with databases and has wide functionality: it can change the structure of a document, collect data from the Internet, process statistically different types of information, build graphs, create tag clouds, etc. To work with Excel files, you will have to download special libraries, but it is most convenient to save tables from Excel in csv format and work in them. By the way, it is R that the program was written with which we make TeamRoulette in our championships. Thanks to her, we manage to scatter people on teams in five minutes instead of two hours. To learn how to work in R, first of all, download a visual and intuitive programming environment - RStudio .

Python

Python is an even more powerful and popular programming language (by the way, it really has nothing to do with python). Like R, Python has special libraries that work with Excel files, and it also knows how to collect information from the Internet (forget about manually driving data into tables!). You can write endlessly about Python, but if in a nutshell - it's a really convenient and quick tool that is worth mastering if you want to automate routine operations, develop your own algorithmic thinking and generally keep up with technical progress.

Unlike R, Python does not have one of the most convenient programming environments - here everyone is free to choose to taste. For example, we recommend IDLE, Jupyter Notebook, Spyder, for more advanced programmers - PyCharm.

You_can learn how to program in Python and analyze data using it in our online course "Python. Data Analysis". The consultants from Big4 and Big3 will tell you how to work with libraries, create programs and algorithms for processing information.

Well, as it were, let's go

Well, if you (You, He, She, It, They) are reading this means we are starting our first Python lesson. Hooray (...) Today you will learn how to code. And what's more, you'll learn how to code in Python.

But to start coding you need Python. Where to get it?

Where to get Python?

But you think that now you can just sit down and cod. Well actually yes. BUT usually real hackers and programmers code in code editors. For working with Python We (I) recommend using a Jupyter Notebook or JupyterLab or Visual Studio Code. We (I) Will code in Visual Studio Code, but the other editors are no different.

Well, it's CODING time.

I'm too old for that

Everyone always writes the first code that displays "Hello World". Well, are we some kind of gifted? No, and therefore we will begin with this. In Python, the print () function is used to output text. To output "Hello World" we need to write the following:

```
1    print("Hello world!!!")
```

It's alife

Yes, you just wrote your first program. Now you are a programmer (NO).

Let's look at the structure of the print function. This function consists of the name - print, and the place where we throw what this function should output. If you want to display any text, you need to write it in quotation mark, either in single or double. But now let's enter some text. For this, Python has an input function. To accept something, you need to write the following:

```
1    a=input()
2    print(a)
```

What does this program do for us? First we introduce something, at the moment we don't care what it is, text or numbers. After, our program displays what you wrote.

But how to make sure that we write the text before entering something? Really simple. There are two ways to do this.

```
1    print('          )
2    a=input()
3    print(a)
```

How can, but not necessary

If you run the second program you will notice that you have to enter data in the same line in which the text is written.

```
1    a=input(          )
2    print(a)
```

How to do

But this is not aesthetically pleasing. We are here with you all the aesthetes. And so in order for you to enter values on a separate line, you can do the following:

```
1    a=input(          )
2    print(a)
```

Like cool, but why?

As we can see, \ n appeared at the end. This is a control character that indicates the passage to the next line. But it's too lazy for me to write it down every time, and therefore I prefer to type everything in the line where the text is written.

But where to apply it? Very simple, you can take math. There are some simple arithmetic operations in Python that I will tell you about now.

Python has the following arithmetic operations: addition, subtraction, multiplication, division, integer division, exponentiation, and the remainder of division. As everything is recorded, you can see below:

```
1    6+2
2    6-2
3    6*2
4    6/2
5    3//2
6    3**2
7    3%2
```

I will finally learn how to multiply

If you want to immediately print the result, then you just need to write an arithmetic operation in print:

```
1    print(6+2)
```

The result of this program will be 8

But how do we carry out operations with numbers that the user enters? We need to use input. But by default in Python, the values that input passes are a string. And most arithmetic operations cannot be performed on a line. In order for our program to work as we intended, we need to specify what type of value Python should use.

To do this, we use the int function:

```
1    a=int(input("        :  "))
2    b=int(input("        :  "))
3    print(a+b)
```

We add up the two numbers that the user enters. (Wow, I found out how much 2 + 2 will be)

Python code optimization with ctypes

Content:

Basic optimizations

Styles

Python compilation

Structures in Python

Call your code in C

Pypy

Basic optimizations

Before rewriting the Python source code in C, consider the basic optimization methods in Python.

Built-in Data Structures

Python's built-in data structures, such as set and dict, are written in C. They work much faster than your own data structures composed as Python classes. Other data structures besides the standard set, dict, list, and tuple are described in the collections module documentation.

List expressions

Instead of adding items to the list using the standard method, use list expressions.

```python
#Slow
    mapped = []
    for value in originallist:
    mapped.append (myfunc (value))

    # Faster
    mapped = [myfunc (value) in originallist]
```

ctypes

The ctypes module allows you to interact with C code from Python without using a module subprocessor another similar module to start other processes from the CLI.

There are only two parts: compiling C code to load in quality shared object and setting up data structures in Python code to map them to C types.

In this article, I will combine my Python code with LCS.c, which finds the longest subsequence in two-line lists. I want the following to work in Python:

```python
list1 = ['My', 'name', 'is', 'Sam', 'Stevens', '!']
    list2 = ['My','name', 'is', 'Alex', 'Stevens', '.']

    common = lcs (list1, list2)

    print (common)
    # ['My', 'name', 'is', 'Stevens']
```

One problem is that this particular C function is the signature of a function that takes lists of strings as argument types and returns a type that does not have a fixed length. I solve this problem with a sequence structure containing pointers and lengths.

Compiling C code in Python

First, C source code (lcs.c) is compiled in lcs.soto load in Python.

```
gcc -c -Wall -Werror -fpic -O3 lcs.c -o lcs.o
    gcc -shared -o lcs.so lcs.o
```

Wall will display all warnings:

Werror will wrap all warnings in errors:

fpic will generate position-independent instructions that you will need if you want to use this library in Python:

O3 maximizes optimization:

And now we will begin to write Python code using the resulting shared object file.

Structures in Python

Below are two data structures that are used in my C code.

```
struct sequence
    {
        char ** items:
        int length:
    }:

    struct cell
    {
      int index:
      int length:
      struct Cell * prev:
    }:
```

And here is the translation of these structures into Python.

```python
import ctypes
    class SEQUENCE (ctypes.Structure):
        _fields_ = [('items', ctypes.POINTER (ctypes.c_char_p)),
                ('length', ctypes.c_int)]

    class CELL (ctypes.Structure):
        pass

    CELL._fields_ = [('index', ctypes.c_int), ('length',
ctypes.c_int),
                ('prev', ctypes.POINTER (CELL))]
```

A few notes:

All structures are classes that inherit from ctypes.Structure.

The only field _fields_is a list of tuples. Each tuple is (<variable-

name>, <ctypes.TYPE>).

There ctypesare similar types in c_char (char) and c_char_p (* char) .

There is ctypesalso one POINTER()that creates a type pointer from each type passed to it.

If you have a recursive definition like in CELL, you must pass the initial declaration, and then add the fields _fields_in order to get a link to yourself later.

Since I did not use CELLPython in my code, I did not need to write this structure, but it has an interesting property in the recursive field.

Call your code in C

In addition, I needed some code to convert Python types to new structures in C. Now you can use your new C function to speed up Python code.

```python
def list_to_SEQUENCE (strlist: List [str]) -> SEQUENCE:
    bytelist = [bytes (s, 'utf-8') for s in strlist]
    arr = (ctypes.c_char_p * len (bytelist)) ()
    arr [:] = bytelist
    return SEQUENCE (arr, len (bytelist))


def lcs (s1: List [str], s2: List [str]) -> List[str]:
    seq1 = list_to_SEQUENCE(s1)
    seq2 = list_to_SEQUENCE(s2)

# struct Sequence * lcs (struct Sequence * s1, struct Sequence *
s2)
common = lcsmodule.lcs (ctypes.byref (seq1), ctypes.byref
(seq2)) [0]

    ret = []

    for i in range (common.length):
        ret.append (common.items [i] .decode ('utf-8'))
    lcsmodule.freeSequence (common)

    return ret

lcsmodule = ctypes.cdll.LoadLibrary ('lcsmodule / lcs.so')
lcsmodule.lcs.restype = ctypes.POINTER (SEQUENCE)

list1 = ['My', 'name', 'is', 'Sam', 'Stevens', '!']
list2 = ['My', 'name', 'is', 'Alex', 'Stevens', '.']

common = lcs (list1, list2)

print (common)

# ['My', 'name', 'is', 'Stevens']
```

A few notes:

**char (list of strings) matches directly to a list of bytes in Python.

There lcs.cis a function lcs()with the signature struct Sequence * lcs (struct Sequence * s1, struct Sequence s2) . To set up the return type, I use lcsmodule.lcs.restype = ctypes.POINTER(SEQUENCE).

To make a call with a reference to the Sequence structure, I use ctypes.byref()one that returns a "light pointer" to your object (faster than ctypes.POINTER()).

common.items- this is a list of bytes, they can be decoded to get retin the form of a list str.

lcsmodule.freeSequence (common) just frees the memory associated with common. This is important because the garbage collector (AFAIK) will not automatically collect it.

Optimized Python code is code that you wrote in C and wrapped in Python.

Something More: PyPy

Attention: I myself have never used PyPy.

One of the simplest optimizations is to run your programs in the PyPy runtime, which contains a JIT compiler (just-in-time) that speeds up the work of loops, compiling them into machine code for repeated execution.

Finding the Perfect Toolkit: Analyzing Popular Python Project Templates

The materials, the translation of which we publish today, is dedicated to the story about the tools used to create Python applications. It is designed for those programmers who have already left the category of beginners but have not yet reached the category of experienced Python developers.

For those who can't wait to start practice, the author suggests using Flake8,pytest, and Sphinx in existing Python projects. He also recommends a look at pre-commit,Black, and Pylint. Those who plan to start a new project, he advises paying attention to Poetry and Dependable.

Overview

It has always been difficult for me to form an objective opinion about the "best practices" of Python development. In the world of technology, some popular trends are continually emerging, often not existing for long. This complicates the extraction of the "useful signal" from the information noise.

The freshest tools are often only good, so to speak, on paper. Can they help the practical programmer with something? Or their application only leads to the introduction of something new in the project, the performance of which must be maintained, which carries more difficulties than benefits?

I didn't have a clear understanding of what exactly I considered the "best practices" of development. I suppose I found something useful, based mainly on episodic evidence of "utility," and on the occasional mention of this in conversations. I decided to put things in order in this matter. To do this, I began to analyze all the templates of Python projects that I could find (we are talking about templates used by the cookiecutter command-line utility to create Python projects based on them).

It seemed to me that it was fascinating to learn about what auxiliary tools the template authors consider worthy of getting these tools into new Python projects created based on these templates.

I analyzed and compared the 18 most popular template projects (from 76 to 6300 stars on GitHub), paying particular attention to what kind of auxiliary tools they use. The results of this examination can be found in this table.

Below I want to share the main conclusions that I have made while analyzing popular templates.

De facto standards

The tools discussed in this section are included in more than half of the templates. This means that they are perceived as standard in a large number of real Python projects.

Flake8

I have been using Flake8 for quite some time, but I did not know about the dominant position in the field of linting that this tool occupies. I thought that it exists in a kind of competition, but the vast majority of project templates use it.

Yes, this is not surprising. It is difficult to oppose something to the convenience of linting the entire code base of the project in a matter of seconds. Those who want to use cutting-edge development can recommend a look at us make-python-style guide. This is something like "Flake8 on steroids." This tool may well contribute to the transfer to the category of obsolete other similar tools (like Pylint).

Pytest and coverage.py

The vast majority of templates use pytest. This reduces the use of the standard unit test framework. Pytest looks even more attractive when combined with tox. That's precisely what was done in about half of the templates. Code coverage with tests is most often checked using coverage.py.

Sphinx

Most templates use Sphinx to generate documentation. To my surprise, MkDocs is rarely used for this purpose.

As a result, we can say that if you do not use Flake8, pytest, and Sphinx in your current project, then you should consider introducing them.

Promising tools

In this section, I collected those tools and techniques, the use of which in the templates suggested some trends. The point is that although all this does not appear in most project templates, it is found in many relatively recent templates. So - all this is worth paying attention to.

Pyproject.toml

File usage is pyproject.tomlsuggested in PEP 518. This is a modern mechanism for specifying project assembly requirements. It is used in most fairly young templates.

Poetry

Although the Python ecosystem isn't doing well in terms of an excellent tool for managing dependencies, I cautiously optimistic that Poetry could be the equivalent of npm from the JavaScript world in the Python world.

The youngest (but popular) project templates seem to agree with this idea of mine. Real, it is worth saying that if someone is working on some kind of library that he can plan to distribute through PyPI, then he will still have to use setup tools. (It should to be noted that after the publication of this material, I was informed that this is no longer a problem).

Also, be careful if your project (the same applies to dependencies) relies on Conda. In this case, Poetry will not suit you, since this tool, in its current form, binds the developer to pip and virtualenv.

Dependabot

Dependabot regularly checks project dependencies for obsolescence and tries to help the developer by automatically opening PR.

I have recently seen this tool more often than before. It seems like to me that it is an excellent tool: the addition of which to the project affects the project very positively. Dependabot helps reduce security risks by pushing developers to keep dependencies up to date.

As a result, I advised you not to lose sight of Poetry and Dependabot. Consider introducing these tools into your next project.

Personal recommendations

Analysis of project templates gave me a somewhat ambivalent perception of the tools that I will list in this section. In any case, I want to use this section to tell about them, based on my own experience. At one time, they were beneficial to me.

Pre-commit

Even if you are incredibly disciplined - do not waste your energy on performing simple routine actions such as additional code run through the linter before sending the code to the repository. Similar tasks can be passed to Pre-commit. And it's better to spend your energy on TDD and teamwork on code.

Pylint

Although Pylint is criticized for being slow, although this tool is criticized for the features of its settings, I can say that it allowed me to grow above myself in the field of programming.

He gives me specific instructions on those parts of the code that I can improve, tells me how to make the code better comply with the rules. For a free tool, this alone is already very much.

Therefore, I am ready to put up with the inconvenience associated with Pylint.

Black

Black at the root of the debate over where to put spaces in the code. This protects our teams from an empty talk and meaningless differences in files caused by different editors' settings.

In my case, it brightens up what I don't like about Python (the need to use a lot of spaces). Moreover, it should be noted that the Black project in 2019 joined the Python Software Foundation, which indicates the seriousness and quality of this project.

As a result, I want to say that if you still do not use pre-commit, Black, and Pylint - think about whether these tools can benefit your team.

Subtotals

Twelve of the eighteen investigated templates were created using the cookiecutter framework. Some of those templates where this framework is not used have exciting qualities.

But given the fact that cookiecutter is the leading framework for creating project templates, those who decide to use a template that did not use a cookiecutter should have excellent reasons for this. Such a decision should be very well justified.

Those who are looking for a template for their project should choose a template that most closely matches his view of things.

If you, when creating projects according to a precise template, continuously have to reconfigure them in the same way, think about how to fork such a template and refine it, inspired by examples of templates from my list.

And if you are attracted to adventure - create your template from scratch. Cookiecutter is an excellent feature of the Python ecosystem, and the simple process of creating Jinja templates allows you to quickly and easily do something your own.

Bonus: Template Recommendations

Django

Together with the most popular Django templates, consider using we make-django-template. It gives the impression of a deeply thought out product.

Data Processing and Analysis

In most projects aimed at processing and analyzing data, the Cookiecutter Data Science template is useful. However, data scientists should also look at Kedro.

This template extends Cookiecutter Data Science with a mechanism for creating standardized data processing pipelines. It supports loading and saving data and models. These features are very likely to be able to find a worthy application in your next project.

Here I would also like to express my gratitude to the creators of the shablona template for preparing very high- quality documentation. It can be useful to you even if you end up choosing something else.

General Purpose Templates

Which general-purpose template to choose in some way depends on what exactly you are going to develop based on this template - a library or a regular application. But I, selecting a similar template, along with the most popular projects of this kind, would look very closely at Jace's Python Template.

This is not a well-known pattern, but I like the fact that it has Poetry, isort , Black, pylint, and mypy .

PyScaffold is one of the most popular non-cookiecutter based templates. It has many extensions (for example, for Django, and Data Science projects). It also downloads version numbers from GitHub using setuptools-scm. Further, this is one of the few templates supporting Conda.

Here are a couple of templates that use GitHub Actions technology:

The Python Best Practices Cookiecutter template, which, I want to note, has most of my favorite tools.

The Blueprint / Boilerplate For Python Projects template, which I find pretty interesting, as the ability it gives them to find common security problems with Bandit, looks promising. Also, this template has a remarkable feature, which consists in the fact that the settings of all tools are collected in a single file setup.cfg.

And finally - I recommend taking a look at we make-python-package template. I think it's worth doing it anyway. In particular, if you like the Django template of the same developer, or if you are going to use the advanced, we make-python-style guide instead of pure Flake8.

How are broad integer types implemented in Python?

When you write in a low-level language such as C, you are worried about choosing the right data type and qualifiers for your integers, at each step, you analyze whether it will be enough to use it simply intor whether you need to add longor even long double. However, when writing code in Python, you don't need to worry about these "minor" things, because Python can work with numbers of integerany size type .

In C, if you try to calculate 220,000 using the built-in function

```
#include <stdio.h>
#include <math.h>

int main (void) {
  printf ("%Lf\n", powl (2, 20000));
  return 0;
}

$ ./a.out
inf
```

powl, you will get the output inf.

But in Python, making this easier than ever is easy:

```
>>> 2 ** 20,000
398027684033796659235430720619120245370477727804924259387134 ...

...
... 6021 digits long ...

...
6309376
```

It must be under the hood that Python is doing something very beautiful, and today we will find out the exactly what it does to work with integers of arbitrary size!

Presentation and Definition

Integer in Python, this is a C structure defined as follows:

```
struct _longobject {
   PyObject_VAR_HEAD
   digit ob_digit [1];
};
PyObject_VAR_HEADIs a macro, it expands to PyVarObject, which has the following structure:
typedef struct {
   PyObject ob_base;
   Py_ssize_t ob_size; /* Number of items in variable part */
} PyVarObject;
```

Other types that have PyObject_VAR_HEAD:

PyBytesObject

PyTupleObject

PyListObject

This means that an integer, like a tuple or a list, has a variable length, and this is the first step to understanding how Python can support work with giant numbers. Once expanded, the macro _longobjectcan be considered as:

```
struct _longobject {
   PyObject ob_base;
   Py_ssize_t ob_size; /* Number of items in variable part */
   digit ob_digit [1];
};
```

There PyObjectare some meta fields in the structure that are used for reference counting (garbage collection), but to talk about this, we need a separate article. The field on which we will focus this ob_digitand in a bit ob_size.

Decoding ob_digit

ob_digitIs a statically allocated array of unit length of type digit (typedef для uint32_t). Since this is an array, it ob_digitis a pointer primarily to a number, and therefore, if necessary, it can be increased using the malloc function to any length. This way, python can represent and process very large numbers. Typically, in low-level languages such as C, the precision of integers is limited to 64 bits. However, Python supports integers of arbitrary precision. Starting with Python 3, all numbers are presented in the form bignum and are limited only by the available system memory.

Decoding ob_size

ob_sizestores the number of items in ob_digit. Python overrides and then uses the value ob_sizeto to determine the actual number of elements contained in the array to increase the efficiency of allocating memory to the array ob_digit.

Storage

The most naive way to store integer numbers is to store one decimal digit in one element of the array. Operation such as additional and subtractions can be performed according to the rules of mathematics from elementary school.

With this approach, the number 5238 will be saved like this:

This approach is inefficient because we will use up to 32-bit digits (uint32_t) for storing a decimal digit, which ranges from 0 to 9 and can be easily represented with only 4 bits. After all, when writing something as universal like python, the kernel developer needs to be even more inventive.

So, can we do better? Of course, otherwise, we would not have posted this article. Let's take a closer look at how Python stores an extra-long integer.

Python path

Instead of storing only one decimal digit in each element of the array ob_digit, Python converts the numbers from the number system with base 10 to the numbers in the system with base 230 and calls each element as a number whose value ranges from 0 to 230 - 1.

In the hexadecimal number system, the base 16 ~ 24 means that each "digit" of the hexadecimal number ranges from 0 to 15 in the decimal number system. In Python, it's similar to a "number" with a base of 230, which means that the number will range from 0 to 230 - 1 = 1073741823 in decimal.

In this way, Python effectively uses almost all of the allocated space of 32 bits per digit, saves resources, and still performs simple operations, such as adding and subtracting at the math level of elementary school.

Depending on the platform, Python uses either 32-bit unsigned integer arrays or 16-bit unsigned integer arrays with 15-bit digits. To perform the operations that will be discussed later, you need only a few bits.

Example: 1152921504606846976

As already mentioned, for Python, numbers are represented in a system with a base of 230, that is, if you convert 1152921504606846976 into a number system with a base of 230, you will get 100.

1152 9215 0460 6846 976 = 1 * ((230) 2 + 0) * ((230) 1 + 0) *((230) 0)

Since it is the ob_digitfirst to store the least significant digit, it is stored as 001 in three digits. The structure _longobjectfor this value will contain:

ob_size like 3

ob_digit like [0, 0, 1]

We created a demo REPL that will show how Python stores an integer inside itself, and also refers to structural members such as ob_size, ob_refcountetc.

Integer Long Operations

Now that we have a pure idea of how Python implements integers of arbitrary precision, it is time to understand how various mathematical operations are performed with them.

Addition

Integers are stored "in numbers," which means that addition is as simple as in elementary school, and the Python source code shows us that this is how addition is implemented. A function with a name x_addin a file longobject.cadds two numbers.

```
For (i = 0; i < size_b; ++i) {
    carry += a->ob_digit [i] + b->ob_digit [i];
    z->ob_digit [i] = carry & PyLong_MASK
    carry >> = PyLong_SHIFT;
}
For ( ; i < size_a; ++i) {
    carry += a->ob_digit [i];
    z->ob_digit [i] = carry & PyLong _MASK
    carry >> = PyLong_SHIFT
}
z->ob_digit [i] = carry
```

The code snippet above is taken from a function x_add. As you can see, it iterates over a number by numbers and performs the addition of numbers, calculates the result and adds hyphenation.

It becomes more interesting when the result of addition is a negative number. The sign ob_sizeis an integer sign, that is, if you have a negative number, then it ob_sizewill be a minus. The value ob_sizemodulo will determine the number of digits in ob_digit.

Subtraction

Just as addition takes place, subtraction also takes place. A function with a name x_subin the file longobject.csubtracts one number from another.

```
For (i = 0: i < size_b: ++i) {
    borrow = a -> ob_digit [i] - b-> ob_digit [i] - borrow:
    z-> ob_digit [i] = borrow & PyLong_MASK:
    borrow >> = PyLong_SHIFT:
    borrow & = 1: /* Keep only one sign bit */
}
for (: i <size_a: ++i) {
    borrow = a-> ob_digit [i] - borrow:
    z-> ob_digit [i] = borrow & PyLong_MASK:
    borrow >> = PyLong_SHIFT:
    borrow & = 1: /* Keep only one sign bit */
}
```

The code snippet above is taken from a function x_sub. In it, you see how the enumeration of numbers occurs and subtraction is performed, the result is calculated and the transfer is distributed. Indeed, it is very similar to addition.

Multiplication

And again, the multiplication will be implemented in the same naive way that we learned from the lessons of mathematics in elementary school, but it is not very efficient. To maintain efficiency, Python implements theKaratsuba algorithm, which multiplies two n-digit numbers in O (nlog23) simple steps. The algorithm is not simple and its implementation is beyond the scope of this article, but you can find its implementation in functions and in the file .k_mul k_lopsided_mullongobject.c

Division and other operations

All operations on integers are defined in the file longobject.c, they are very simple to find and trace the work of each. Attention: A detailed understanding of the work of each of them will take time, so pre-stock up with popcorn.

Optimizing Frequently Used Integers

Python preallocates a small number of integers in memory ranging from -5 to 256. This allocation occurs during initialization, and since we cannot change integers (immutability), these pre-allocated numbers are singleton and are directly referenced instead of being allocated. This means that every time we use/create a small number, Python instead of reallocation simply returns a reference to the previously allocated number.

Such optimization can be traced in the macro IS_SMALL_INTand function get_small_intc longobject.c. So Python saves a lot of space and time in calculating commonly used integer numbers.

Create a bot in Python to learn English

No, this is not one of the hundreds of articles on how to write your first Hello World bot in Python. Here you will not find detailed instructions on how to get an API token in BotFather or launch a bot in the cloud. In return, we will show you how to unleash the full power of Python to the maximum to achieve the most aesthetic and beautiful code. We perform a song about the appeal of complex structures - we dance and dance. Under the cut asynchrony, its system of saves, a bunch of useful decorators, and a lot of beautiful code.

Disclaimer: People with brain OOP and adherents of the "right" patterns may ignore this article.

Idea

To understand what it is like not to know English in modern society, imagine that you are an 18th-century nobleman who does not know French. Even if you are not very well versed in history, you can still imagine how hard it would be to live under such circumstances. In the modern world, English has become a necessity, not a privilege, especially if you are in the IT industry. The project is based on the catechism of the future: the development of a neural network as a separate unit, and education, which is based on games and sports spirit. Isomorphic paradigms have been hanging in the air since ancient times, but it seems that over time, people began to forget that the most straightforward solutions are the most effective.

Here is a shortlist of the basic things I want to put together:

Be able to work with three user dictionaries

Ability to parse youtube video/text, and then add new words to the user's dictionary

Two basic skills training modes

Flexible customization: full control over user dictionaries and the environment in general

Built-in admin panel

Naturally, everything should work quickly, with the ability to easily replenish existing functionality in the future. Putting it all together, I thought that the best embodiment of my idea into reality would be a Telegram bot. My tale is not about how to write handlers for the bot correctly - there are dozens of such articles, and this is simple mechanical work. I want the reader to learn to ignore the typical dogmas of programming. Use what is profitable and effective here and now.

"I learned to let out the cries of unbelievers past my ears because it was impossible to suppress them."

Base structure

The bot will be based on the python-telegram-bot (ptb) library. I use loguru as a logger , though there is one small snag here. The fact is that ptb by default uses a different logger (standard logging) and does not allow you to connect your own. Of course, it would be possible to intercept all journal messages globally and send them to our registrar, but we will do it a little easier:

```python
from loguru import logger
import sys

# Configure dual-stream output to the console and to the file
config = {
    'handlers': [
        {'sink': sys.stdout, 'level': 'INFO'},
        {'sink': 'logs.log', 'serialize': False, 'level': 'DEBUG'},
    ]
}

logger.configure(**config)

# ...

updater = Updater('YOUR_TOKEN')
dp = updater.dispatcher

# Roughly fasten your logger. Cheap and cheerful
updater.logger = logger
dp.logger = logger
```

Unfortunately, I don't have the opportunity to deploy my bot on stable data centers, so data security is a priority. For these purposes, I implemented my system of saves. It provides flexible and convenient work with data - statistics collection, as an example of easy replenishment of functionality in the future.

```python
from __future__ import annotations  # In the future, I will omit this import
from loguru import logger

import inspect
import functools
import os

def file_is_empty (path: str) -> bool:
    return os.stat (path) .st_size == 0

def clear_file (path: str) -> None:
    with open (path, 'w'): pass

def cache_decorator (method):
    @ functools.wraps (method)
    def wrapper (self, * args, ** kwargs):
        res = method (self, * args, ** kwargs)
        Cache.link recess (self, {'method_name': method __name__}) # (1)
        # During testing, multiple calls can slow down
        # program work: opt avoids this
        logger.opt (lazy = True) .debug (f'Decorator for {method __name__} was end ')
        return res
    return wrapper

class cache:
    """
```

+ cache_si ze - Std thfDtlgh 'hi ch dl data will be su'ed

+ cache_files - Dump file in w'hich all intermediate operations on

data are stored

link = None

def   init   (self. cache_si ze =10):

= Save all screw'ed cl asses. Thi s all or's you t o fl exibl>' vork with

data.

sel f. cl asses = []

=Files matching classes

 sel f._cache_fi1es = []

= (1). A sm dl hack that dl or's you to cd1 a specifi c instance

thrDtlgh a common class

= Thi s w'wks because w'e oril \' have one instance Df the cl ass. 'hi ch

= implements d 1 the logic of 'orking with data. In additi on. it is convenient ari d all o 's

= st gum cantl›' expand the functl Dflallt›' in the future

sel f. cl ass .link = self

self._counter = 0

self.CACHE SIZE = cache st ze

def add (self, d s: class, file: str) -> NDne:

All or's to fasten a class to a sa ver

+ cls - Inst an ce of the class

+ file - The fi1 e the instari ce is 'orking with

self._cache_files.append (file)

self._cl asses.append (cls)

if fi1e i s eotptl' (fi1e): return hDne

1ogger.opt dan.'=True).debug(fTor{cls.   class names) file (file) is not empty' ')

fa data in sells oad(file):
    is.save nDn Caclti ng (data)

cl ear_file (file)

sel f._counter = 0

def recess (self, cls: ct ass, data diet) —>Ncri e:

The main method that performs the basi c l o c of saves

if self. counter + 1/ = self.CACHE SIZE:

    self.save all 0

el se:

self._counter + = l

fil ename = self._cache_files [self._classes.index (cls)]

self.save (data. fil enam e = filename)

= For simplicit›', save_d1, save, load methods are omitted

Now we can create any methods that can modify data, without

fear of losing important data:

```
@cache_decorator
def add_smth_important (* args, ** kwargs) -> Any:
    # ...
    # We make some important actions on the data ...
    # ...
```

Now that we have figured out the basic structure, the main

question remains: how to put everything together. I

implemented the main class - EnglishBot, which brings together the entire primary structure: PTB, work with the database, the save system, and which will manage the whole business logic of the bot. If the implementation of Telegram commands were simple, we could easily add them to the same class. But, unfortunately, their organization occupies most of the code of the entire application, so adding them to the same class would be crazy. I also did not want to create new classes/subclasses, because I suggest using a very simple structure:

```python
# Import the main class
from modules import EnglishBot
# Import classes that implement Telegram commands
from modules.module import start
# ...

if __name__ == '__main__':
    # Initialize the bot
    tbot = EnglishBot (
        # ...
    )

    # Add handlers to the stack
    tbot.add_command_handler (start, 'start')
    # ...
```

How command modules get access to the main class, we will consider further.

All out of nothing

Ptb handlers have two arguments - update and context, which store all the necessary information stack. Context has a wonderful chat_data argument that can be used as a data storage dictionary for chat. But I do not want to constantly refer to it in a format context.chat_data['data']. I would like something light and beautiful, say context.data. However, this is not a problem.

```python
from telegram.ext import CommandHandler

def a (self, key: str):
    # First, check if the class has the required value
    # If not, then try to return it from chat_data
    try:
        return object __getattribute__ (self, key)
    except:
        return self.chat_data[key]

def b (self, key: str, data = None, replace = True):
    #Small hack: if replace = False and data exists, then overwriting does not occur
    # In this case, if the data is not specified, then they are put in None
    if replace or not self.chat_data.get (key, None):
        self.chat_data [key] = data


# Bind in context to receive data in the format context.data
CallbackContext.__getattribute__ = a
# As well as a convenient setter for your needs
CallbackContext.set = b
```

We continue to simplify our lives. Now I want all the necessary information for a specific user to be in quick access context.

```python
def bind_context (func):
    def wrapper (update, context):
        context._bot.bind_user_data (update, context) # (2)
        return func (update, context)
    return wrapper

class EnglishBot:
    # ...

    def bind_user_data (self, update, context) -> dict:
        context.set ('t_id', update.message.chat_id, replace = False)
        context.set ('t_ln', update.message.from_user.language_code, replace = False)
        # ...
        # Set all the necessary information that we want to have quick access from context
        # For example, something from the database
        # ...
```

Now we'll completely become impudent and fasten our bot instance to context:

```python
class EnglishBot:
    # ...

    def __init__ (self, *args, **kwargs):
        # ...
        # (2): Now we can access the instance in the format context._bot
        CallbackContext._bot = self
```

We put everything in place and get a citadel of comfort and convenience in just one call.

```python
from EnglishBot import bind_context

@bind_context
def start (update, context):
    # Now we have access to everything from one place
    # For example, we can easily add a new user to the database
    # Check if the user is in our database
    if not context._bot.user_exist (context.t_id):
        # For example, add some important notifications
        context.set ('push_notification', True)
        # And then add the user to the database
        context._bot.new_user (context.t_id, context.t_ln)

    return update.message.reply_text ('Welcome')
    # ...
```

Decorators are our everything

Most often, it turns out that the name of the function coincides with the name of the command to which we want to add a handler. Why not use this statistical feature for your selfish purposes.

```python
class EnglishBot:
    # ...

    def add_command_handler (self, func: function, name = None) -> None:
        """
        Function that adds a command handler
        """

        name = name or func.__name__
        self.dp.add_handler (CommandHandler (name, func))

    # ...

# In the main file:
tbot.add_command_handler (start) # Instead of tbot.add_command_handler (start, 'start')
```

It looks cool, but it doesn't work. It's all about the bind_context decorator, which will always return the name of the wrapper function. Correct this misunderstanding.

```python
import functools

def bind_context (func):
    # functools.wraps from stdlib saves signatures since Python 3.4
    @ functools.wraps (func)
    def wrapper (update, context):
        context._bot.bind_user_data (update, context)
        return func (update, context)
    return wrapper
```

There are many message handlers in the bot, which, by design, should cancel the command when entering zero. Also I need to discard all edited posts.

```python
import functools

END = -1

def zero_exiter (func):
    @ functools.wraps (func)
    def wrapper (update, context):
        if update.to_dict () ['message']. get ('text', None) == '0':
            update.message.reply_text ('Sending some message')
            return END

        return func (update, context)
    return wrapper

def skip_edited (func):
    @ functools.wraps (func)
    def wrapper (update, context):
        # This works in all cases, because None returned
        # in the conversation_handler stack, leaves the function in its current state
        if not update.to_dict (). get ('edited_message', None):
            return func (update, context)
    return wrapper
```

We do not forget at the same time about the most important decorator - @run_asyncon which asynchrony is based. Now we collect the heavy function.

```python
from telegram.ext.dispatcher import run_async
from EnglishBot import skip_edited

@run_async
@skip_edited
def heavy_function (update, context):
    # ...
    # A heavy computing function that needs asynchrony
    # Has post edit protection
    # ...
```

Remember that asynchrony is a Jedi sword, but with this sword,
you can quickly kill yourself.

Sometimes programs freeze without sending anything to the log.
@logger.catch, the last decorator on our list, ensures that any
error is correctly reported to a logger.

```python
from loguru import logger

@ logger.catch
def heavy_function2 (update, context):
    # ...
    # Another heavy computing function on which a program may hang
    # ...
```

Admin panel

Let's implement an admin panel with the ability to
receive/delete logs and send a message to all users.

```python
from EnglishBot import bind_context
from Cache import file_is_empty
from telegram import ReplyKeyboardMarkup
from loguru import logger

LOG_FILE = 'logs.log'
SENDING, MAIN, END = range (1, -2, -1)

buttons = ReplyKeyboardMarkup (
    [('Get logs', 'logs'), ('Clear logs', 'clear')],
    [('Send message', 'send')],
    # [...],
)

@bind_context
def admin_panel (update, context):
    # Check user admin rights
    if not context._bot.acess_check (context.t_id):
        # A good security practice is to show the user that such a command does not exist
        return update.message.reply_text (f'Unknown command {update.message.text} ')

    update.message.reply_text ('Choose an option', reply_markup = buttons)

    return MAIN
```

!fi ero exiter
def send d1 (updast   context).
    count = 0

!fi ero exiter
def send d1 (updast   context).
    count = 0

logsmethods

def get logs (update context).
    if fil e is empU.' (LOG FILE).
        update.cd1back quo.'.repl>' text
            are empU.") else.
      = Show' document loading
        context.bot.send chat acti ‹xi
        (chat id = context.t icL action
        = 'upload docum cut')
        context.bot.sendDocument (chat i
        d = context.t icL docimi cut =
        open (L OG FILE 'rb') name = L
        Ohr FILE
time‹xit = 1000)

  = Since we do not cl ose the admin
    panel you need to rem ove the
    dourload icon on the button
    update.cd1back quell'.answer (text
    = ")
  = B asicd1\' thi s is urin ecessm.'. As I
sai d earli er None does not change the
positi on of the hand er
  = But this was' the code locks much
    m‹xe readabl e return ñIAIN

def logs d ear (update context).
    with open (LOG FILE 'u") as fi1 e.
        update.cd1back quo.'.repl>' text
        ('O ear ed) update.cd1back
        quo.'.answer (text = ")

    return ñIAIN

=   Send methods

def take message (update context).
    update.cd1back quell'.repl>' text
    ('Send m essag e) update.cd1back
    quell'.answer (text = ")

    return SENDING

```
!fi ero exiter
def send dl (updast    context).
    count = 0

    Get user identifi cfs from the
    database for id in li st (context.
    bot.get user ids Q).
      = It may' happen that some user
      has added a bet to the em ergenc\'
      = Then when to.'ing to send him a
      message  an error u411 be  caught
      to.'.
        = fi'e do not  setid  a message to
        oursel ves if i d   context.t icL
        continue
        = Be sure to use ñlarkdour to
      save message formatting
        context.bet.send message
        (context.t icL text =
        update.message.text markdour
        parse mode =  ñlarkdour')
        count + = 1
      except. pass

    update.cd1back quell'.rep1>' text
    (£Sent to { count) pecpl e ')
    update.cd1back quell'.answer (text
    = ")
```

```
#

# In the main file
tbot.add_conversation_handler (
    entry_points = [('admin', admin)],
    # The regularity for send_alk allows you to process any message that does not start with /
    states = [[(logs, " logs $'), (logs_clear, " clear $'), (send, " send $')], [(send_alk, '@ ^ ((?t * (( ^ \/) +)). *)( +) $
')]]
)
```

The add_conversation_handler function allows you to add a

conversation handler in a minimalistic way:

```python
class EnglishBot:
    # ...

    def add_conversation_handler (self, entry_points: list, states: list, fallbacks: list) -> None:
        fallbacks = [CommandHandler (name, func) for name, func in fallbacks]
        entry_points = [CommandHandler (name, func) for name, func in entry_points]
        r_states = {}

        for i in range (len (states)):
            r_states [i] = []

            # Each array describes functions of one state
            for func, pattern in states [i]:
                # If the regular starts with the @ symbol, then we add a message handler
                # Otherwise, a regular button handler
                if pattern [0] == '@':
                    r_states [i] .append (MessageHandler (Filters.regex (pattern [1 ]), func))
                else:
                    r_states [i] .append (CallbackQueryHandler (func, pattern = pattern))

        conv_handler = ConversationHandler (entry_points = entry_points, states = r_states, fallbacks = fallbacks)
        dp.add_handler (conv_handler)
```

Main functionality

Let's teach our bot to add new words to user dictionaries.

```python
from EnglishBot import bind_context, skip_edited, zero_exiter
from youtube_transcript_api import YouTubeTranscriptApi
from telegram.ext.dispatcher import run_async

START_OVER, ADDING, END = range (1, -2, -1)

re_youtube = re.compile ('^ (http (s)? \/\ /)? ((w) {3} .)? youtu (be | .be)? (. com)? \ /.+' )
re_text = re.compile ('^ [az] {3,20} $')

def is_youtube_link (link: str) -> bool:
    if re_youtube.match (link) is not None: return True

def clear_text (text: str) -> str:
    bad_symbols = '! @ #% $ ^ & * () _ + 1234567890 - = /| \?> <, ":' ~ [] {}'
```

```python
        text = text.replace (s. ")

    return  text. strw    ()  IDS'& ()


!@skip_edited
:@bind_context
def add_w'ords (update. context).
    update.message.reply' text ('Enter text:')
    return ADDING


:H uri_asx'nc
:@skip_edit ed
:@zero_exiter
def parse_text (update. context):
        DDDM DZténg takes soote titzte, sD ñ'ou need tD T1ctT1' the user that e\' .'thing is fine
    message = update.message.repl>'_text ('L oad rig ...')

    if is 'outube_link (update.message.text):
      = If the video is irivdid or there are no subtitl es in it, then we will catch ari  error
        to.':
            transcript list = Y en TubeTranscriptApi list transcripts (get ski deD id (update.message.text))
            t = tr ariscript_listfnd_transcript (['en'])
            _tmt = clear_tmt  ('.' .j » ([i [tmt']  fur i in tletJ  0])} split ()
        except:
            otessag z edtt text ('k\'âtid x'ideD. To.' again:')
            return ADD UG
    else:
        _text = clear_tnt (update.message.text) .split ()

    =  ¥Ve get a link to the words the user alread>' has
        T'& ds.' CDotext. bDt.get ck ct  'ords (cDlttWt.t id)
        1 'ards tD be ad6ed
        good_w'ords = []
    = Discarded words
        bad_words = Q

    = First, w'e discard duplicates
        for word in set    text):
        =  Then w'e check the correctness of the w'ord regular
            z = re_text.match (word)
            if z.
            = Add a vord onl>' if it is n ot already' in the user ñ ation m.'
                if z.group () net in _w'ords:
                    good_wcrds.append (word)
            el se:
                bad_words.append ( 'ord)

    = The Dnl >' thi Hg left 1 S tD suggest the user tD Add en ds
    = And then add them t o the di cti Dfl .'




.. In the main file:

    tbot.add_coriversation_handler (
        entr>'  oints = [('add_wcrds', add_ 'crds)],
```

```python
states = [
    [(parse_text, '@ ^ ((?!. * (( ` | ( ) +)). ") (. +) $')],
    #
])
```

We pack the bot

Before we pack our bot, add proxy support and change log levels
from the console.

```python
# In the main file:

import argparse

parser = argparse.ArgumentParser ()
parser.add_argument ('-l', '--level', default = 'INFO',
            choices = ['TRACE', 'DEBUG', 'INFO', 'SUCCESS', 'WARNING', 'ERROR', 'CRITICAL'],
            help = 'Allows you to enable the bot in a given mode')
parser.add_argument ('-p', '--proxy', help = 'Allows you to enable bot with proxy')
args = parser.parse_args ()

config = {
  'handlers': [
     {'sink': sys.stdout, 'level': args.level},
     # It's not a mistake. In the file I collect logs of level DEBUG and higher
     {'sink': 'logs.log', 'serialize': False, 'level': 'DEBUG'},
  ],
}

logger.configure (** config)

if args.proxy:
    t_proxy = {'proxy_url': args.proxy, 'read_timeout': 1000, 'connect_timeout': 1000}
    # ...
    # Proxies for other services
    # ...
else:
    t_proxy = None
```

Python 3.5+ supports the ability to pack a directory into a single
executable file. Let's take this opportunity to be able to deploy
your work environment on any VPS easily. First, get the
dependency file. If you are using a virtual environment, it can be
done with one command: pip freeze > requirements.txt. If the

project does not have a virtual environment, then you will have to tinker a bit. You can try to use pip freeze and manually isolate all the necessary packages. Still, if too many packages are installed on the system, then this method will not work. The second option is to use ready-made solutions, for example, pipreqs.

Now that our dependency file is ready, we can pack our directory into a .pyzfile. To do this, enter the command py - m zipapp "ПУТЬ_К_КАТАЛОГУ" -m "ИМЯ_ГЛАВНОГО_ФАЙЛА:ГЛАВНАЯ_ФУНКЦИЯ" -o bot.pyz, it will create the bot.pyz file in the project folder. Please note that the code in init .py must be wrapped in some function, otherwise the executable file will be impossible to compile.

```
# Sample __init__ py file
# py -m zipapp "PATH_TO_CATALOG" -m "__init__.py:main" -o bot.pyz

def main ():
    #

if __name__ == '__main__':
    main ()
```

We wrap the files in the archive zip bot.zip requirements.txt bot.pyzand send it to our VPS.

The thermal imager on the Raspberry PI

Well-known thermal imaging modules appeared on the famous Chinese site. Is it possible to assemble an exotic and, possibly, even useful thing - a home-made thermal imager? Why not, like Raspberry was lying somewhere. What came of it – I will tell you under the cut.

MLX90640. What is it?

And this, in fact, is a thermal imaging matrix with a microcontroller on board. Production of the previously unknown company Melexis. The thermal imaging matrix has a dimension of 32 by 24 pixels. This is not much, but when interpolating the image, it seems to be enough to make out something, at least.

There are two type of sensor is available version, the cases of which differ in the viewing angle of the matrix. A more squat structure A overlooks the outside world at an angle of 110 (horizontal) at 75 (vertical) degrees. B - under 55 by 37.5 degrees, respectively. The device case has only four outputs - two for power, two for communicating with the control device via the I2C interface. Interested datasheets can be downloaded here.

And then what is the GY-MCU90640?

Chinese comrades put the MLX90640 on board with another microcontroller on board (STM32F103). Apparently, for easier matrix management. This whole farm is called GY-MCU90640. And it costs at the time of acquisition (end of December 2018) in the region of 5 thousands $. As follows:

As you see, there are two types of boards, with a narrow or wide-angle version of the sensor onboard.

Which version is best for you? A good question, unfortunately, I had it only after the modules was already ordered and received.

For some reason, at this time of the orders, I did not pay attention to these nuances. But in vain.

A wider version will be useful on self-propelled robots or in security system (the field of view will be larger). According to the datasheets, it also has less noise and higher measurement accuracy.

But for visualization tasks, I would more recommend a more "long-range" version of B. For one very significant reason. In the future, when shooting, it can be deployed (manually or on a platform with a drive) and take composite "photos," thereby increasing the more than a modest resolution of 32 by 24 pixels. Collects thermal images 64 by 96 pixels, for example. Well, all right, in the future, the photos will be from the wide-angle version A.

Connect to Raspberry PI

There are two ways to control the thermal imaging module: Shorten the "SET" jumper on the board and use I2C to contact the internal microcontroller MLX90640 directly.

Leave the jumper alone and communicate with the module through a similar interface installed on the STM32F103 board via RS-232.

If you write in C ++, it will probably be more convenient to ignore the extra microcontroller, short-circuit the jumper and use the API from the manufacturer, which lies here.

Humble pythonists can also go the first way. It seems like that there are a couple of Python libraries (here and here). But unfortunately, not a single one worked for me.

Advanced pythonists can write a module control driver in Python. The procedure for obtaining a frame is described in detail in the datasheet. But then you will have to prescribe all the calibration procedures, which seems slightly burdensome. Therefore, I had to go the second way. It turned out to be moderately thorny, but quite passable.

Thanks to the insight of Chinese engineers or just a happy coincidence, the shawl turned out to have a perfect location of the conclusions:

It remains only to put the block and insert the scarf into the raspberry connector. A 5 to 3 Volt converter is installed on the board, so it seems that nothing threatens Raspberry's delicate Rx and Tx terminals.

It should be added that the connection according to the first option, is also possible, but requires more labor and solder skill. The board must be installed on the other side of the Raspberry connector (shown in the title photo of this post).

Soft

On a well-known Chinese site, such a miracle is offered to access the GY-MCU90640:

Most likely, there should be some description of the interaction protocol with the microcontroller installed on the board, according to which this software product works! After a brief conversation with the seller of scarves (respect to these respected gentlemen), such a protocol was sent to me. It appeared in pdf and pure Chinese.

Thanks to Google's translator and active copy-paste, after about an hour and a half, the protocol was decrypted, anyone can read it on Github. It turned out that the scarf understands six basic commands, among which there is a frame request on the COM port.

Each pixel of the matrix is, in fact, the temperature value of the object that this pixel is looking at. The temperature in degrees Celsius times 100 (double-byte number). There is even a special mode in which the scarf will send frames from the matrix to the Raspberry 4 times per second.


```python
import numpy as np
import cv2

# function to get Emissivity from MCU
def get_emissivity():
```

```python
ser.write (semi d .to_bytes ([0xA5,Dx55 ,0xOl ,OxFB]))

read = ser.read (4) return read [2] / 100

d function to ga temperatures from MCU (Celsius degree x 100)

‹Ref ga_temp_oray (d):


# getting ambient tame

T_a = (iot (d[1540]) + int (d [1541]) • 256) / 100


# getting raw array of pixels temperie

raw_data = d [4: 1540]

T_array =npJrombtdfa(raw_          . ‹type = up.intl6)


rctura T_a,T_anay


#fiioaiontoconverttemplestopixelsoaimage

def td_to_image(f).

norm = up.nint8 ((f. 100 - Twin) • 255, (Tmax-Tmin))

norm.shy = (24.32)
```

#================================= Main cycle =================================

Color map range

```python
Tn        =40

Tmin =20
```

```python
print ('Corifi guring Seri d port')
ser = seri d .Seri d (' dev ." seri d 0')
ser.baucYate = 115200


= set frequency' of module to 4 Hz
ser.site (seri d.to baies ([0xA5  0x25  0x01  0xCB]))
time.sleep  (0.1)


= Starting automati c data colecti on
ser.site (seri d.to baies ([0xA5  0x35  0x02  0xD/])
t0 = time.time  Q



while True.
= waiting for data frame
data = ser.read  (1544)


= The data is ready' l et's handle it!
To tanp array' = get temp  array' (data)
ta img = td to image  (temp array')


= Guage processing
img = cv2.appl vColorñlap (ta img cv2.COL ORñfAP JE T)
img = cv2.rest ze (inn g (320 240) interpolati on = cv2.IhMR  GB  IC)
img = cv2 Hi p (inn g l)


text = Tmin = {. +. lf) Tmax  = {. +. lf) FPS = {. .2f)'. format (temp
array'.min () ." 100 temp array'.max Q ." 100
l ." (time .time Q - t0))
cv2. putText (img text (5 15) cv2.FONT HERSHEY SET&LE X 0.45 (0
0 0) 1)
cv2.imshou' ('Output' img)

* if 's' is pressed - savi ng of picture key' = cv2.waitKe\' (1) & 0xFF
if key'    ord (" s").
fname = 'pic ' + dt.datetime.now' Q. strfli me (". o Y-°. o m-°. » d °. » H-°. » ñl-
°. » S) + '.jpg' cv2.imuñte (fnam e img)
print ('Savi rig image' fnam e) t0 = time.time  Q




except KevboardInterrupt.
* to terminate the cycle
ser.site (seri d.to baies ([0xA5  0x35  0x01  0xDB])) ser.close  Q
cv2.destrovAl l fi'indows  Q print ('Stopped)

= just in case ser.close Q
cv2.destrovAl l fi'indows Q
```

Results

The script polls the thermal imaging matrix and outputs the frames to the monitor console on which the Raspberry PI is connected, four times per second. This is enough not to experience significant discomfort when shooting objects. To visualize the frame, the OpenCV package is used. When the "s" button is pressed, the thermal imaging "heat maps" in jpg format are saved in the folder with the script.

For more information, I deduced the minimum and maximum temperatures on the frame. That is, looking at the color, you can see what approximately the temperature of the most heated or chilled objects. The measurement error is approximately a degree with a larger side. The thermal range is set from 20 to 40 degrees. Exit the script by pressing Ctrl + C.

The script works approximately the same on both the Raspberry Pi Zero W and the Pi 3 B +. I installed the VNC server on the smartphone. Thus, picking up raspberries connected to a power bank and a smartphone with VNC running, you can get a portable thermal imager with the ability to save thermal images. Perhaps this is not entirely convenient, but quite functional. After the first start, an incorrect measurement of the maximum temperature is possible. In this case, you need to exit the script and rerun it.

That is all for today. The experiment with a home-made thermal imager turned out to be successful. With the helping of this device, it is quite possible to conduct a thermal imaging inspection of the house on your own, for example.

Due to the lower temperature contrast than indoors, the pictures were not very informative. In the photo above, the whole house is on two sides. On the bottom - photos of different windows.

In the code, I changed only the temperature range. Instead of +20 ... + 40, I set -10 ... + 5.

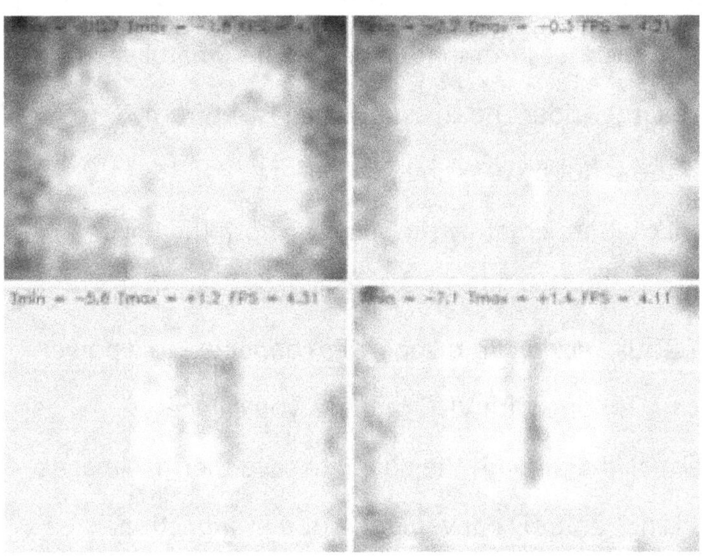

Finding a Free Parking Space with Python

I live in a proper city. But, like in many others, the search for a parking space always turns into a test. Free spaces quickly occupy, and even if you have your own, it will be difficult for friends to call you because they will have nowhere to park.

So I decided to point the camera out the window and use deep learning so that my computer tells me when the space is available:

It may sound complicated, but writing a working prototype with deep learning is quick and easy. All the necessary components are already there - you just need to know where to find them and how to put them together.

So let's have some fun and write an accurate free parking notification system using Python and deep learning

Decomposing the task

When we have a difficult task that we want to solve with the help of machine learning, the first step is to break it down into a sequence of simple tasks. Then we can use various tools to solve each of them. By combining several simple solutions, we get a system that is capable of something complex.

Here is how I broke my task:

The video stream from the webcam directed to the window enters the conveyor input: Through the pipeline, we will transmit each frame of the video, one at a time.

The first point is to recognize all the possible parking spaces in the frame. Before we can look for unoccupied places, we need to understand in which parts of the image there is parking.

Then on each frame you need to find all the cars. This will allow us to track the movement of each machine from frame to frame.

The third step is to determine which places are occupied by machines and which are not. To do this, combine the results of the first two steps.

Finally, the program should send an alert when the parking space becomes free. This will be determined by changes in the location of the machines between the frames of the video.

Each of the step can be completed in different ways using different technologies. There is no single right or wrong way to compose this conveyor: different approaches will have their advantages and disadvantages. Let's deal with each step in more detail.

We recognize parking spaces

Here is what our camera sees:

We need to scan this image somehow and get a list of places to park:

The solution "in the forehead" would be to simply hardcode the locations of all parking spaces manually instead of automatically recognizing them. But in this case, if we move the camera or want to look for parking spaces on another street, we will have to do the whole procedure again. It sounds so-so, so let's look for an automatic way to recognize parking spaces.

Alternatively, you can search for parking meters in the image and assume that there is a parking space next to each of them:

However, with this approach, not everything is so smooth. Firstly, not every parking space has a parking meter, and indeed, we are more interested in finding parking spaces for which you do not have to pay. Secondly, the location of the parking meter does not tell us anything about where the parking space is, but it only allows us to make an assumption.

Another idea is to create an object recognition model that looks for parking space marks drawn on the road:

But this approach is so-so. Firstly, in my city, all such trademarks are very small and difficult to see at a distance, so it will be difficult to detect them using a computer. Secondly, the street is full of all sorts of other lines and marks. It will be challenging to separate parking marks from lane dividers and pedestrian crossings.

When you encounter a problem that at first glance seems complicated, take a few minutes to find another approach to solving the problem, which will help to circumvent some technical issues. What is the parking space? This is just a place where a car is parked for a long time. Perhaps we do not need to recognize parking spaces at all. Why don't we acknowledge only cars that have stood still for a long time and not assume that they are standing in a parking space?

In other words, parking spaces are located where cars stand for a long time:

Thus, if we can recognize the cars and find out which of them do not move between frames, we can guess where the parking spaces are. Simple as that - let's move on to recognizing cars!

Recognize cars

Recognizing cars on a video frame is a classic object recognition task. There are many machine learning approaches that we could use for recognition. Here are some of them in order from the "old school" to the "new school":

You can train the detector based on HOG (Histogram of Oriented Gradients, histograms of directional gradients) and walk it through the entire image to find all the cars. This old approach, which does not use deep learning, works relatively quickly but does not cope very well with machines located in different ways.

You can train a CNN-based detector (Convolutional Neural Network, a convolutional neural network) and walk through the entire image until you find all the cars. This approach works precisely, but not as efficiently since we need to scan the image several times using CNN to find all the machines. And although we can find machines located in different ways, we need much more training data than for a HOG detector.

You can use a new approach with deep learning like Mask R-CNN, Faster R-CNN, or YOLO, which combines the accuracy of CNN and a set of technical tricks that significantly increase the speed of recognition. Such models will work relatively quickly (on the GPU) if we have a lot of data for training the model.

In the general case, we need the simplest solution, which will work as it should and require the least amount of training data. This is not required to be the newest and fastest algorithm. However, specifically in our case, Mask R- CNN is a reasonable choice, even though it is unique and fast.

Mask R-C-N-N architecture is designed in such a way that it recognizes objects in the entire image, effectively spending resources, and does not use the sliding window approach. In other words, it works pretty fast. With a modern GPU, we can recognize objects in the video in high resolution at a speed of several frames per second. For our project, this should be enough.

Also, Mask R-CNN provides a lot of information about each recognized object. Most recognition algorithms return only a bounding box for each object. However, Mask R-CNN will not only give us the location of each object but also its outline (mask):

To train Mask R-CNN, we need a lot of images of the objects that we want to recognize. We could go outside, take pictures of cars, and mark them in photographs, which would require several days of work. Fortunately, cars are one of those objects that people often want to recognize, so several public datasets with images of cars already exist.

One of them is the popular SOCO dataset (short for Common Objects In Context), which has images annotated with object masks. This dataset contains over 12,000 images with already labeled machines. Here is an example image from the dataset:

Such data is excellent for training a model based on Mask R-CNN.

But hold the horses, there is news even better! We are not the first who wanted to train their model using the COCO dataset - many people had already done this before us and shared their results. Therefore, instead of training our model, we can take a ready-made one that can already recognize cars. For our project, we will use the open-sourcemodel from Matterport.

If we give the image from the camera to the input of this model, this is what we get already "out of the box":

The model recognized not only cars but also objects such as traffic lights and people. It's funny that she recognized the tree as a houseplant.

For each recognized object, the Mask R-CNN model returns four things:

Type of object detected (integer). The pre-trained COCO model can recognize 80 different everyday objects like cars and trucks. A complete list is available here.

The degree of confidence in the recognition results. The higher the number, the stronger the model is confident in the correct recognition of the object.

Abounding box for an object in the form of XY-coordinates of pixels in the image.

A "mask" that shows which pixels within the bounding box are part of the object. Using the mask data, you can find the outline of the object.

Below is the Python code for detecting the bounding box for machines using the pre-trained Mask R-CNN and OpenCV models:

```
import nump\' as up

import mrcnn config import mrcnn.utils
from mrcnn.model import ñlaskRCNN from pathli b import Path


= The corfi gur ati on that the flask-RCNN librm.' u41 l use. class
ñlaskRCNNCorfi g (mrcnn config Colt g.
    DUE   = " coco   retr ained model corifi g" EvfAGES PER GPL = 1
    GPL COLNT   1
    h     I CLASSES = 1 + 80= in the COCO dataset there are 80 classes +
    1 background class. DETECTION UHN CONFIDENCE = 0.6
```

= fi'e filter the list of r ecogniti on results so that on1\' cars remain. def get
car boxes (boxes class i ds).
    car boxes = Q

    for i box in enumerate (boxes).
        = If the found obj eO is not a car them skip it. if class ids [i] in [3 8
        6].
            car boxes.append (box) return up.array' (car boxes)

= The root direct α\' of the project. ROOT DIR = Path (".")

= Dir eO w.' for savi rig logs and trained model. ñIODEL DIR = ROOT DIR
 ." " logs"

* Locd path to the fi le with trained weights.
COCO ñIODEL PATH = ROOT DIR ." " mask rem coco.h5"

= Dourload COCO dataset if necessary'. if not COCO ñIODEL
PATH.exists Q.
    mrcnn.utils.dourload trained weights (COCO ñIODEL PATH)

= Dir eO w.' with images for processing. EvfAGE DIR = ROOT DIR ."
 "images"

= \'i deo fi le or camera for processing - insert a vd ue of 0 if you want to use a
cam era not a video file. VIDEO SOFF CE   " test images ." parking.m@"

= Create a flask-RCNN model in output mode.
model = ñlaskR W U (mode = " inference" model dir = ñIODEL DIR corifi g
= ñlaskR C UCorifi g Q)

= Dourload the pre-train ed model.
modd. l oad weights (COCO ñIODEL PATH b\' name = True)

* Locati αi of parking spaces.
pznked cr boies=hone

```python
# Download the video file for which we want to run recognition.
video_capture = cv2.VideoCapture (VIDEO_SOURCE)

# We loop through each frame.
while video_capture.isOpened ():
    success, frame = video_capture.read ()
    if not success:
        break

    # Convert the image from the BGR color model (used by OpenCV) to RGB.
    rgb_image = frame [:, :, ::-1]

    # We supply the image of the Mask R-CNN model to get the result.
    results = model.detect ([rgb_image], verbose = 0)

    # Mask R-CNN assumes that we recognize objects in multiple images.
    # We transmitted only one image, so we extract only the first result.
    r = results [0]

    # The variable r now contains recognition results:
    # - r ['rois'] - bounding box for each recognized object.
    # - r ['class_ids'] - identifier (type) of the object.
    # - r ['scores'] - degree of confidence.
    # - r ['masks'] - masks of objects (which gives you their outline).

    # Filter the result to get the scope of the car.
    car_boxes = get_car_boxes (r ['rois'], r ['class_ids'])

    print ("Cars found in frame of video:")

    # Display each frame on the frame.
    for box in car_boxes:
        print ("Car", box)

        y1, x1, y2, x2 = box

        # Draw a frame.
        cv2.rectangle (frame, (x1, y1), (x2, y2), (0, 255, 0), 1)

    # Show the frame on the screen.
    cv2.imshow ('Video', frame)

    # Press 'q' to exit.
    if cv2.waitKey (1) & 0xFF == ord ('q'):
        break

# We clear everything after completion.
video_capture.release ()
cv2.destroyAllWindows ()
```

After running this script, an image with a frame around each detected machine will appear on the screen: Also, the coordinates of each machine will be displayed in the console:

Cars found in frame of video:
Car: [492 871 551 961]
Car: [450 819 509 913]
Car: [411 774 470 856]

So we learned to recognize cars in the image.

We recognize empty parking spaces

We know the pixel coordinates of each machine. Looking through several consecutive frames, we can quickly determine which of the cars did not move and assume that there are parking spaces. But how to understand that the car left the parking lot?

The problem is that the frames of the machines partially overlap each other:

Therefore, if you imagine that each frame represents a parking space, it may turn out that it is partially occupied by the machine, when in fact it is empty. We need to find a way to measure the degree of intersection of two objects to search only for the "most empty" frames.

We will use a measure called Intersection Over Union (ratio of intersection area to total area) or IoU. IoU can be found by calculating the number of pixels where two objects intersect and divide by the number of pixels occupied by these objects:

So we can understand how the very bounding frame of the car intersects with the frame of the parking space. make it easy to determine if parking is free. If the IoU is low, like 0.15, then the car takes up a small part of the parking space. And if it is high, like 0.6, then this means that the car takes up most of the space and you can't park there.

Since IoU is used quite often in computer vision, it is very likely that the corresponding libraries implement this measure. In our library Mask R-CNN, it is implemented as a function mrcnn.utils.compute_overlaps ().

If we have a list of bounding boxes for parking spaces, you can add a check for the presence of cars in this framework by adding a whole line or two of code:

```
# Filter the result to get the scope of the car.
car_boxes = get_car_boxes (r ['rois'], r ['class_ids'])

# We look how much cars intersect with well-known parking spaces.
overlaps = mrcnn.utils.compute_overlaps (car_boxes, parking_areas)

print (overlaps)
```

The result should look something like this:

```
[
[1. 0.07040032 0. 0.]
[0.07040032 1. 0.07673165 0.]
[0. 0. 0.02332112 0.]
]
```

In this two-dimensional array, each row reflects one frame of the parking space. And each column indicates how strongly each of the places intersects with one of the detected machines. A result of 1.0 means that the entire space is entirely occupied by the car, and a low value like 0.02 indicates that the car has climbed into place a little, but you can still park on it.

To find unoccupied places, you just need to check each row in this array. If all numbers are close to zero, then most likely, the place is free!

However, keep in mind that object recognition does not always work correctly with real-time video. Although the model based on Mask R-CNN is wholly accurate, from time to time, it may miss a car or two in one frame of the video. Therefore, before asserting that the place is free, you need to make sure that it remains so for the next 5-10 next frames of video. This way, we can avoid situations when the system mistakenly marks a place empty due to a glitch in one frame of the video. As soon as we make sure that the place remains free for several frames, you can send a message!

Send SMS

The last part of our conveyor is sending SMS notifications when a free parking space appears.

Sending a message from Python is very easy if you use Twilio.

Twilio is an accessible API that allows you to send SMS from almost any programming language with just a few lines of code.

Of course, if you prefer a different service, you can use it. I have nothing to do with Twilio: it's just the first thing that come to brain .

To using Twilio, sign-up for a trial account, create a Twilio phone number, and get your account authentication information. Then install the client library:

```
pip install twilio
```

After that, use the following code to send the message:

```python
from twilio.rest import Client

# Twilio account details
twilio_account_sid = 'Your Twilio SID'
twilio_auth_token = 'Your Twilio Authentication Token'
twilio_source_phone_number = 'Your Twilio Phone Number'

# Create a Twilio client object
client = Client (twilio_account_sid, twilio_auth_token)

# Send SMS
message = client.messages.create (
    body = "Message body",
    from_ = twilio_source_phone_number,
    to = "Your number where the message will come"
)
```

To add the ability to send messages to our script, just copy this code there. However, you need make sure that the message is not sent on every frame, where you can see the free space. Therefore, we will have a flag that in the installed state will not allow sending messages for some time or until another place is vacated.

Putting it all together

```python
import numpy as np
import cv2
import mrcnn.config
import mrcnn.utils
```

```python
from mrcnn.model import MaskRCNN
from pathlib import Path
from twilio.rest import Client

# The configuration that the Mask-RCNN library will use.
class MaskRCNNConfig (mrcnn.config.Config):
    NAME = "coco_pretrained_model_config"
    IMAGES_PER_GPU = 1
    GPU_COUNT = 1
    NUM_CLASSES = 1 + 80 # in the COCO dataset there are 80 classes + 1 background class.
    DETECTION_MIN_CONFIDENCE = 0.6

# We filter the list of recognition results so that only cars remain.
def get_car_boxes (boxes, class_ids):
    car_boxes = []

    for i, box in enumerate (boxes):
        # If the found object is not a car, then skip it.
        if class_ids [i] in [3, 8, 6]:
            car_boxes.append (box)

    return np.array (car_boxes)

# Twilio configuration.
twilio_account_sid = 'Your Twilio SID'
twilio_auth_token = 'Your Twilio Authentication Token'
twilio_phone_number = 'Your Twilio Phone Number'
destination_phone_number = 'Number where the message will come'
client = Client (twilio_account_sid, twilio_auth_token)

# The root directory of the project.
ROOT_DIR = Path (".")

# Directory for saving logs and trained model.
MODEL_DIR = ROOT_DIR / "logs"

# Local path to the file with trained weights.
COCO_MODEL_PATH = ROOT_DIR / "mask_rcnn_coco.h5"

# Download COCO dataset if necessary.
if not COCO_MODEL_PATH.exists ():
    mrcnn.utils.download_trained_weights (COCO_MODEL_PATH)

# Directory with images for processing.
IMAGE_DIR = ROOT_DIR / "images"

# Video file or camera for processing - insert the value 0 if using a camera, not a video file.
VIDEO_SOURCE = "test_images / parking.mp4"

# Create a Mask-RCNN model in output mode.
model = MaskRCNN (mode = "inference", model_dir = MODEL_DIR, config = MaskRCNNConfig ())

# Download the pre-trained model.
model.load_weights (COCO_MODEL_PATH, by_name = True)
```

Location of parking spaces.

parked_car_boxes= None

    Douml oad the st deo file for vhlch ve vant t D run recDgM ti or.
video_capture = eve.\'ideoCapture /fiDE O_S OURCE)

.=. How' mans' frames in a row' math an mnpR.' place we have already' seen.
free space frames = 0

.=. Have w'e d ready sent SMS?
sms sent = Fd se

  "e l cop thfDugh each frame.
whil e s4 deD Capture.isOpened 0
    success, frame = video_capture.read ()
    if not success:
       break

    Corivert the image from the BGR col or model to RGB .
rgb_ mage = frame [.... .: − I]

    # fi'e supply' the image of the flask R—Ch   model to get the result.
results = mDdel.detect ([r gb image], s erbDse = 0)

    flask R-CA assumes that 'e recognize objects in multiple images.
= fi'e tr aris iitted onl>' one imag e, sD we extract Ofll\' the fir st result.
  r = results [0]

= The variable r now' contains recogniti on results.
   = - r rois'] - bounding box for each recognized object:
    - r class ids'] - identifier (type) of the object:
     - r § scar est - degree Df cDn 1 dence:
= -r masks   masks of objects ('hich gi yes von their outline).

  if parked car boxes i s None:
    = Thi s is the first frame Df the videD - let's say' that all detected cars are in the parking l ot.
   = Save the locad on of each car as a parking space and move on tD the next fratne.
    parked_car_boxes = get_car_boxes (• L•ois'], r cl ass_i ds'])
  else:
    = XVe dread>' knor' where the places are. Check if there are an>'.

    = U'e ar e l DDki fly for KOf.S Dn the oirr cut fram e.
    car_boxes = get_car_boxes (r ['r<x sd . L+   '])

     1'e l Dok hDT' rauch these cars I ntersect a'tth 'ell -knDTW parking
     DS'erl aps = rarcnn.uti ls.co tpute_a'erl aps {parked_car_bDxes, car_boxes)

    = XVe assume that there are no emph.' seats until 'e find at l east one.
    free_space = Fal se

    = XVe go through the cycle for each well-known parking space.
    fa parking_area. overl ap_areas in zip (parked_car_boxes. overl aps):

```python
        # Here we look for the maximum value of the intersection with any detected
        # car in the frame by the machine (no matter which).
        max_IoU_overlap = np.max(overlap_areas)


    # We get the upper left and lower right coordinates of the parking space.
    y1, x1, y2, x2 = parking_area

        # Check if space is free by checking the IoU value.
        if max_IoU_overlap < 0.15:
            # Place is free! Draw a green frame around it.
            cv2.rectangle(frame, (x1, y1), (x2, y2), (0, 255, 0), 3)
            # We note that we found at least it is free space.
            free_space = True
        else:
            # The place is still taken - we draw a red frame.
            cv2.rectangle(frame, (x1, y1), (x2, y2), (0, 0, 255), 1)

        # Write the IoU value inside the frame.
        font = cv2.FONT_HERSHEY_DUPLEX
        cv2.putText(frame, f"{max_IoU_overlap:0.2}", (x1 + 6, y2 - 6), font, 0.3, (255, 255, 255))

    # If at least one place was free, we begin to count frames
    # This is to make sure that the place is really free
    # and do not send another notification.
    if free_space:
        free_space_frames += 1
    else:
        # If everything is busy, reset the counter.
        free_space_frames = 0

    # If the place is free for several frames, we can say that it is free.
    if free_space_frames > 10:
        # Display SPACE AVAILABLE !! at the top of the screen.
        font = cv2.FONT_HERSHEY_DUPLEX
        cv2.putText(frame, f"SPACE AVAILABLE!", (10, 150), font, 3.0, (0, 255, 0), 2, cv2.FILLED)

        # Send a message if you have not done so already.
        if not sms_sent:
            print("SENDING SMS !!!")
            message = client.messages.create(
                body="Parking space open - go go go!",
                from_=twilio_phone_number,
                to=destination_phone_number
            )
            sms_sent = True

    # Show the frame on the screen.
    cv2.imshow('Video', frame)

    # Press 'q' to exit.
    if cv2.waitKey(1) & 0xFF == ord('q'):
        break

# Press 'q' to exit.
video_capture.release()
cv2.destroyAllWindows()
```

To run that code, you first need to install Python 3.6+, Matterport Mask R-CNN, and OpenCV.

I specifically wrote the code as simple as possible. For example, if he sees in the first frame of the car, he concludes that they are all parked. Try experiment with it and see if you can improve its reliability.

Just by changing the identifiers of the objects that the model is looking for, you can turn the code into something completely different. For example, imagine that you are working at a ski resort. After making a couple of changes, you can turn this script into a system that automatically recognizes snowboarders jumping from a ramp and records videos with cool jumps. Or, if you work in a nature reserve, you can create a system that counts zebras. You are limited only by your imagination.

Creating games on the Pygame framework | Part 1

Hi, Python lover!

This is the first of a third-part tutorial on creating games using Python 3 and Pygame. In the second part, we examined the class TextObjectused to render text to the screen is created to the main window, and learned how to draw objects: bricks, ball, and racket.

In this part, we will the dive deeper into the heart of Breakout, and learn how to handle events, get acquainted with the main Breakout class, and see how to move various objects in the game.

Event handling

Breakout has three types of events: keystroke events, mouse events, and timer events. The main loop in the Game class handles keystrokes and mouse events and passes them to subscribers (by calling a handler function).

Although the Game class is very general and does not have knowledge about Breakout implementation, the subscription and event handling methods are very specific.

Breakout class

The Breakout class implements most of the knowledge about how Breakout is controlled. In this tutorial series, we will meet the Breakout class several times. Here are the lines that various event handlers register.

It should be noted that all key events (for both the left and right "arrows") are transmitted to one racket handler method.

```python
# Register the handle_mouse_event () method of the button object
self.mouse_handlers.append (b.handle_mouse_event)

# Register racket handle () method for handling key events
self.keydown_handlers [pygame.K_LEFT] .append (paddle.handle)
self.keydown_handlers [pygame.K_RIGHT] .append (paddle.handle)
self.keyup_handlers [pygame.K_LEFT] .append (paddle.handle)
self.keyup_handlers [pygame.K_RIGHT] .append (paddle.handle)
```

Keystroke handling

The Game class calls registered handlers for each key event and passes the key. Note that this is not a Paddle

class. Into Breakout, the only object that is interested in such events is a racket. When you press or release a key, its method is handle()called. The Paddle object does not need to know if this was a key press or release event, because it controls the current state using a pair of Boolean variables: moving_left and moving_right. If moving_left True, it means that the "left" key was pressed, and the next event will be the release of the key, which will reset the variable. The same applies to the right key. The logic is simple and consists of switching the state of these variables in response to any event.

```python
def handle (self, key):
    if key == pygame.K_LEFT:
        self.moving_left = not self.moving_left
    else:
        self.moving_right = not self.moving_right
```

Mouse event handling

Breakout has a game menu that we will meet soon. The menu button controls various mouse events, such as movement and button presses (mouse down and mouse up events). In the response to these events, the button updates the internal state variable. Here is the mouse processing code:

```python
def handle_mouse_event (self, type, pos):
    if type == pygame.MOUSEMOTION:
        self.handle_mouse_move (pos)
    elif type == pygame.MOUSEBUTTONDOWN:
        self.handle_mouse_down (pos)
    elif type == pygame.MOUSEBUTTONUP:
        self.handle_mouse_up (pos)

def handle_mouse_move (self, pos):
    if self.bounds.collidepoint (pos):
        if self.state! = 'pressed':
            self.state = 'hover'
    else:
        self.state = 'normal'

def handle_mouse_down (self, pos):
    if self.bounds.collidepoint (pos):
        self.state = 'pressed'

def handle_mouse_up (self, pos):
    if self.state == 'pressed':
        self.on_click (self)
        self.state = 'hover'
```

Notice that the method handle_mouse_event() registered to receive mouse events checks the type of event and redirects it to the appropriate method that processes this type of event.

Handling Timer Events

Timer events are not processed in the main loop. However, since the main loop is called in each frame, it is easy to check whether the time has come for a particular event. You will see this later when we discuss temporary special effects.

Another situation is the need to pause the game. For example, when displaying a message that the player must read and so that nothing distracts him. The show_message()Breakout class method takes this approach and to calls time.sleep(). Here is the relevant code:

```python
import config as c

class Breakout (Game):
    def show_message (self,
            text,
            color = colors.WHITE,
            font_name = 'Arial',
            font_size = 20,
            centralized = False):
        message = TextObject (c.screen_width // 2,
                c.screen_height // 2,
                lambda: text, color,
                font_name, font_size)
        self.draw ()
        message.draw (self.surface, centralized)
        pygame.display.update ()
        time.sleep (c.message_duration)
```

Game process

Gameplay (gameplay) is where the Breakout rules come into play. The gameplay consists in moving various objects in response to events and in changing the state of the game based on their interactions.

Moving racket

You saw earlier that the Paddle class responds to arrow keys by updating its

fields *moving_left* and *moving_right*. The movement itself occurs in a method *update()*. Certain calculations are performed here if the racket is close to the left or right edge of the screen. We do not want the racket to go beyond the boundaries of the screen (taking into account a given offset).

Therefore, if the movement moves the object beyond the borders, then the code adjusts the movement so that it stops right at the border. Since the racket only moves horizontally to the vertical component of the movement is always zero.

```python
import pygame

import config as c
from game_object import GameObject


class Paddle(GameObject):
    def __init__(self, x, y, w, h, color, offset):
        GameObject.__init__(self, x, y, w, h)
        self.color = color
        self.offset = offset
        self.moving_left = False
        self.moving_right = False

    ...

    def update(self):
        if self.moving_left:
            dx = -(min(self.offset, self.left))
        elif self.moving_right:
            dx = min(self.offset, c.screen_width - self.right)
        else:
            return

        self.move(dx, 0)
```

Moving ball

The ball simply uses the functionality of the base class
GameObject, which moves objects based on their speed (its
horizontal and vertical components). As we will soon see, the
speed of a ball is determined by many factors in the Breakout
class. Since the movement consists simply of adding speed to the
current position, the direction in which the ball moves is
completely determined by the speed along the horizontal and
vertical axes.

Setting the initial speed of the ball

The Breakout ball comes out of nowhere at the very beginning of
the game every time a player loses his life. It simply materializes

from the ether and begins to fall either exactly down or at a slight angle. When the ball is created in the method create_ball(), it gets the speed with a random horizontal component in the range from - 2 to 2 and the vertical component specified in the config.py module (the default value is 3).

```python
def create_ball (self):
    speed = (random.randint (-2, 2), c.ball_speed)
    self.ball = Ball (c.screen_width // 2,
                c.screen_height // 2,
                c.ball_radius,
                c.ball_color,
                speed)
    self.objects.append (self.ball)
```

Summarize

In this part, we looked at handling events such as keystrokes, mouse movements, and mouse clicks. We also examined some elements of Breakout gameplay: moving the racket, moving the ball, and controlling the speed of the ball.

In the fourth part, we will consider the important topic of collision recognition and see what happens when the ball hits different game objects: a racket, bricks, walls, ceiling, and floor. Then we will pay attention to the game menu. We will create our buttons, which we use as a menu, and will be able to show and hide if necessary.

Creating games on the Pygame framework | Part 2

This is the Second of a Thired-part tutorial on the creating games using Python 3 and Pygame. In the third part, we delved to the heart of Breakout, and learned how to handle events, got acquainted within the main Breakout class and saw how to move different game objects.

In this part, we will learn the how to recognize collisions and what happens to when a ball hits different object: a racket, bricks, walls, ceiling, and floor. Finally, we will look at the important topic of the user interface, and in particular, how to create the menu from your buttons.

Collision Recognition

In games, the objects collide with each other, and Breakout is no exception. The ball is collides with objects. The main method handle_ball_collisions()has a built-in function is called intersect()that is used to the check whether the ball hit the object and where it collided with the object. It returns 'left,' 'right,' 'top,' 'bottom,' or None if the ball does not collide with an object.

```python
def handle_ball_collisions (self):
    def intersect (obj, ball):
        edges = dict (
            left = Rect (obj.left, obj.top, 1, obj.height),
            right = Rect (obj.right, obj.top, 1, obj.height),
            top = Rect (obj.left, obj.top, obj.width, 1),
            bottom = Rect (obj.left, obj.bottom, obj.width, 1))
        collisions = set (edge for edge, rect in edges.items () if
                ball.bounds.colliderect (rect))
        if not collisions:
            return none

        if len (collisions) == 1:
            return list (collisions) [0]

        if 'top' in collisions:
            if ball.centery> = obj.top:
                return 'top'
            if ball.centerx < obj.left:
                return 'left'
            else:
                return 'right'

        if 'bottom' in collisions:
            if ball.centery> = obj.bottom:
                return 'bottom'
            if ball.centerx < obj.left:
                return 'left'
            else:
                return 'right'
```

Collision of a ball with a racket.

When the ball hit the racket, it bounces. If it hit the top of the racket, it bounces back up, but retains same components horizontal fast speed.

But if he hit the side of the racket, it bounces to the opposite side (right or left) and continues to move down until it hits the floor. The code uses a function intersect().

```python
# Kick on the racket
s = self.ball.speed
edge = intersect (self.paddle, self.ball)
if edge is not None:
    self.sound_effects ['paddle_hit'].play ()
if edge == 'top':
 speed_x = s [0]
 speed_y = -s [1]
 if self.paddle.moving_left:
  speed_x -= 1
 elif self.paddle.moving_left:
  speed_x += 1
 self.ball.speed = speed_x, speed_y
elif edge in ('left', 'right'):
 self.ball.speed = (-s [0], s [1])
```

Collision with the floor.

The ball hits to the racket from the side, the ball continues fall and then hits the floor. At this moment, the player to loses his life and the ball is recreated so that game can continue. The game ends when player runs out of life.

```python
# Hit the floor
if self.ball.top> c.screen_height:
    self.lives -= 1
 if self.lives == 0:
  self.game_over = True
 else:
  self.create_ball ()
```

Collision with ceiling and walls

When a ball hits the wall or ceiling, it simply bounces off them.

```python
# Hit the ceiling
if self.ball.top <0:
    self.ball.speed = (s [0], -s [1])

# Kick against the wall
if self.ball.left <0 or self.ball.right> c.screen_width:
 self.ball.speed = (-s [0], s [1])
```

Collision with bricks

When ball hits a brick, this is the main event the Breakout game - the brick disappeared, the player receives a point, the ball bounce back, and several more events occur (sound effect, and sometimes a special effect), which we will consider later.

To determine that the ball has hit a brick, the code will check if any of the bricks intersects with the ball:

```
#Bump on a brick
for brick in self.bricks:
    edge = intersect (brick, self.ball)
if not edge
 continue

self.bricks.remove (brick)
self.objects remove (brick)
self.score + = self.points_per_brick

if edge in ('top', 'bottom'):
 self.ball speed = (s [0], -s [1])
else:
 self.ball speed = (-s [0], s [1])
```

Game Menu Design Program

Most games have some kind of U.I. Breakout has simple menu with two buttons, 'PLAY' and 'QUIT.' The menu is display at the beginning of the game and disappears when the player clicks on 'PLAY.'

Let's see how the button and menu are implemented, as well as how they integrate into the game.

Button Creation

Pygame has no built-in UI library. The third-party extensions, but for the menu, we decided to create our buttons. that has three states: normal, highlighted, and press. The normal state when the mouse is not above the buttons, and the highlight state is when the mouse is above the button, the left mouse button not yet press. The press state is when the mouse is above the button, and the player pressed the left mouse button.

The buttons implement as a rectangle with a back ground color and text display on top of it. The button also receive the (onclick function), which is called when the button is clicked.

```python
import pygame

from game_object import GameObject
from text_object import TextObject
import config as c


class Button (GameObject):
    def __init__(self,
                 x,
                 y,
                 w,
                 h,
                 text,
                 on_click = lambda x: None,
                 padding = 0):
        super().__init__(x, y, w, h)
        self.state = 'normal'
        self.on_click = on_click

        self.text = TextObject(x + padding,
                   y + padding, lambda: text,
                   c.button_text_color,
                   c.font_name,
                   c.font_size)

    def draw(self, surface):
        pygame.draw.rect(surface,
                   self.back_color,
                   self.bounds)
        self.text.draw(surface)
```

The button process its own mouse events and changes its internal state based on these events. When the button is in the press state and receives the event *MOUSE BUTTONUP*, this means that the player has press the button and the function is called *on _ click()*.

```
def handle_mouse_event (self, type, pos):
    if type == pygame.MOUSEMOTION:
        self.handle_mouse_move (pos)
    elif type == pygame.MOUSEBUTTONDOWN:
        self.handle_mouse_down (pos)
    elif type == pygame.MOUSEBUTTONUP:
        self.handle_mouse_up (pos)

def handle_mouse_move (self, pos):
    if self.bounds.collidepoint (pos):
        if self.state! = 'pressed':
            self.state = 'hover'
    else:
        self.state = 'normal'

def handle_mouse_down (self, pos):
    if self.bounds.collidepoint (pos):
        self.state = 'pressed'

def handle_mouse_up (self, pos):
    if self.state == 'pressed':
        self.on_click (self)
        self.state = 'hover'
```

The property *back _ color* used to draw on the background rectangle to always returns the color corresponding to current form of the button, so that it is clear to the player that the button is active:

```
@property
def back_color (self):
    return dict (normal = c.button_normal_back_color,
        hover = c.button_hover_back_color,
        pressed = c.button_pressed_back_color) [self.state]
```

Menu Design

The function *create_menu* ()create a menu with two buttons with the text 'PLAY' and 'QUIT.' It has two built- in function, *on _* *play* ()and *on _ quit* ()which it pass to the correspond button. Each button is add to the list *objects* (for rendering), as well as in the field *menu _ buttons*.

```python
def create_menu (self):
    for i, (text, handler) in enumerate ((('PLAY', on_play),
                        ('QUIT', on_quit))):
        b = Button (c.menu_offset_x,
            c.menu_offset_y + (c.menu_button_h + 5) * i,
            c.menu_button_w,
            c.menu_button_h,
            text
            handler
            padding = 5)
    self.objects.append (b)
    self.menu_buttons.append (b)
    self.mouse_handlers.append (b.handle_mouse_event)
```

When PLAY the button is prese *onplay()*, a function is called that removes the button from the list *object* so that the no longer drawn. In adding, the values of the Boolean field that trigger the starting of the game - *is_gamerunningand startlevel*- Thats OK When the button is press, QUIT is _ game_ runningtakes on value (False)(in fact, pausing the game), it set game_ over to True, which triggers the sequence of completion of the game.

```python
def on_play (button):
    for b in self.menu_buttons
    self.objects.remove (b)

    self.is_game_running = True
    self.start_level = True

def on_quit (button):
    self.game_over = True
    self.is_game_running = False
```

Show and hide GameMenu

The display and hiding the menu are performed implicitly. When the buttons are in the list object, the menu is visible : when they removed, it is hidden. Everything is very simple.

Create built-in menu with its surface that renders its subcomponents (buttons and other objects) and then simply add or remove these menu components, but this is not required for such a simple menu.

To summarize

We examined the collision recognition and what happens when the ball collides with the different objects: a racket, bricks, walls, floor, and ceiling. We also created a menu with our buttons, which can be hidden and displayed on command.

In last part of the series, we will consider completion of the game, tracking points, and lives, sound effects, and music. We develop complex system of special effects that add few spices to game. Finally, we will the discuss further development and possible improvements.

Creating games on the Pygame framework| Part 3

This is the last of the Thired parts of the tutorial on creating games using Python 3 and PyGame. In the fourth part, we learned to recognize collisions, respond to the fact that the ball collides with different game objects, and created a game menu with its buttons.

In last part, we will look at various topics: the end of the game, managing lives and points, sound effects, music, and even a flexible system of special effects. For dessert, we will consider possible improvements and directions for further development.

End of the game

Sooner or later, the game should end. In this form of Breakout, the game ends in one of two ways: the player either loses all his life or destroys all the bricks. There is no next level in the game (but it can easily be added).

Game over!

The game_overclass of the Game class is set to False in the method init ()of the Game class. The main loop continues until the variable game_overchanges to True :

```python
class Game:
    def __init__ (self,
            caption
            width
            height
            back_image_filename,
            frame_rate):

        self.game_over = False


def run (self):
    while not self.game_over:
    self.surface.blit (self.background_image, (0, 0))

    self.handle_events ()
    self.update ()
    self.draw ()

    pygame.display.update ()
    self.clock.tick (self.frame_rate)
```

All this happens in the Breakout class in the following cases:

The player presses the QUIT button in the menu.

The player loses his last life.

The player destroys all bricks.

```python
def on_quit (button):
    self.game_over = True
self.is_game_running = False

def handle_ball_collisions (self):

    # Hit the floor
    if self.ball.top > c.screen_height:
    self.lives -= 1
    if self.lives == 0:
    self.game_over = True

        if not self.bricks:
            self.show_message ('YOU WIN !!!', centralized = True)
            self.is_game_running = False
            self.game_over = True
            return

def update (self):

    if not self.bricks:
    self.show_message ('YOU WIN !!!', centralized = True)
    self.is_game_running = False
    self.game_over = True
    return
```

Game End Message Display

Usually, at the end of the game, we do not want the game window to disappear silently. An exception is a case when we click on the QUIT button in the menu. When a player loses their last life, Breakout displays the traditional message 'GAME OVER!', And when the player wins, it shows the message 'YOU WIN!'

In both cases, the function is used show_message(). It displays text on top of the current screen (the game pauses) and waits a few seconds to before returning. The next iteration of the game loop, checking the field game_overwill determine that it is True, after which the program will end.

This is what the function looks like show_message():

```python
def show_message (self,
        text,
        color = colors.WHITE,
        font_name = 'Arial',
        font_size = 20,
        centralized = False):
    message = TextObject (c.screen_width // 2,
                c.screen_height // 2,
                lambda: text,
                color,
                font_name,
                font_size)
    self.draw ()
    message.draw (self.surface, centralized)
    pygame.display.update ()
    time.sleep (c.message_duration)
```

Saving records between games

In this version of the game, we do not save records, because there is only one level in it, and the results of all players after the destruction of the bricks will be the same. In general, saving records can be implemented locally, saving records to a file and displaying another message if a player breaks a record.

Adding Sound Effects and Music

Games are an audiovisual process. Many games have sound effects - short audio clips that are played when a player kills monsters finds a treasure, or a terrible death. Some games also have background music that contributes to the atmosphere. There are only sound effects in Breakout, but we will show you how to play music in your games.

Sound effects

To play sound effects, we need sound files (as is the case with image files). These files can be.wav, .mp3, or .ogg format. Breakout stores its sound effects in a folder sound_effects:

```
~/git/pygame-breakout> tree sound_effects/
sound_effects/
+-- brick_hit.wav
+-- effect_done.wav
+-- level_complete.wav
+-- paddle_hit.wav
```

Let's see how these sound effects load and play at the right time.

First, play sound effects (or background music), we need to initialize the Pygame sound system. This is done in the Game class:pygame.mixer.pre_init(44100, 16, 2, 4096)

Then, in the Breakout class, all sound effects are loaded from config into the object pygame mixer Soundand stored in the dictionary:

```python
# In config.py
sounds_effects = dict (
    brick_hit = 'sound_effects / brick_hit.wav',
    effect_done = 'sound_effects / effect_done.wav',
    paddle_hit = 'sound_effects / paddle_hit.wav',
    level_complete = 'sound_effects / level_complete.wav',
)

# In breakout.py
class Breakout (Game):
    def __init__(self):
        ...

        self.sound_effects = {
            name: pygame.mixer.Sound (sound)
            for name, sound in c.sounds_effects.items ()}
        ...
```

Now we can play sound effects when something interesting happens. For example, when a ball hits a brick:

```python
#Bump on a brick
for brick in self.bricks:
    edge = intersect (brick, self.ball)
    if not edge:
        continue

    self.sound_effects ['brick_hit']. play ()
```

The sound effect is played asynchronously: that is, the game does not stop while it is playing. Several sound effects can be played at the same time.

Record your sound effects and messages

Recording your sound effects can be a simple and fun experience. Unlike creating visual resources, it does not require much talent. Anyone can say "Boom!" or "Jump," or shout, "They killed you. Get lucky another time! "

Playing background music

Background music should play continuously. Theoretically, a very long sound effect can be created, but the looped background music is most often used. Music files can be in .wav, .mp3, or .midi format. Here's how the music is implemented:

```
music = pygame.mixer.music.load ('background_music.mp3')
pygame.mixer.music.play (-1, 0.0)
```

Only one background music can play at a time. However, several sound effects can be played on top of background music. This is what is called mixing.

Adding Advanced Features

Let's do something curious. It is interesting to destroy bricks with a ball, but it quickly bothers. What about the overall special effects system? We will develop an extensible special effects system associated with some bricks, which is activated when the ball hits the brick.

This is what the plan will be. Effects have a lifetime. The effect begins when the brick collapses and ends when the effect expires. What happens if the ball hits another brick with a special effect? In theory, you can create compatible effects, but to simplify everything in the original implementation, the active effect will stop, and a new effect will take its place.,

Special effects system

In the most general case, a special effect can be defined as two purposes. The first role activates the effect, and the second reset it. We want attach effects to bricks and give the player a clear understanding of which bricks special , so they can try to hit them or avoid them at certain points.

Our special effects are determined by the dictionary from the module breakout.py. Each effect has a name (for example, long_paddle) and a value that consists of a brick color, as well as two functions. Functions are defined a lambda functions that take a Game instance, which includes everything that can change the special effect in Breakout.

```python
special_effects = dict (
    long_paddle = (
        colors.ORANGE,
        lambda g: g.paddle.bounds.inflate_ip (
                c.paddle_width // 2, 0),
        lambda g: g.paddle.bounds.inflate_ip (
                -c.paddle_width // 2, 0)),
    slow_ball = (
        colors.AQUAMARINE2,
        lambda g: g.change_ball_speed (-1),
        lambda g: g.change_ball_speed (1)),
    tripple_points = (
        colors.DARKSEAGREEN4,
        lambda g: g.set_points_per_brick (3),
        lambda g: g.set_points_per_brick (1)),
    extra_life = (
        colors.GOLD1,
        lambda g: g.add_life (),
        lambda g: None))
```

When creating bricks, they can be assigned one of the special
effects. Here is the code:

```python
def create_bricks (self):
    w = c.brick_width
    h = c.brick_height
    brick_count = c.screen_width // (w + 1)
    offset_x = (c.screen_width - brick_count * (w + 1)) // 2

    bricks = []
    for row in range (c.row_count):
        for col in range (brick_count):
            effect = None
            brick_color = c.brick_color
            index = random.randint (0, 10)
            if index < len (special_effects):
                x = list (special_effects.values ()) [index]
                brick_color = x [0]
                effect = x [1:]

            brick = Brick (offset_x + col * (w + 1),
                    c.offset_y + row * (h + 1),
                    w,
                    h,
                    brick_color,
                    effect)
            bricks.append (brick)
            self.objects.append (brick)
    self.bricks = bricks
The Brick class has an
```

effect field, which usually has the value None, but (with a probability of 30%) may contain one of the special effects defined above. Note that this code does not know what effects exist. He simply receives the effect and color of the brick and, if necessary, assigns them.

In this version of Breakout, we only trigger effects when we hit a brick, but you can come up with other options for triggering events. The previous effect is discarded (if it existed), and then a new effect is launched. The reset function and effect start time are stored for future use.

```python
if brick.special_effect is not None:
    # Reset the previous effect, if any
    if self.reset_effect is not None:
        self.reset_effect (self)

    # Triggering a special effect
    self.effect_start_time = datetime.now ()
    brick.special_effect [0] (self)
    # Setting the current effect reset function
    self.reset_effect = brick.special_effect [1]
```

If the new effect is not launched, we still need to reset the current effect after its lifetime. This happens in the method update(). In each frame, a function to reset the current effect is assigned to the field reset_effect. If the time after starting the current effect exceeds the duration of the effect, then the function is called reset_effect(), and the field reset_effecttakes the value None (meaning that there are currently no active effects).

```python
# Reset special effect if necessary
if self.reset_effect:
    elapsed = datetime.now () - self.effect_start_time
    if elapsed >= timedelta (seconds = c.effect_duration):
        self.reset_effect (self)
        self.reset_effect = None
```

Racket increase

The effect of a long racket is to increase the racket by 50%. Its reset function returns the racket to its normal size. The brick has the color Orange.:

```python
long_paddle = (
    colors.ORANGE,
    lambda g: g.paddle.bounds.inflate_ip (
        c.paddle_width // 2, 0),
    lambda g: g.paddle.bounds.inflate_ip (
        -c.paddle_width // 2, 0)),
```

Ball slowdown

Another effect that helps in chasing the ball is slowing the ball, that is, reducing its speed by one unit. The brick has an Aquamarine color.

```python
slow_ball = (colors.AQUAMARINE2,
    lambda g: g.change_ball_speed (-1),
    lambda g: g.change_ball_speed (1)),
```

More points

If you want great results, then you will like the effect of tripling points, giving three points for each destroyed brick instead of the standard one point. The brick is dark green.

```
tripple_points = (colors.DARKSEAGREEN4,
      lambda g: g.set_points_per_brick (3),
      lambda g: g.set_points_per_brick (1)),
```

Extra lives

Finally, a very useful effect will be the effect of extra lives. He just gives you another life. It does not need a reset. The brick has a gold color.

```
extra_life = (colors.GOLD1,
      lambda g: g.add_life (),
      lambda g: None))
```

Future Features

There are several logical directions for expanding Breakout. If you are interested in trying on yourself in adding new features and functions, here are a few ideas.

Go to the next level

To turn Breakout into a serious game, you need levels: one is not enough. At the beginning of each level, we will reset the screen, but save points and lives. To complicate the game, you can slightly increase the speed of the ball at each level or add another layer of bricks.

Second ball

The effect of temporarily adding a second ball will create enormous chaos. The difficulty here is to treat both balls as equal, regardless of which one is the original. When one ball disappears, the game continues with the only remaining. Life is not lost.

Lasting records

When you have levels with increasing difficulty, it is advisable to create a high score table. You can store records in a file so that they are saved after the game. When a player breaks a record, you can add small pizzas or let him write a name (traditionally with only three characters).

Bombs and bonuses

In the current implementation on, all special effects are associated with bricks, but you can add effects (good and bad) falling from the sky, which the player can collect or avoid.

Summarize

Developing Breakout with Python 3 and Pygame has proven to be an enjoyable experience. This is a compelling combination for creating 2D games (and for 3D games too). If you love Python and want to create your games, then do not hesitate to choose Pygame.

Object-Oriented Programming (OOP) in Python 3

Algorithms and data structures

Hi, Python lover!

<u>Table of contents</u>

What is object-oriented programming (OOP)?

Python classes

Python Object (Instances)

How to define class in Python Instance Attribute Class Attributes

Object CreationWhat's it? Exercise Overview (# 1)

Instance MethodsChanging Attributes

Python object inheritance Example of a dog park Expansion of parent class functionality Parent and child classes Overriding parent class functionality Exercise overview (# 2)

Conclusion

you will become familiars with the following basic concepts of OOP in Python:

Python Classes

Object Instances

Definition and work with methods

OOP Inheritance

What is object-oriented programming (OOP)?

Object-oriented programming, or, in short, OOP, is a programming paradigm that provides a means of structuring programs in such a way that properties and behavior are combined into separate objects.

For example, an object can represent a person with a name, age, address, etc., with behaviors such as walking, talking, breathing, and running. Or an email with properties such as a recipient list, subject, body, etc., as well as with behaviors such as adding attachments and sending.

In other words, object-oriented programming is an approach for modeling specific real things, such as cars, as well as the relationships between things like companies and employees, students and teachers, etc. OOP models real objects as program objects that have some data that are associated with it and can performs certain function.

Another common program para-digm is procedural program, which structure a program like a recipe in the sense that it provides a set of steps in the form of functions and blocks of code that are executed sequentially to complete a task.

The key conclusion is that objects are at the center of the paradigm of object-oriented programming, representing not only data, as in procedural programming, but also in the general structure of the program.

NOTE Since Python is a programming language with many paradigms, you can choose the paradigm that is best suited to the problem in question, mix different para-digms in one program or switching from one para-digm to another as your program develops.

Python classes

Focusing first on the data, each object or thing is an instance of some class.

The primitive data structures available in Python, such as numbers, strings, and lists, are designed to represent simple things, such as the value of something, the name of the poem, and your favorite colors, respectively.

What if you want to imagine something much more complex? For example, let say you wanted to track several different animals. If you use a list, the first element may be the name of the animal, while the second element may represent its age. How would you know which element should be? What if you had 100 different animals? Are you sure that every animal has a name, age, and so on? What if you want to add other properties to these animals? This is not enough organization, and this is exactly what you need for classes.

Classes are used to create new user data structure that contain arbitrary informations abouts some thing. In this case of an animal, we could creates an Animal()class to track animal properties such as name and age.

It is importants to note that a class simply provides structure - it is an example of how something should be defined, but in fact, it does not provide any real content. Animal()The class may indicate that the name and age are required to determine the animal, but it will not claim that the name or age of a particular animal is.

This can help present the class as an idea of how something should be defined.

Python Objects (Instances)

While a class is a plan, an instance is a copy of a class with actual values, literally an object belonging to a particular class. This is no longer an idea: it's a real animal, like a dog named Roger, which is eight years old.

In other words, a class is a form or profile. It determines the necessary informations. After you fullfill out the form, your specific copy is an instance of the class: it contains up-to-date information relevant to you.

You can fill out several copies to create many different copies, but without a form, as a guide, you would be lost without knowing what information is required. Thus, before you can create separate instances of an object, we must first specify what you need by defining a class.

How to define a class in Python

Defining a class is simple in Python:

```
class Dog:
    pass
```

You start with a classkeyword to indicate that you are creating a class, then you add the class name (using theCamelCase notation starting with a capital letter).

Also here we used the Python keyword pass. This is huge often used as a placeholder where the code will eventually go. This allows us to run this code without generating an error.

Note: the above code is correct in Python 3. On Python 2.x ("deprecated Python"), you would use a slightly different class definition:

```
# Python 2.x Class Definition
class Dog (object):
    pass
```

Not the (object)parts in parentheses indicate the parent class that you are inheriting from (more on this below). In Python-3, this is no longer necessary because it is implicit by defaulting.

Instance attribute

All class create objects, and all objects contain characteristics called attributes (called properties in the first paragraph). Use the init ()method to initialize (for example, determine) the initial attributes of an object by giving them a default value (state). This method must have atleast one argument, as well as a self variable that refers to the object itself (for example, Dog).

```
class Dog:

    # Initializer / Instance Attributes
    def __init__ (self, name, age):
        self.name = name
        self.age = age
```

In our Dog()class, each dog has a specific name and age, which is certainly important to know when you start creating different dogs. Remember: the class is intended only to define a dog, and not to create instances of individual dogs with specific names and ages: we will come back to this soon.

Similarly, a self variable is also an instance of a class. Since class instances have different meanings, we could argue, Dog.name = namenot self.name = name. But since not all dogs have the same name, we must be able to assign different values for different instances. Hence the need for a special self variable that will help track individual instances of each class.

NOTE: you will never have to call a init ()method: it is called automatically when a new instance of Dog is created.

Class attributes

Although instance attributes are specific to each object, class attributes are the same for all instances, in this case, all dogs.

```python
class Dog:

    # Class Attribute
    species = 'mammal'

    # Initializer / Instance Attributes
    def __init__ (self, name, age):
        self.name = name
        self.age = age
```

Thus, although each dog has a unique name and age, each dog will be a mammal. Let's create some dogs ...

Create Objects

Instantiating is an unusual term for creating a new unique instance of a class.

For example: >>>

```
>>> class Dog:
...     pass
...
>>> Dog()
<__main__.Dog object at 0x1004ccc50>
>>> Dog()
<__main__.Dog object at 0x1004ccc90>
>>> a = Dog()
>>> b = Dog()
>>> a == b
False
```

We started by definea new Dog()class, then created two new

dogs, each of which was assigned to different

objects. So, to create an instance of the class, you use the class

name follow by parentheses. Then, to demonstration that each

instance is actually different, we created two more dogs,

assigning each variable, and then checking to see if these

variables are equal.

What do you think is the type of class instance? >>>

```
>>> class Dog:
...     pass
...
>>> a = Dog()
>>> type(a)
<class '__main__.Dog'>
```

Let's look at the more complex example ...

```python
class Dog:

    # Class Attribute
    species = 'mammal'

    # Initializer / Instance Attributes
    def __init__(self, name, age):
        self.name = name
        self.age = age


# Instantiate the Dog object
philo = Dog("Philo", 5)
mikey = Dog("Mikey", 6)

# Access the instance attributes
print("{} is {} and {} is {}.".format(
    philo.name, philo.age, mikey.name, mikey.age))

# Is Philo a mammal?
if philo.species == "mammal":
    print("{0} is a {1}!".format(philo.name, philo.species))
```

NOTE Notice how we use point records to access the attributes of each objects. Save as (dog_class.py), then run program. You should see:

```
Philo is 5 and Mikey is 6.
Philo is a mammal!
```

What's the matter?

We create a new instance of the Dog()class and assigned it to a variable Philo. Then we passed him two arguments, "Philo" and 5, which represent the name and age of this dog, respectively. These attribute are pass to the init method, which is called every time you creates a new attaching, instance the name and age to the object. You may be wondering why we should not have given self arguments.

This is the magic of Python: when you create a new instance of the class, Python automatically determines what selfies (in this case, Dog), and passes it to the init method.

Review of exercises (# 1)

Exercise: "The oldest dog"

Using the same Dogclass, create three new dogs, each with a different age. Then write a function with a name get_biggest_number()that takes any number of ages (*args) and returns the oldest. Then print the age of the oldest dog something like this:

 The oldest dog is 7 years old. Solution: "The oldest dog"

Solution "The oldest dog."

```python
class Dog:

    # Class Attribute
    species = 'mammal'

    # Initializer / Instance Attributes
    def __init__(self, name, age):
        self.name = name
        self.age = age


# Instantiate the Dog object
jake = Dog("Jake", 7)
doug = Dog("Doug", 4)
william = Dog("William", 5)


# Determine the oldest dog
def get_biggest_number(*args):
    return max(args)


# Output
print("The oldest dog is {} years old.".format(
    get_biggest_number(jake.age, doug.age, william.age)))
```

Instance Methods

Instance methods are defined inside the class and are used to get the contents of the instance. They can also be used to perform operation with the attribute of our objects. Like a init method, the first argument is always self:

```python
class Dog:

    # Class Attribute
    species = 'mammal'

    # Initializer / Instance Attributes
    def __init__(self, name, age):
        self.name = name
        self.age = age

    # instance method
    def description(self):
        return "{} is {} years old".format(self.name, self.age)

    # instance method
    def speak(self, sound):
        return "{} says {}".format(self.name, sound)

# Instantiate the Dog object
mikey = Dog("Mikey", 6)

# call our instance methods
print(mikey.description())
print(mikey.speak("Gruff Gruff"))
```

Save as dog_instance_methods.py , then run it:

```
Mikey is 6 years old
Mikey says Gruff Gruff
```

In the last method, speak()we define the behavior. What other types of behavior can you assign to a dog? Go back to the beginning of the paragraph to see examples of the behavior of other objects.

Attribute Change

You can changes the value of attributes based on some behavior:

```
>>>
```

```python
>>> class Email:
... def __init__ (self):
... self.is_sent = False
... def send_email (self):
... self.is_sent = True
...
>>> my_email = Email ()
>>> my_email.is_sent
False
>>> my_email.send_email ()
>>> my_email.is_sent
True
```

Here we added a method for sending an email that updates the is_sentvariable to True.

Python object inheritance

Inheritance is a processing in which one class accepts the attributes and methods of another. Newly created classes are called child classes, and the classes from which the child classes derive are called parent classes.

It is importants to note that child classes override or extend the functionality (for example, attributes and behavior) of parent classes. In other words, child classes inherit all the attributes and behavior of the parent, but can also define other behavior to be followed. The most basic type of class is the class object, which usually all other classes inherit as the parents.

When you defining a new class, Python 3 implicitly uses its object as the parent class. Thus, the following two definitions are equivalent:

```python
class Dog (object):
    pass

# In Python 3, this is the same as:

class Dog:
    pass
```

Note. In Python 2.x, there is a difference between the new and old-style classes. I will not go into details, but you will usually want to specify an object as the parent class to make sure that you define a new style class if you are writing Python 2 OOP code.

Dog Park Example

Let's imagine that we are in a dog park. There are several Dog objects involved in Dog behavior, each with different attributes. In ordinary conversation, this means that some dogs are running, and some are stretched, and some are just watching other dogs. Besides, each dog was named its owner, and since each dog lives and breathes, each is aging.

How else can you distinguish one dog from another? How about a dog breed: >>>

```python
>>> class Dog:
... def __init__ (self, breed):
... self.breed = breed
...
>>> spencer = Dog ("German Shepard")
>>> spencer.breed
'German Shepard'
>>> sara = Dog ("Boston Terrier")
>>> sara.breed
'Boston Terrier'
```

Each dog breed has slightly different behaviors. To take this into account, let's create separate classes for each breed. These are child classes of the parent Dogclass.

Extending parent class functionality

Create new file this called dog_inheritance.py :

```python
# Parent class
class Dog:

    # Class attribute
    species = 'mammal'

    # Initializer / Instance attributes
    def __init__(self, name, age):
        self.name = name
        self.age = age

    # instance method
    def description(self):
        return '{} is {} years old'.format(self.name, self.age)

    # instance method
    def speak(self, sound):
        return '{} says {}'.format(self.name, sound)


# Child class (inherits from Dog class)
class RussellTerrier(Dog):
    def run(self, speed):
        return '{} runs {}'.format(self.name, speed)


# Child class (inherits from Dog class)
class Bulldog(Dog):
    def run(self, speed):
        return '{} runs {}'.format(self.name, speed)


# Child classes inherit attributes and
# behaviors from the parent class
jim = Bulldog("Jim", 12)
print(jim.description())

# Child classes have specific attributes
# and behaviors as well
print(jim.run("slowly"))
```

Read the comments aloud while you are working with this program to help you understand what is happening, and then, before you run the program, see if you can predict the expected result.

You should see:

```
Jim is 12 years old
Jim runs slowly
```

We did not add any special attributes or methods to distinguish between a RussellTerrierand a Bulldog. Still, since they are now two different classes, we could, for example, give them different class attributes that determine their respective speeds.

Parent and child classes

isinstance()The function is used to determine if the instance is also an instance of a specific parent class. Save this as dog_isinstance.py :

```python
# Parent class
class Dog:

    # Class attribute
    species = 'mammal'

    # Initializer / Instance attributes
    def __init__ (self, name, age):
        self.name = name
        self.age = age

    # instance method
    def description (self):
        return '{} is {} years old'.format (self.name, self.age)

    # instance method
    def speak (self, sound):
        return '{} says {}'.format (self.name, sound)


# Child class (inherits from Dog () class)
class RussellTerrier (Dog):
    def run (self, speed):
        return '{} runs {}'.format (self.name, speed)


# Child class (inherits from Dog () class)
class Bulldog (Dog):
    def run (self, speed):
        return '{} runs {}'.format (self.name, speed)


# Child classes inherit attributes and
# behaviors from the parent class
jim = Bulldog ("Jim", 12)
print (jim.description ())

# Child classes have specific attributes
# and behaviors as well
print (jim.run ("slowly"))

# Is jim an instance of Dog ()?
print (isinstance (jim, Dog))

# Is julie an instance of Dog ()?
julie = Dog ("Julie", 100)
print (isinstance (julie, Dog))

# Is johnny walker an instance of Bulldog ()
johnnywalker = RussellTerrier ("Johnny Walker", 4)
print (isinstance (johnnywalker, Bulldog))

# Is julie and instance of jim?
print (isinstance (julie, jim))
```

Conclusion: >>>

```
('Jim', 12)
Jim runs slowly
True
True
False
Traceback (most recent call last):
  File "dog_isinstance.py", line 50, in <module>
    print (isinstance (julie, jim))
TypeError: isinstance () arg 2 must be a class, type, or tuple of classes and types
```

It makes sense? Both jimand julieare instances of the Dog()class and johnnywalkerare not instances of Bulldog()the class. Then, as a health check, we checked juliewhether the instance is an instance jim, which is impossible, since jimit instancedoes not belong to the class itself, but to the class TypeError.

Overriding parent class functionality

Remember that child classes can also override the attributes and behavior of the parent class. For example: >>>

```
>>> class Dog:
... species = 'mammal'
...
>>> class SomeBreed (Dog):
... pass
...
>>> class SomeOtherBreed (Dog):
... species = 'reptile'
...
>>> frank = SomeBreed ()
>>> frank.species 'mammal'
>>> beans = SomeOtherBreed ()
>>> beans.species 'reptile'
```
The SomeBreed()class inherits speciesfrom the parent class, while the SomeOtherBreed()class overrides speciesby setting it reptile.

Review of exercises (# 2)

Exercise: "Legacy of the dogs"

Create a Petsclass that contains dog instances: this class is completely separate from the Dogclass. In other words, a Dogclass is not inherited from the Petsclass. Then assign three instances of the dog to the Petsclass instance . Start with the following code below. Save the file as pets_class.py . Your output should look like this:

```
I have 3 dogs.
Tom is 6.
Fletcher is 7.
Larry is 9.
And they're all mammals, of course.
```

Start Code:

```python
# Parent class
class Dog:

    # Class attribute
    species = 'mammal'

    # Initializer / Instance attributes
    def __init__ (self, name, age):
        self.name = name
        self.age = age

    # instance method
    def description (self):
        return '{} is {} years old'.format (self.name, self.age)

    # instance method
    def speak (self, sound):
        return '{} says {}'.format (self.name, sound)

# Child class (inherits from Dog class)
class RussellTerrier (Dog):
    def run (self, speed):
        return '{} runs {}'.format (self.name, speed)

# Child class (inherits from Dog class)
class Bulldog (Dog):
    def run (self, speed):
        return '{} runs {}'.format (self.name, speed)
```

Solution: "Dog Inheritance"

```python
# Parent class
class Pets:

    dogs = []

    def __init__(self, dogs):
        self.dogs = dogs


# Parent class
class Dog:

    # Class attribute
    species = 'mammal'

    # Initializer / Instance attributes
    def __init__(self, name, age):
        self.name = name
        self.age = age

    # Instance method
    def description(self):
        return self.name, self.age

    # Instance method
    def speak(self, sound):
        return "%s says %s" % (self.name, sound)

    # Instance method
    def eat(self):
        self.is_hungry = False


# Child class (inherits from Dog class)
class RussellTerrier(Dog):
    def run(self, speed):
        return "%s runs %s" % (self.name, speed)


# Child class (inherits from Dog class)
class Bulldog(Dog):
    def run(self, speed):
        return "%s runs %s" % (self.name, speed)

# Create instances of dogs
my_dogs = [
    Bulldog("Tom", 6),
    RussellTerrier("Fletcher", 7),
    Dog("Larry", 9)
]

# Instantiate the Pets class
my_pets = Pets(my_dogs)

# Output
print("I have {} dogs.".format(len(my_pets.dogs)))
for dog in my_pets.dogs:
    print("{} is {}.".format(dog.name, dog.age))

print("And they're all {}s, of course.".format(dog.species))
```

Exercise: Hungry Dogs

Use the same files, add an instance attribute is_hungry = Truein the Dogclass. Then add the called method, eat()which when called changes the value is_hungryto False. Find out how best to feed each dog, and then print "My dogs are hungry." if everyone is hungry or "My dogs are not hungry." if everyone is not hungry. The final result should look like this:

```
I have 3 dogs.
Tom is 6.
Fletcher is 7.
Larry is 9.
And they're all mammals, of course.
My dogs are not hungry.
```

Solution: Hungry Dogs

```python
# Parent class
class Pets:

    dogs = []

    def __init__(self, dogs):
        self.dogs = dogs


# Parent class
```

```python
class Dog.

    * Oass attribute
    sped es = 'mamm d '

    * Initi d i zer ." In stance attributes
    def   iriit    (self name age).
       self.name  = name
       self.age  = age
       self.is hungo.' = True


=  mist ance method
   def descripti on (self).
       return self.name  self.age

= mist ance method
  def speak (self sound).
      return " °. o s says°. o s" °. o (self.name sound)
```

= mist ance method
    def cat (self).
        self.is hungo.' = Fd se

= Oiild class (inherits from Dog cl ass)
  class RussellT erri er (Dog).
      def mn (self speed).
          return " °. o s runs°. o s" °. o (self.name speedt

= Oiild class (inherits from Dog cl ass)
  class Bulldog (Dog.
      def run (self speed).
          return " °. o s runs°. o s" °. o (self.name speedt

= Create instances of dogs
  m\' dogs = [
      Bulldog (" Tom" 6)
      Ru ssellT erri er (" FI ct cher" Tt
      Dog ("L are.'" 9)

          stanttate the Pets class
      ate'   ts = Pets (ate' dogs)

= Output
  print (" I have {) dogs.". format (len (m\'   ets.dogs)))
  for dog in m\'   ets.dogs.
      dog.eat ()
      print (" {) is {).". format (dog.name dog.age))

  print ("And the\"re d1 {) s of ccxirse." . format (dog.species))

  are m\' dogs hungo.' = Fdse
  for dog in m\'   ets.dogs.
      if dog.i s hungo.'.

  are_my_dogs_hungry = True

if are_my_dogs_hungry.
  print (" My dogs are hungry.")
else:
  print (" My dogs are not hungry.")

Exercise: "Dog Walking"

Next, add a walk()method like Petsand Dogclasses, so that when you call a method in the Petsclass, each instance of a dog is assigned to Petsa class walk(). Save this as dog_walking.py . This is a little trickier.

Start by implementing a method just like a speak()method. As for the method in the Petsclass, you will need to iterate over the list of dogs and then call the method itself.

The output should look like this:

```
Tom is walking!
Fletcher is walking!
Larry is walking!
```

Solution: "dog walking"

# Parent class
class Pets:

    dogs = []

    def __init__ (self, dogs):
        self.dogs = dogs

    def walk (self):
        for dog in self.dogs:
            print (dog.walk ())

# Parent class
class Dog:

    # Class attribute
    species = 'mammal'
    is_hungry = True

    # Initializer / instance attributes
    def __init__ (self, name, age):
        self.name = name
        self.age = age

    # Instance method
    def description (self):
        return self.name, self.age

    # Instance method
    def speak (self, sound):
        return "%s says %s" % (self.name, sound)

    # Instance method
    def eat (self):
        self.is_hungry = False

```python
    def walk (self):
        return "%s is walking!" % (self.name)


# Child class (inherits from Dog class)
class RussellTerrier (Dog):
    def run (self, speed):
        return "%s runs %s" % (self.name, speed)


# Child class (inherits from Dog class)
class Bulldog (Dog):
    def run (self, speed):
        return "%s runs %s" % (self.name, speed)

# Create instances of dogs
my_dogs = [
    Bulldog ("Tom", 6),
    RussellTerrier ("Fletcher", 7),
    Dog ("Larry", 9)
]

# Instantiate the Pet class
my_pets = Pets (my_dogs)

# Output
my_pets.walk ()
```

Exercise: "Testing Understanding"

Answer the following OOP questions to verify your learning progress:

What class?

What an example?

What is the relationship between class and instance?

What Python syntax is used to define a new class?

What is the spelling convention for a class name?

How do you create or create an instance of a class?

How do you access the attributes and behavior of an instance of a class?

What kind of method?

What is the purpose self?

What is the purpose of the init method?

Describe how inheritance helps prevent code duplication.

Can child classes override the properties of their parents?

Solution: "Test of understanding" Show hide

A class mechanism used to create new custom data structures. It contains data, as well as methods used to process this data.

An instance is a copy of a class with actual values, literally an object of a particular class.

While a class is a plan used to describe how to create something, instances are objects created from these drawings.

class PythonClassName:

Capitalized CamelCase designation - i.e. PythonClassName()

You use the class name followed by parentheses. So if the name of the class Dog(), the instance of the dog will be - my_class = Dog().

With dot notation - for example, instance_name.attribute_name

A function that defined inside a class.

The first argument of each method refers to the current instance of the class, which is called by the convention self. The init method self refers to a newly created object, while in other methods, it a self refers into the instance whose method was called. For more on the init con self, check out this article.

init The method initializes an instance of the class.

Child classes inherit all the attributes and behavior of the parent.

Yes.

Conclusion

Now you should know what classes are, why you want or should use them, and how to create parent and child classes to better structure your programs.

Remember that OOP is a programming paradigm, not a Python concept. Most modern programming languages, such as Java, C #, C ++, follow the principles of OOP. So the good news is that learning the basics of object-oriented programming will be useful to you in a variety of circumstances - whether you work in Python or not.

Now the industry does not stand still and there are more and more web sites, services and companies that need specialists. Demand for developers is growing, but competition among them is growing.

To be the best in your business, you need to be almost an absolutely universal person who can write a website, create a design for it, and promote it yourself.

In this regard, even a person who has never sat at this computer begins to think, but should I try?

But very often it turns out that such enthusiasts burn out at the initial stage, without having tried themselves in this matter.

Or maybe he would become a brilliant creator of code? Would create something new? This we will not know.

Every day, the threshold for entering programming is growing. You can never predict what new language will come out.

Such an abundance breaks all the desire of a newly minted programmer and he is lost in this ocean of information.

All these javascripts of yours ... pythons ... what fear ..

A great misconception is the obligation to know mathematics. Yes, it is needed, but only in a narrow field, but it is also useful for understanding some aspects.

The advice that can be given to people who are just starting their activity is not to chase everything at once. Allow yourself time to think.

What do I want to do? Create a program for everyone to be useful? Create additional services to simplify any tasks? Or do you really have to go make games?

The second advice will be to answer my question how much time am I ready to devote to this? The third point is to think about how fast you want to achieve your intended result.

So, there is no "easy way" to start programming, it all depends on you - your interest, what you want to do and your tasks.

In any case, you need to try and do everything possible in your power. Good luck in your endeavors!

PYTHON

CRASH COURSE

Beginner guide to computer programming, web coding and data mining. Learn in 7 days machine learning, artificial intelligence, NumPy and Pandas packages with exercises for data analysis.

JASON TEST

What Is Python?

Python is a high-level, object-oriented, construed programming language with complex semblance. Combined with dynamic typing and dynamic binding, its high-level data structures make it very attractive for Rapid Application Development as well as for use as a scripting or glue language for connecting existing components. Python's quick, easy to understand syntax, stresses readability, and hence reduces the expense of running the software. Python connects modules and packages that promote the modularity of the software and reuse of code. For all major platforms, the Python interpreter and the comprehensive standard library are available free of charge in source or binary form and can be freely distributed.

Programmers also fall in love with Python because of the increased productivity it brings. The edit-test-debug process is amazingly quick since there is no compilation phase. Python debugging programs are simple: a mistake or bad feedback would never trigger a segmentation fault. Alternatively, it creates an exception when the translator detects an error. If the program miscarries to catch the exception, the parser will print a stack trace. A source-level debugger allows you to inspect local and global variables, check arbitrary expressions, set breakpoints, walk through the code one line at a time, etc. The debugger itself is written in Python, testifying to the introspective power of Python. On the other side, often the fastest way to debug a system is to add a few print statements to the source: the quick process of edit-test-debug renders this simple approach quite efficient.

Who is the Right Audience?

The resolve of this book is to get you up to speed with Python as easy as possible so that you can create programs that work — games, data analysis, and web applications — while building a programming base that will serve you well for the rest of your life. Python Crash Course is designed for people of any age who have never programmed in or worked in Python before. This book is for you if you want to learn the basics of programming quickly, so you can focus on interesting projects, and you like to test your understanding of new concepts by solving meaningful issues. Python Crash Course is also great for middle and high school teachers who would like to give a project-based guide to programming to their pupils.

What You Will Learn?

The sole purpose of this book is to make you generally a good programmer and, in particular, a good programmer for Python. As we provide you with a solid foundation in general programming concepts, you can learn quickly and develop good habits. You should be prepared to move on to more sophisticated Python methods after working your way through the Python Crash Course, and it will make the next programming language much easier to grasp. You will learn basic programming concepts in the first part of this book, which you need to know to write Python programs. These concepts are the same as those you would learn in almost any programming language when starting out.

You can learn about the different data types and ways you can store data within your applications in lists and dictionaries. You'll learn how to build data collections and work efficiently through those collections. You'll learn to use while and when loops to check for certain conditions so that you can run certain sections of code while those conditions are true and run certain sections when they aren't true — a strategy that can significantly automate processes. To make your programs accessible and keep your programs going as long as the user is active, you'll have to accept input from users. You're going to explore how to apply functions as reusable parts of your software, and you only have to write blocks of code that execute those functions once, which you can use as many times as you want. You will then extend this concept with classes to more complicated behavior, making programs fairly simple to respond to a variety of situations.

You must learn how to write programs to handle common errors graciously. You will write a few short programs after going on each of these basic concepts, which will solve some well-defined problems. Finally, you can take the first step towards intermediate programming by learning how to write checks for your code so that you can further improve your programs without thinking about bugs being implemented. For Part I, all the details will allow you to take on bigger, more complicated tasks.

Why Python?

Every year we consider whether to continue using Python or move on to another language — maybe one that is newer to the programming world. But for a lot of reasons, I keep on working on Python. Python is an incredibly efficient language: the programs will do more than many other languages will need with fewer lines of code. The syntax of Python, too, should help write clean code. Compared to other languages, the code will be easy to read, easy to debug, and easy to extend and expand on.

People use Python for many purposes: making games, creating web applications, solving business problems, and developing internal tools for all types of applications interesting ventures. Python is also heavily utilized for academic research and theoretical science in scientific fields.

One of the main reasons I keep on using Python is because of the Python community, which includes an incredibly diverse and welcoming group of people. Community is important for programmers since programming is not a practice of solitude. Most of us will ask advice from others, even the most seasoned programmers, who have already solved similar problems. Getting a well-connected and supportive community is essential to help you solve problems and the Python community fully supports people like you who are using Python as your first programming language.

What Is Machine Learning?

Machine-learning algorithms use correlations in massive volumes of data to identify patterns. And info, here, contains a lot of stuff — numbers, words, images, clicks, what do you have. This can be fed into a machine-learning system because it can be digitally processed.

Machine learning is the procedure that powers many of today's services — recommendation programs such as those on Netflix, YouTube, and Spotify; search engines such as Google and Baidu; social media channels such as Facebook and Twitter; voice assistants such as Siri and Alexa. The collection continues.

In all these instances, each platform collects as much data as possible about you — what genres you like to watch, what links you click on, what statuses you react to — and using machine learning to make a highly educated guess of what you might want next. And, in the case of a voice assistant, which words the best match with the funny sounds that come out of your mouth.

Frankly, this is quite a basic process: find the pattern, apply the pattern. But the world runs pretty much that way. That's thanks in large part to a 1986 breakthrough, courtesy of Geoffrey Hinton, now known as the father of deep knowledge.

What is Deep Learning?

Deep knowledge is machine learning on steroids: it uses a methodology that improves the capacity of computers to identify – and reproduce – only the smallest patterns. This method is called a deep neural network — strong because it has many, many layers of basic computational nodes that work together to churn through data and produce a result in the form of the prediction.

What are Neural Networks?

Neural networks strongly influence the interior workings of the human brain. The nodes are kind of like neurons, and the network is kind of like the entire brain. (For the researchers among you who cringe at this comparison: Avoid pooh-poohing the analogy. It's a good analogy.) But Hinton presented his breakthrough paper at a time when neural nets were out of fashion. Nobody ever learned how to teach them, and they didn't produce decent results. The method had taken nearly 30 years to make a comeback. And boy, they made a comeback!

What is Supervised Learning?

The last thing you need to know is that computer (and deep) learning comes in three flavors: controlled, unmonitored, and enhanced. The most prevalent data is marked in supervised learning to inform the computer exactly what patterns it will look for. Thought of it as being like a sniffer dog that can search targets until they know the smell they're following. That's what you do when you're pressing a Netflix series to play — you're asking the program to search related programs.

What is Unsupervised Learning?

In unsupervised learning, the data does not have any names. The computer is only searching for whatever trends it can locate. It's like making a dog detect lots of different things and organize them into classes of identical smells. Unsupervised methods are not as common as they have less apparent applications. Interestingly, they've achieved traction in cybersecurity.

What is Reinforcement Learning?

Finally, we have the enhancement of learning, the new field of machine learning. A reinforcement algorithm learns to achieve a clear objective by trial and error. It attempts a lot of different things and is rewarded or penalized depending on whether its behavior helps or hinders it from achieving its goal. It's like giving and denying treats as you show a puppy a new trick. Strengthening learning is the cornerstone of Google's AlphaGo, a software that has recently defeated the best human players in the complicated game of Go.

What Is Artificial Intelligence (AI)?

Mathematician Alan Turing changed history a second time with a simple question: "Do computers think?" Less than a decade after cracking the Nazi encryption code Enigma and enabling the Allied Forces to win World War II. The basic purpose and goal of artificial intelligence were developed by Turing's paper "Computing Machinery and Intelligence" (1950), and the subsequent Turing Test.

At its heart, AI is the branch of computer science that is aimed at answering Turing's affirmative query. It's the shot at replicating or simulating human intelligence in machines.

The expansive purpose of artificial intelligence has led to numerous questions and debates. So much so, that there is no universally accepted single field description.

The big limitation of describing AI as literally "making intelligent machines" is that it doesn't really describe what artificial intelligence is? Who makes an Intelligent Machine?

Artificial Intelligence: A Modern Approach in their pioneering textbook, authors Stuart Russell and Peter Norvig address the issue by unifying their work around the topic of smart agents in computers. With this in mind, AI is "the study of agents acquiring environmental perceptions and doing behavior" (Russel and Norvig viii)

Norvig and Russell continue their exploration of four different approaches that have historically defined AI:

1.	Thinking humanly

2.	Thinking rationally

3.	Acting humanly

4.	Acting rationally

The first two theories are about thought patterns and logic, while the rest are about behavior. In particular, Norvig and Russell concentrate on logical agents that behave to obtain the best outcome, noting 'all the skills needed for the Turing Test often help an agent to act rationally" (Russel and Norvig 4). Patrick Winston, MIT's Ford Professor of Artificial Intelligence and Computer Science, describes AI as "algorithms allowed by constraints, revealed by representations that help loop-focused models that bind together thought, interpretation and behavior."

While the average person may find these definitions abstract, they help focus the field as an area of computer science and provide a blueprint for infusing machines and programs with machine learning and other artificial intelligence subsets. When addressing an audience at the 2017 Japan AI Experience, Jeremy Achin, CEO of DataRobot, started his speech by presenting the following description of how AI is used today: "AI is a computational system capable of executing activities typically involving human intelligence ... Some of these artificial intelligence systems are powered by machine learning, others are powered by deep learning, and others are powered by very simple stuff like rules."

What Is Data Science?

Data science continues developing as one of the most exciting and challenging career options for qualified professionals. Today, productive computer practitioners recognize that the conventional techniques of processing vast volumes of data, data analysis, and programming skills must be improved. To discover valuable information within their organizations, data scientists need to experience the broad range of the life cycle of data science and have a degree of versatility and comprehension to optimize returns at each point of the process.

What Is Data Mining?

Data mining is investigating and analyzing big data to find concrete patterns and laws. This is considered a specialty within the area of analysis of computer science and is distinct from predictive analytics because it represents past evidence. In contrast, data mining attempts to forecast future outcomes. Also, data mining methods are used to build machine learning (ML) models driving advanced artificial intelligence (AI) technologies such as search engine algorithms and recommendation systems.

How to Do Data Mining

The accepted data mining process involves six steps:

1.   Business understanding

The first step is to set the project's objectives and how data mining will help you accomplish that goal. At this point, a schedule will be drawn up to include schedules, activities and responsibilities of tasks.

2.   Data understanding

In this phase, data is gathered from all available data sources. At this point, data visualization applications are also used to test the data's properties and ensure it helps meet business goals.

3.   Data Preparation

Data is then washed, and it contains lost data to ensure that it can be mined. Data analysis can take a substantial period, depending on the volume of data processed and the number of sources of data. Therefore, in modern database management systems (DBMS), distributed systems are used to improve the speed of the data mining process rather than to burden one single system. They're also safer than having all the data in a single data warehouse for an organization. Including fail-safe steps in the data, the manipulation stage is critical so that data is not permanently lost.

4.   Data Modeling

Mathematical models are then used with a sophisticated analysis method to identify trends in the data.

5.   Evaluation

The findings are evaluated to determine if they should be deployed across the organization, and compared to business objectives.

6.   Deployment

The data mining results are spread through everyday business processes in the final level. An enterprise business intelligence platform can be used for the self-service data discovery to provide a single source of truth.

Benefits of Data Mining

- **Automated Decision-Making**

Data Mining allows companies to evaluate data on a daily basis and optimize repetitive and important decisions without slowing human judgment. Banks can identify fraudulent transactions immediately, request verification, and even secure personal information to protect clients from identity theft. Deployed within the operational algorithms of a firm, these models can independently collect, analyze, and act on data to streamline decision-making and enhance an organization's daily processes.

- **Accurate Prediction and Forecasting**

For any organization, preparing is a vital operation. Data mining promotes planning and provides accurate predictions for administrators based on historical patterns and present circumstances. Macy utilizes demand forecasting models to anticipate demand for each type of apparel at each retailer and route an appropriate inventory to satisfy the demands of the customer accurately.

- **Cost Reduction**

Data mining enables more efficient use and resource allocation. Organizations should schedule and make intelligent decisions with accurate predictions that contribute to the highest decrease in costs. Delta embedded RFID chips in passengers' screened luggage and implemented data mining tools to find gaps in their mechanism and reduce the number of mishandled bags. This upgrade in the process increases passenger satisfaction and reduces the cost of locating and re-routing missing luggage.

- **Customer Insights**

Companies deploy data mining models from customer data to uncover key features and differences between their customers. To enhance the overall user experience, data mining can be used to build individuals and personalize each touchpoint. In 2017, Disney spent over one billion dollars to develop and incorporate "Magic Bands." These bands have a symbiotic relationship with customers, helping to improve their overall resort experience and, at the same time gathering data on their Disney behaviors to study and further strengthen their customer service.

What Are Data Analytics?

Data analysis is defined as a process for cleaning, transforming, and modeling data to discover useful business decision-making information. Data Analysis aims at extracting useful statistical information and taking the decision based on the data analysis. Whenever we make any decision in our daily life, it is by choosing that particular decision that we think about what happened last time, or what will happen. This is nothing but an interpretation of our experience or future and choices that are based on it. We accumulate thoughts of our lives, or visions of our future, for that. So this is nothing but an analysis of the data. Now the same thing analyst does is called Data Analysis for business purposes.

Here you'll learn about:

- Why Data Analysis?
- Data Analysis Tools
- Types of Data Analysis: Techniques and Methods
- Data Analysis Process

Why Data Analysis?

Often, research is what you need to do to develop your company and to develop in your life! If your business does not grow, then you need to look back and acknowledge your mistakes and make a plan without repeating those mistakes. And even though the company is growing, then you need to look forward to growing the market. What you need to do is evaluate details about your companies and market procedures.

Data Analysis Tools

Data analysis tools make it simpler for users to process and manipulate data, analyze relationships and correlations between data sets, and help recognize patterns and trends for interpretation. Here is a comprehensive list of tools.

Types of Data Analysis; Techniques and Methods

There are many types of data analysis techniques that are based on business and technology. The main types of data analysis are as follows:

- Text Analysis
- Statistical Analysis
- Diagnostic Analysis
- Predictive Analysis
- Prescriptive Analysis

Text Analysis

Text Analysis is also known as Data Mining. Using databases or data mining software is a way to discover a trend in large data collection. It used to turn the raw data into information about the market. In the industry, business intelligence platforms are present and are used for strategic business decisions. Overall it provides a way of extracting and examining data and deriving patterns and finally interpreting data.

Statistical Analysis

Statistical Analysis shows "What happens?" in the form of dashboards using the past data. Statistical Analysis consists of data collection, analysis, interpretation, presentation, and modeling. It analyzes a data set or a data sample. This type of analysis has two categories-Descriptive Analysis and Inferential Analysis.

Descriptive Analysis

Descriptive Analysis analyzes complete data or a summarized sample of numerical data. For continuous data, it shows mean and deviation, while percentage and frequency for categorical data.

Inferential Analysis

This analyzes full data from samples. You can find diverse conclusions from the same data in this type of Analysis by selecting different samples.

Diagnostic Analysis

Diagnostic research reveals, "Why did this happen?" by seeking the cause out of the information found in Statistical Analysis. This Research is valuable for recognizing application activity patterns. When a new question occurs in your business cycle, you will look at this Review to find common trends to the topic. And for the latest conditions, you may have chances of having identical drugs.

Predictive Analysis

Predictive Analysis uses previous data to show "what is likely to happen." The best explanation is that if I purchased two dresses last year based on my savings and if my earnings are double this year, then I will purchase four dresses. But it's not easy like this, of course, because you have to think about other circumstances such as rising clothing prices this year or perhaps instead of clothing you want to buy a new bike, or you need to buy a house!

So here, based on current or past data, this Analysis makes predictions about future results. Projections are a pure calculation. Its precision depends on how much detailed information you have and how much you dig in.

Prescriptive Analysis

Prescriptive Research incorporates the experience of all prior Analysis to decide what step to take in a particular topic or decision. Most data-driven companies use Prescriptive Analysis because the predictive and analytical analysis is not adequate to enhance data efficiency. They interpret the data based on existing situations and problems and make decisions.

Data Analysis Process

Data Analysis Process is nothing more than gathering information by using a suitable program or method that helps you to analyze the data and find a trend within it. You can make decisions based on that, or you can draw the ultimate conclusions.

Data Processing consists of the following phases:

- Data Requirement Gathering
- Data Collection
- Data Cleaning
- Data Analysis
- Data Interpretation
- Data Visualization

Data Requirement Gathering

First of all, you need to wonder why you want to do this data analysis? What you need to figure out the intent or intention of doing the Study. You have to determine what sort of data analysis you want to carry out! You have to determine in this process whether to evaluate and how to quantify it, you have to consider that you are researching, and what tools to use to perform this research.

Data Collection

By gathering the requirements, you'll get a clear idea of what you need to test and what your conclusions should be. Now is the time to collect the data based on the requirements. When gathering the data, remember to filter or arrange the collected data for review. As you have collected data from different sources, you must keep a log with the date and source of the data being collected.

Data Cleaning

Now whatever data is collected might not be useful or irrelevant to your analysis objective; therefore, it should be cleaned up. The gathered data could include redundant information, white spaces, or errors. The data should be cleaned without error. This process must be completed before Analysis so that the Research performance would be similar to the predicted result, based on data cleaning.

Data Analysis

Once the data is collected, cleaned, and processed, Analysis is ready. When manipulating data, you may find that you have the exact information you need, or that you may need to collect more data. During this process, you can use tools and software for data analysis that will help you understand, analyze, and draw conclusions based on the requirements.

Data Interpretation

It's finally time to interpret your results after analyzing your data. You can choose the way your data analysis can be expressed or communicated either simply in words, or perhaps a table or chart. Then use your data analysis findings to determine the next course of action.

Data Visualization

Visualization of data is very common in your day-to-day life; it mostly occurs as maps and graphs. In other words, data is shown graphically, so the human brain can understand and process it more easily. Visualization of data is used to spot hidden information and patterns. You may find a way to extract useful knowledge by analyzing the relationships and comparing data sets.

Who Is This Book For?

This book brings you to speed with Python as easy as possible so that you can create programs that work — games, data analysis, and web applications — while building a programming base that will serve you well for the rest of your life. Python Crash Course is for people of any age who have never previously programmed in Python or who have not programmed to anything. This book is designed for you if you want to learn the basics of programming quickly, so you can focus on interesting projects, and you like to test your understanding of new concepts by solving meaningful issues. Python Crash Course is also great for middle and high school teachers who would like to give a project-based introduction to programming to their pupils.

What Can You Expect to Learn?

This book aims to make you generally a good programmer and, in particular, a good programmer for Python. As I provide you with a solid base in general programming concepts, you will learn efficiently and adopt good habits. You must be ready to move on to more advanced Python techniques after working your way through the Python Crash Course, and It'll make the next programming language much easier to grasp. You will learn basic programming concepts in the first part of this book, which you need to know to write Python programs. Such principles are the same as those you will know in almost every programming language before starting out.

You can learn about the different data types and ways you can store data within your applications in lists and dictionaries. You'll learn how to build data collections and work efficiently through those collections.

You'll learn to use while and when loops to check for certain conditions so that you can run certain sections of code while those conditions are true and run certain sections when they aren't true — a strategy that can significantly automate processes. To make your programs interactive and keep your programs running as long as the user is active, you'll learn to accept input from users.

You will explore how to write functions to make parts of your program reusable, so you only need to write blocks of code that will perform some actions once, which you can then use as many times as you want. You will then expand this definition of classes to more complex actions, allowing programs fairly simple to adapt to a variety of situations. You must learn how to write programs to handle common errors graciously. You will write a few short programs after going on each of these basic concepts, which will solve some well-defined problems. Finally, you will take your first step towards intermediate programming by learning how to write tests for your code so that you can further develop your programs without worrying about bugs being introduced. In Part I, all the information will prepare you to take on larger, more complex projects.

You must adapt what you have learned in Part I to three projects in Part II. You can do any or all of those tasks that work best for you in any order. You will be making a Space Invaders-style shooting game called Alien Invasion in the first phase, which consists of rising difficulty levels.

DAY 3

Getting Started

You will run the first Python script, hello world.py, in this chapter. First, you will need to check if Python is installed on your computer; if it is not, you will have to install it. You can also need a text editor for your Python programs to work on. Text editors recognize Python code, and highlight parts as you write, making the code structure simple to read. Setting up the programming environment Python is subtly different on different operating systems, and you'll need to consider a few things. Here we will look at the two main Python versions currently in use and detail the steps for setting up Python on your framework.

Python 2 and Python 3

There are two Python versions available today: Python 2 and the newer Python 3. Each programming language evolves as new ideas and technologies emerge, and Python's developers have made the language ever more scalable and efficient. Most deviations are incremental and barely noticeable, but code written for Python 2 may not be used in some cases, it function properly on installed Python 3 systems. Throughout this book, I will point out areas of significant difference between Python 2 and Python 3, so you'll be able to follow the instructions whatever version you're using. Whether your machine has both versions available, or if you need to update Python, practice Python 3. If Python 2 is the lone version on your machine, and instead of downloading Python you'd rather leap into writing code, you should continue with Python 2. But the sooner you upgrade to use Python 3, the better you'll work with the latest release.

Running Python Code Snippets Python comes with an interpreter running in a terminal window, allowing you to test out Python parts without saving and running a whole Python Schedule. You'll see fragments throughout this novel, which look like this:

u >>> print("Hello Python interpreter!")

Hello Python Interpreter!

The bold text is what you will type in and then perform by clicking enter. Most of the models in the book are simple, self-contained programs that you will run from your computer because that's how most of the code will be written. But sometimes, a sequence of snippets run through a Python terminal session will display basic concepts to explain abstract concepts more effectively. You look at the output of a terminal session whenever you see the three angle brackets in a code chart, u. Within a second, we will try to cod in the interpreter for your program.

Hello World!

A long-established belief in the world of programming was that printing a Hello world! The message on the screen, as your first new language program, will bring you luck.

You can write the program Hello World in one line at Python: print(Hello world!) Such a simple program serves a genuine purpose. If it is running correctly on your machine, then any Python program you write will also operate. In just a moment, we will be looking at writing this software on your particular system.

Python on Different Operating Systems

Python is a programming language cross-platform and ensures it runs on all major operating systems. Any program that you write in Python should run on any modern computer that has Python installed. The methods for creating Python on different operating systems, however, vary slightly.

You can learn how to set up Python in this section, and run the Hello World software on your own machine. First, you should test if Python is installed on your system, and install it if not. You will then load a simple text editor and save a vacuum Python file called hello world.py. Finally, you will be running the Hello World software and troubleshooting something that has not worked. I'll go

Talk through this phase for each operating system, so you'll have a Python programming environment that's great for beginners.

Python on Linux

Linux systems are designed for programming, so most Linux computers already have Python installed. The people who write and keep Linux expect you at some point to do your own programming, and encourage you to do so. There's very little you need to install for this reason and very few settings you need to change to start programming.

Checking Your Version of Python

Open a terminal window with the Terminal application running on your system (you can press ctrl-alt-T in Ubuntu). Enter python with a lowercase p to find out if Python is installed. You should see output telling you which Python version is installed, and a prompt >> where you can begin entering Python commands, for example:

$ python Python 2.7.6 (default, Mar 22 2014, 22:59:38) on linux2

[GCC 4.8.2]

To get more information, type "help," "copyright," "credits" or

"license."

This result tells you that Python 2.7.6 is the default version of

Python currently installed on that computer. To leave the Python

prompt and reappearance to a terminal prompt, press ctrl-D or

enter exit() when you have seen this output.

You may need to specify that version to check for Python 3; so

even if the output displayed Python 2.7 as the default version,

try the python3 command:

$python3 Python 3.5.0 (default, Sep 17 2015, 13:05:18)

On Linux [GCC 4.8.4]

To get more information, type "help," "copyright," "credits" or

"license."

This performance means you've built Python 3, too, so you can

use either version. Whenever you see the command to python in

this book, instead, enter python3. Most Linux distributions

already have Python installed, but if your system came with

Python 2 for some reason or not, and you want to install Python

3, see Appendix A.

Installing a Text Editor

Geany is an understand text editor: it is easy to install, will let you run almost all of your programs directly from the editor instead of through a terminal, will use syntax highlighting to paint your code, and will run your code in a terminal window, so you'll get used to using terminals. Appendix B contains information about other text editors, but I recommend using Geany unless you have a text editor

Running the Hello World Program

Open Geany to commence your first program. Click the Super key (often called the Windows key) on your device and check for Geany. Drag the icon onto your taskbar or desktop to make a shortcut. Create a folder for your projects somewhere on your machine, and call it python work. (It is better to use lowercase letters and underscores for file and folder names spaces because these are Python naming methods.) Go back to Geany and save a blank Python file (Save As) named hello world.py in your python work tab. The .py extension tells Geany to have a Python program in your file. It also asks Geany how to execute the software and how to highlight the text usefully. Once your data has been saved, enter the following line:

Print("Hello world Python!)

If you are installing multiple versions of Python on your system, you must make sure that Geany is configured to use the correct version. Go to Create Commands for the Building Package. With a button next to each, you should see the terms Compile and execute. Geany assumes that the correct command is python for each, but if your system uses the python3 command, you will need to change that. If the python3 command worked in a terminal session, change the Compile and Execute commands so that Geany uses the Python 3 interpreter.

Your Order to Compile will look like this:

Python3 -m py compile% "f"

You have to type this command exactly as shown here. Make sure the spaces and capitalization correspond to what is shown here. Your Command to Execute should look like this:

Python 3% "f"

Running Python in a Terminal Session

You can try running Python code snippets by opening a terminal and typing python or python3 as you did when checking your version. Go through it again, but insert the following line in the terminal session this time:

>>> print("Hello Python interpreter!")

Hello Python interpreter! >>>

You will display your message directly in the latest terminal window. Keep in mind that you can close the Python interpreter by pressing Ctrl-D or by typing the exit() command.

Installing a Text Editor

Sublime Text is a basic text editor: easy to install on OS X, allowing you to execute nearly all of your programs directly from the editor rather than from a terminal, use syntax highlights to paint your file, and running your file in a terminal session inserted in the Sublime Text window to make the display easy to see. Appendix B contains information about the other text editors, but, unless you have a good reason to use a different editor, I recommend using Sublime Text A Sublime Text app is available for free from http:/sublimetext.com/3. Click on the download link and look for an OS X installer. Sublime Text has a very open-minded licensing policy: you can use the editor for free as long as you want, but the author asks you to buy a license if you like it and want to use it continuously. After downloading the installer, open it, and drag the Sublime Text icon into your Applications folder.

Configuring Sublime Text for Python 3

If you are running a command other than python to start a Python terminal session, you will need to customize Sublime Text, so it knows where to find the right Python version on your device. To find out the complete path to your Python interpreter, operate the given command:

$type -a python3 python3 is /usr / local / bin / python3

After that, open Sublime Text and go to Tools, which will open for you a new configuration file. Remove what you see and log in as follows:

{.sublime-build "cmd": ["/usr / local / bin / python3", "-u," "$file"],}

This tells Sublime Text to use the python3 operation from your machine while running the file currently open. Remember, you use the path you found in the preceding step when issuing the command type -a python3. Save the file as Python3.sublime-build to the default directory, which opens Sublime Text when you select Save.

Running the Hello World Program

Python on Windows

Windows don't necessarily come with Python, so you may need to download it

Then install a text editor, import, and then update.

Installing Python

First, search if you have Python installed on your system. Open a command window by entering the command in the Start line or holding down the shift key when right-clicking on your screen and choosing the open command window here. Pass python in the lowercase, in the terminal tab. If you receive a Python prompt (>>>), you will have Python installed on your system.

Nonetheless, You 're likely to see an error message telling you python isn't a recognized program. Download a Windows Python installer, in that case. Go to python.org/downloads/ Http:/. Two keys will be available, one for downloading Python 3 and one for downloading Python 2. Click the Python 3 button which will start installing the right installer for your device automatically Installation. After downloading the file, run the installer. Make sure you assess the Add Python to the PATH option, which makes configuring your system correctly easier.

Variables and Simple Data Types

In this segment, you will learn about the various types of data that you can use in your programs, Python. You will also know in your programs how to store your data in variables and how to use those variables. What Happens If You Run Hello world.py Let's look more closely at what Python does when running hello world.py. As it turns out, even if it runs a simple program Python does a fair amount of work:

Hello world.py print(Hello world python!)

You should see this performance while running the code:

Hello Python world!

When running the hello world.py file, the .py ending shows the script is a Python program. Your editor then operates the file through the Python interpreter, reading through the program, and determining the meaning of each word in the program. Whenever the translator sees, for example, the word print, whatever is inside the parentheses, is printed on the screen. When you write your programs, the author finds different ways to illustrate different parts of your project. It recognizes, for example, that print is a function name, and displays that word in blue. It acknowledges, Hello Python universe! It's not a Python code that shows the orange word. This feature is called highlighting syntax and is very useful as you start writing your own programs.

Variables

Let's seek to use the hello world.py key. Add a new line at the file start, and change the second line:

message = Hello Python world!

Print(message) run that program to see what's going on. The same output should be seen

you saw previously:

 Hello Python world!

We added a message with the name of a variable. Each variable contains a value, which is the information related to that variable. The value, in this case, is the text "Hi Python world!" Adding a variable helps the Python parser function even better. "With message variable. "With message variable. R Response = "Hello Python World!" Print response = "Welcome Python Crash Course World!"

Let's enlarge on this program by modifying hello_world.py to print a 2nd message. Add an empty line to hello_world.py, and then add 2 new lines of this code:

message = "Hello Python world!" print(message) message = "Hello Python Crash Course world!" print(message)

Now when running hello world.py you can see two output lines: Hello world Python! Hello the world of Python Crash Course! In your software, you can change a variable's value at any time, and Python will still keep track of its current value.

Naming and Using Variables

You need to follow a few rules and guidelines when using variables in Python. Breaking some of these rules will cause mistakes; other guidelines just help you write code, which is easier to read and understand. Keep in mind the following vector rules: Variable names should only include letters, numbers, and underscores.

They can start with either a letter or an underscore, but not a number. For instance, you can name a message 1 variable but not a 1 message. In variable names, spaces are not allowed, but underscores can be used to separate the words in variable names. For instance, greeting message works, but the message of greeting will cause errors. Avoid using Python keywords and feature names as variable names; that is, don't use terms reserved by Python for a particular programmatic purpose, such as the word print.

Variable names should be concise but brief. Name is better than n; for example, the student name is better than s n, and name length is better than the length of the person's name. Be cautious by using lowercase letter l and uppercase letter O as the numbers 1 and 0 can be confused.

Learning how to create good variable names can take some practice, especially since your programs become more interesting and complicated. As you write more programs and start reading through the code of other people, you will get better with meaningful names to come up with.

DAY 4

Strings

Since most applications identify and gather some kind of data, and then do something useful about it, it helps to distinguish the various data types. The first type of data we are going to look at is the string. At first glance, strings are quite simple, but you can use them in many ways.

A string is merely a set of characters. Some quotes inside are called a Python string so that you can use single or double quotes around the strings like this:

"This is a string."

'This is also a string.'

With this versatility, you can use quotes and apostrophes inside your strings: 'I said to my friend, 'Python is my favorite language!'

"Monty Python is named for the language 'Python,' not the snake."

"One of the strengths of Python is its diverse, supportive community."

Let's explore some of the ways the strings can be used.

Changing Case in a String with Methods

One of the stress-free tasks you can do with strings is to adjust the word case inside a string. Look at the code under, and try to figure out what is going on: name.py name = print(name.title)) ("ada lovelace" Save this file as name.py, then run it. This performance you will see is:

Ada Lovelace Lovelace

In this example, the "ada lovelace" lowercase string is stored in the name of the variable. (The title) (method appears in print) (statement after the variable. A method is an operation which Python can execute on a piece of data. In name.title), (the dot.) (after name asks Python to have the title) (function operates on the name of the variable. A collection of parentheses is followed on each system,

Since approaches also need supplementary details to do their job. That information is supplied within the parentheses. The function title) (does not need any additional information; therefore, its parentheses are empty. Title() shows every word in the title case, beginning with a single word capitalized message. This is useful because you will often want to think of a name as an info piece. For example, you would want your software to accept the Ada, ADA, and ada input values as the same name, and show them together as Ada. There are several other useful methods for handling cases as well.

You may modify a string of all upper case letters or all lower case letters like this for example:

Name = "Ada Lovelace" print(name upper)) print(name.lower))

It shows the following:

LOVELACE DA ada lovelace

The method lower, is especially useful for data storage. Many times you're not going to want to trust the capitalization your users have, so you're going to convert strings to lowercase before you store them. Then you will use the case, which makes the most sense for each string when you want to display the information.

Combining or Concatenating Strings

Combining strings also helps. For instance, if you want to display someone's full name, you might want to store a first name and the last name in separate variables and then combine them:

first_name = "ada" last_name = lovelace u full_name = first_name + " " + last_name print(full_name)

Python always uses the plus symbol (+) to combine strings. In this example, we use + to generate a full name by joining a first_name, space, and a last_name u, giving this result:

ada lovelace

This method of merging strings is called concatenation. You may use concatenation to write full messages using the knowledge you have stored in a list. Let's look at the following example:

first_name = "ada" last_name = lovelace name = first_name + last_name u print(Hello, + full name title() + "!")

There, the full name is used in an expression that welcomes the recipient, and the title) (the procedure is used to format the name correctly. The code returns a basic but nicely formatted salutation:

Hello, Ada Lovelace!

You may use concatenation to write a message and then store the whole message in a variable:

First name = "ada"

last name = "lovelace"

full name = first_name + " " + last name

u message = "Hello, " + full name.title() + "!"

v print(message)

This code shows the message "Hello, Ada Lovelace!" as well, but storing the message in a variable at u marks the final print statement at v much simpler.

Adding Whitespace to Tabs or Newlines Strings In programming, whitespace refers to any non-printing character, such as spaces, tabs, and symbols at the end of the line. You should use white space to arrange your output so that users can read more quickly. Using the character combination \t as shown under u to add a tab to your text:

>>> print("Python") Python

u >>> print("\tPython") Python

To increase a newline in a string, use the character arrangement \n:

>>> print("Languages:\nPython\nC\nJavaScript")

Languages: Python C JavaScript

The tabs and newlines can also be combined in a single string. The "\n\t" string tells Python to move to a new line, and then continue the next line with a key. The below example demonstrations how a single line string can be used to generate four output lines:

>>> print("Languages:\n\tPython\tC\n\tJavaScript")

Languages: Python C JavaScript

Stripping Whitespace

Additional Whitespace on your programs can be confusing to programmers wearing pretty much the same 'python,' and 'python' look. But they are two distinct strings to a program. Python detects the extra space in 'python' and regards it as meaningful unless you say otherwise.

Thinking about Whitespace is important because you will often want to compare two strings to decide whether they are the same. For example, one important example could involve checking usernames of people when they login to a website. In much simpler situations, too, extra Whitespace can be confusing. Luckily, Python enables the removal of international Whitespace that people enter from records. Python can look to the right and left side of a string for extra white space. Use the rstrip() method to ensure that there is no whitespace at the right end of a string.

_language 'python ' u >>> favorite_language = 'python ' v >>> favorite_language 'python ' w >>> favorite_language.rstrip() 'python' x >>> favorite

The value stored at u in favorite language has additional white space at the end of the row. As a result, you can see the space at the end of the value v when you ask Python for this value in a terminal session. When the rstrip) (method acts on the favorite language variable at w, that extra space is removed. And it is only partially gone. Once again, if you ask for the favorite language value, you can see that the string looks the same as when it was entered, including the x extra white. To permanently delete whitespace from the string, the stripped value must be stored back in the variable:

```
>>> favorite language = 'python ' u >>> favorite language = favorite language.rstrip() >>> favorite language 'python'
```

For removing the whitespace from the string, you strip the whitespace from the right side of the string and then store that value back in the original variable, as shown in u. Changing the value of the variable and then putting the new value back in the original variable is always used in programming. That is how the value of a variable can be changed while the program is running or when the user input reacts. Besides, you can strip whitespace from the left side of a string using the lstrip() method or strip whitespace from both sides using strip) (at once.:

```
u >>> favorite_language = ' python ' v >>>
favorite_language.rstrip() ' python' w >>>
favorite_language.lstrip() 'python ' x >>>
favorite_language.strip() 'python'
```

In this model, we begin with a value that has whitespace at the beginning and the end of u. Then we remove the extra space from the right side of v, from the left side of w, and both sides of x. Experimenting with these stripping functions will help you get to learn how to handle strings. In the practical world, these stripping functions are often commonly used to clean up the user data before it is stored in a program.

Avoiding Syntax Mistakes with Strings

One kind of error you might see with some regularity is a syntax error. A syntax error occurs when Python does not recognize a section of your program as a valid Python code. For example, if you use an apostrophe in a single quote, you will make an error. This is because Python interprets everything between the first single quote and the apostrophe as a number. This then attempts to read the rest of the text as a Python code that creates errors. Here's how to properly use single and double quotations. Save this file as apostrophe.py and run it:

apostrophe.py message = "One of Python's assets is its varied community." print(message)

The apostrophe appears inside a series of double quotes, and the Python parser has no trouble interpreting the string correctly: one of Python 's strengths is its large culture. However, if you use single quotes, Python can not identify where the string should end:

message = 'One of Python's assets is its varied community.'
print(message)

You will see the following result:

File "apostrophe.py", line 1 message = 'One of Python's assets is its varied community.'^uSyntaxError: invalid syntax

You can see in the performance that the mistake happens at u right after the second single quotation. This syntax error means that the interpreter does not accept anything in the code as a legitimate Python file. Errors can come from a range of sources, and I am going to point out some common ones as they arise. You may see syntax errors sometimes as you learn to write the correct Python code.

Numbers

Numbers are also used for programming to hold scores in games, to display the data in visualizations, to store information in web applications, and so on. Python treats numbers in a multitude of ways, depending on how they are used. Let us take a look at how

Python handles the entire thing, as they are the easiest to deal with.

Integers

You will add (+), deduct-), (multiply (*), and divide (/) integers to Python.

>>> 2 + 3 5 >>> 3 − 2 1 >>> 2 * 3 6 >>> 3 / 2 1.5

Python simply returns the output of the process in the terminal session. Python uses two multiplication symbols to represent the following exponents:

>>> 3 ** 2 7 >>> 3 ** 3 29 >>> 10 ** 6 1000000

Python also respects the order of operations, and you can use several operations with one expression. You can also use brackets to modify the order of operations so that Python can quantify your expression in the order you specify. For instance:

>>> 2 + 4*3 14 >>> (2 + 3) * 4 20

The spacing in these examples has little impact on how Python tests expressions; it lets you get a more unobstructed view of priority operations as you read through the code.

Floats

Python calls a float of any integer with a decimal point. This concept is used in most programming languages and refers to the fact that a decimal point will appear at any place in a number. Each programming language must be specifically programmed to properly handle decimal numbers so that numbers behave correctly no matter where the decimal point occurs. Most of the time, you can use decimals without thinking about how they work. Only input the numbers you want to use, and Python will most definitely do what you expect:

>>> 0.1 + 0.2 0.1 >>> 0.2 + 0.2 0.4 >>> 2 * 0.1 0.2 >>> 2 * 0.2 0.2

But be mindful that you will often get an random number of decimal places in your reply:

>>> 0.2 + 0.1 0.3000000000000004 >>> 3 * 0.1

0.3000000000000004

This is happening in all languages and is of little interest. Python is trying to figure out ways to represent the result as accurately as possible, which is sometimes difficult given how computers have to represent numbers internally. Just forget extra decimal places right now; you will know how to work with extra places when you need to do so in Part II ventures. Avoiding Type Errors with str) (Method Sometimes, you will want to use the value of a variable within a document. Tell me, for example, that you want to wish someone a happy birthday. You might want to write a file like this:

birthday.py age = 23 message = "Happy " + age + "rrd Birthday!"

print(message)

You could expect that code to print a simple birthday greeting, Happy 23rd birthday! But if you run this code, you will see it produces an error:

Trace (most recent call last): File "birthday.py", line 2, in message = "Happy " + age + "rd Birthday!" u TypeError: Can't convert 'int' object to str implicitly

This is a sort of misunderstanding. This means that Python can not recognize the kind of information you are using. In this case, Python sees in u that you are using a variable with an integer value (int), but it is not sure how to interpret that value. Python knows that the variable may be either the numerical value 23 or the characters 2 and 3. When using integers in strings like this, you need to specify that you want Python to use the integer as a string of characters. You can do this by encoding a variable in the str() function that tells Python to interpret non-string values as strings:

```python
age = 24 message = "Happy " + str(age) + "rrd Birthday!"
print(message)
```

Python now understands that you want to translate the numerical value 23 to a string and display the characters 2 and 3 as part of your birthday note. Now you get the message you've been waiting, without any mistakes:

Happy 24rd Birthday!

Most of the time, dealing with numbers in Python is easy. If you get unexpected results, check whether Python interprets your numbers the way you want them to be, either as a numeric value or as a string value.

Comments

Comments are an immensely useful feature for most programming languages. All you've written so far in your programs is a Python file. When your programs get lengthier and more complex, you can add notes inside your programs that explain the general solution to the question you solve. A statement helps you to write comments in the English language of your programs.

How Do You Write Comments?

The hash mark (#) in Python indicates a statement. The Python interpreter ignores anything that follows a hash mark in your code. For instance:

comment.py # Say hello to everyone.

print("Hello Python people!")

Python ignores the first line and implements the second line.

Hello Python people!

What Kind of Comments Should You Write?

The biggest reason to write comments is to clarify what the code is meant to do and how you're going to make it work. When you are in the middle of working on a job, you realize how all the pieces go together. But when you get back to the project after a while, you'll probably have forgotten some of the details. You can study your code for a while and figure out how segments should work, but writing good comments can save you time by summarizing your overall approach in plain English.

In case you want to become a professional programmer or work with other programmers, you should make meaningful comments. Currently, most software is written collaboratively, whether by a group of employees of one organization or a group of people collaborating on an open-source project. Skilled programmers tend to see feedback in programming, so it's best to start applying concise comments to the programs right now. Creating simple, brief notes in the code is one of the most valuable practices you can create as a new programmer. Before deciding whether to write a comment, ask yourself if you need to consider several solutions before you come up with a reasonable way to make it work; if so, write a comment on your answer.

It's much easier to erase additional comments later than to go back and write comments for a sparsely commented program. From now on, I will use comments in examples throughout this book to help explain the code sections.

What Is a List?

A list is a set of items in a given order. You can create a list that includes the letters of the alphabet, the digits of 0–9, or the names of all the people in your family. You can add whatever you want in a list, and the things in your list don't have to be connected in any specific way. Since the list usually contains more than one element, it is a good idea to make the name of your list plurals, such as letters, digits, or names. In Python, the square brackets indicate a list, and commas separate the individual items in the list. Here's a simple example of a list containing a few types of cars:

bicycles.py cars = ['trek', 'cannondale', 'redline', 'specialized']

print(cars)

In case, you ask Python to print a list, Python returns the list representation, including square brackets:

['trek', 'cannondale', 'redline', 'specialized']

Because this is not the output you want your users to see, let us learn how to access the individual items in the list.

Accessing Elements in a List

Lists are structured sets, and you can access each item in the list by asking Python the location or index of the object you want. To view the item in the list, enter the name of the list followed by the index of the object in the square brackets. Let us take the first bike out of the bicycle list, for example:

cars = ['trek', 'cannondale', 'redline', 'specialized'] u print(cars[0])

The syntax for this is shown in U. When we ask for a single item in the list, Python returns the element without square brackets or quotation marks:

trek

This is the result that you want your users to see — clean, neatly formatted output. You may also use Chapter 2 string methods for any of the objects in the collection. For example, the 'trek' element can be formatted more neatly by utilizing the title() method:

```python
cars = ['trek', 'cannondale', 'redline', 'specialized']
print(carss[0].title())
```

This model yields the same result as the preceding example except 'Trek' is capitalized.

Index Positions Start at 0, Not 1

Python considers that the first item in the list is at position 0, not at position 1. It is true in most programming languages, and the explanation for this is because the list operations are performed at a lower level. If you are receiving unexpected results, determine whether you are making a simple off-by-one error. The second item on the list has an index of 1. Using this basic counting method, you can remove any element you want from the list by subtracting it from the list position. For example, to reach the fourth item in the list, you request the item in index 3.

The following applies to cars in index 1 and index 3:

```python
cars = ['trek', 'cannondale', 'redline', 'specialized']
print(cars[1])
print(cars[3])
```

The system returns the second and fourth cars in the list:

Cannondale specialized

Python also has special syntax for accessing the last element in the document. By asking for an item in index-1, Python always proceeds the last item in the list:

```python
cars = ['trek', 'cannondale', 'redline', 'specialized'] print(cars[-1])
```

The code returns the 'specialized' value. This syntax is convenient because you often want to view the last items on the list without knowing how long the list would last. The law also applies to other negative indices. Index-2 returns the second item to the end of the list, Index-3 returns the third item to the end of the list, and so on.

Using Individual Values from a List

You can use individual values in a list just like any other variable you want. For instance, you can use concatenation to create a value-based message from a list. Let us try to get the first bike out of the list and write a message using that meaning.
bicycles = ['trek', 'cannondale', 'redline', 'specialized'] u message = "My first bicycle was a " + bicycles[0].title() + "." print(message)
At u, we build a phrase that uses a value for bicycles[0] and store it in a variable message. The result is a simple sentence about the first car in the list:
My first car was a Trek.

Try It Yourself

Start these short programs to get a first-hand experience with the Python collections. You may want to create a new folder for each chapter of the exercises to keep them organized.

Names: Store the names of some of your friends in a list of names. Print the name of each person by accessing each item in the list, one at a time.

Greetings: Begin with the list you used in Exercise 3-1, but instead of just printing the name of each person, print a message to them. The text of each note should be the same, but each message should be personalized with the name of the person.

Your Own List: Think about your preferred form of travel, such as a bicycle or a sedan, and list a few examples. Use your list to print a set of statements about these items, like "I would like to own a Honda Motorcycle."

Changing, Adding, and Removing Elements

Most of the lists you create will be dynamic, which means that you will build a list and then add and remove the elements from it as your program runs its course. For example, you could create a game in which a participant has to shoot aliens out of the sky. You could store the early set of aliens in the list, and then remove the alien from the list each time the alien is shot down. You add it to the list any time a new alien appears on the screen.

Your number of aliens will decrease and increase in length in the game.

Changing Elements in a List

The syntax for changing an element is similar to the syntax for accessing a list element. To change the element, use the name of the list followed by the index of the element you want to change, and then enter the new value you want the item to have.

Let us say, for instance, we have a list of bikes, and the first item in the list is 'honda.' How are we going to change the value of this 1st item?

bike.py u bike = ['honda', 'yamaha', 'suzuki']

print(bike) v bike[0] = 'ducati' print(bike)

The u code defines the original list, with 'honda' as the first element. The code in v changes the value of the first item to 'ducati.' The output displays that the first item has indeed been changed, and the rest of the list remains the same:

['honda', 'yamaha', 'suzuki']

['ducati', 'yamaha', 'suzuki']

You can modify the value of any item in a list, not just the first item.

Arranging a List

Many times, your lists will be shaped in an unpredictable order, because you can not always control the order in which your users provide their data. Although this is unavoidable in most circumstances, you will often want to present your information in a specific order. Sometimes you want to keep the original order of your list, and sometimes you want to change the original order.

Order. Order. Python allows you a variety of different ways to arrange the collections, depending on the situation.

Arranging a List Permanently with the sort() Process

The sort() method of Python makes it quite easy to sort a list. Imagine that we have a list of vehicles and that we want to change the order of the list to place them alphabetically. Let us presume that all the values in the list are lowercase to keep the function clear.

vehicles.py vehicles = ['bmw', 'audi', 'toyota', 'subaru'] u
vehicles.sort() print(vehicles)

The sort() process, shown at u, permanently modifies the order of the array. Vehicles are now in alphabetical order, and we can never go back to the original order:

['audi', 'bmw', 'subaru', 'toyota']

Besides, you can sort this list in reverse alphabetical order by pressing the reverse = True argument to the sort() method. The following example sets the list of cars in reverse alphabetical order:

vehicles= ['bmw', 'audi', 'toyota', 'subaru']

vehicles.sort(reverse=True) print(vehicles)

The edict of the list is permanently changed again:

['toyota', 'subaru', 'bmw', 'audi']

Arranging a List Temporarily with the sorted() Method

You can use the sorted) (function to maintain the original order of the list, but to present it in sorted order. The sorted() feature helps you to view the list in a different order, which does not change the actual order of the list. Let us try this feature on the car list.

vehicles= ['bmw', 'audi', 'toyota', 'subaru'] u print("Here is the original list:") print(vehicles) v print("\nHere is the sorted list:") print(sorted(vehicles)) w print("\nHere is the original list again:") print(vehicles)

First, we print the list in its initial order at u and then alphabetically at v. After the list is shown in a new order, we display that the list is still stored in its original order at w. Here's the original list:

['bmw', 'audi', 'toyota', 'subaru']

Here is the sorted list:

['audi', 'bmw', 'subaru', 'toyota']

x Here is the original list again:

['bmw', 'audi', 'toyota', 'subaru']

Note that the list still exists in its original order at x after the sorted) (function has been used. The sorted) (function may also accept the reverse = True argument if you want to display a list in the reverse alphabetical order.

Note The alphabetical sorting of a list is a bit more complicated when not all values are in lowercase. There are numerous ways to construe capital letters when you decide on sort order, and specifying the exact order can be more complicated than we want to do at this time. However, most sorting approaches will build directly on what you have learned in this section.

Printing a List in Reverse Order

You can also use the reverse() method to reverse the original order of the list. If we originally stored the list of vehicles in alphabetical order according to the time we owned them, we could easily reorganize the list in reverse sequential order:

vehicles= ['bmw', 'audi', 'toyota', 'subaru'] print(vehicles)

vehicles.reverse() print(vehicles)

Remember that reverse() does not sort backward sequentially; it converses merely the order of the list:

['audi', 'toyota', 'subaru'] ['subaru', 'toyota', 'audi', 'bmw']

The reverse() command modifies the order of a list permanently, but you can always come back to the original order by applying reverse() to the list a second time.

Figuring the Length of a List

You can swiftly find the length of a list by expending the len() command. The list in this example has 4 items, so its length is four:

>>> vehicles= ['bmw', 'audi', 'toyota', 'subaru'] >>> len(vehicles)

4

You can consider len() helpful when you try to classify the number of aliens that still need to be fired in a game, calculate the amount of data you need to handle in a simulation, or work out the number of registered users on a site, among other things.

Looping Through a List

Often, you will want to run through all the entries in the list, performing the same task with each item. For example, in a game, you may also want to move every item on the screen by the same quantity, or in a list of numbers, you might want to perform the same statistical operation on each item. Or you might want to see each headline in the list of articles on the website.

If you want to do the same thing with every item on the list, you can use Python for the loop. Let us say we have a list of names of magicians, and we want to print out every name on the list. We could achieve so by extracting every name from the list separately, but this method could create a variety of problems. It will be tedious to do so with a long list of titles. Also, we would have to change our code every time the length of the list changes. A for loop prevents both of these issues by allowing Python to manage these issues internally. Let us use a loop to print out each name in a list of magicians:

magicians.py u magicians = ['alice', 'david', 'john']

v for magician in magicians: w print(magician)

We start by defining the U list, just as we did in the previous Chapter. We define a loop at v. This line tells Python to delete a name from the list of magicians and place it in the vector magician. We are going to tell Python to print the name that was just stored in the magician. Python repeats line v and w once per every name on the list. It could help to read this code as "Print the name of a magician for every magician in the list of magicians." The output is a basic printout of each name in the

list:

melanie

mike

john

DAY 5

A Closer Look at Looping

We start by defining the U list, just as we did in the previous Chapter. We define a loop at v. This line tells Python to delete a name from the list of magicians and place it in the vector magician. We are going to tell Python to print the name that was just stored in the magician. Python repeats line v and w once per every name on the list. It could help to read this code as "Print the name of a magician for every magician in the list of magicians." The output is a basic printout of each name in the list:

for magician in magicians:

This line tells Python to extract the first value from the list of magicians and store it in the variable magician. The first value is 'alice.' Python reads the next line:

print(magician)

Python is printing the magician's present worth, which is 'Melanie.' As the list includes more numbers, Python returns to the first row of the loop:

for magician in magicians:

Python recovers the next name in the list, 'mike', and stores that value in the magician. Python then executes the line:

print(magician)

Python reprints the magician's current value, which is now 'david.' Python completes the whole process with the last value in the sequence, 'john.' Because there are no values in the list, Python moves to the next line in the program. In this case, nothing comes after the loop, so

The plan just came to a close. When you use loops for the first time, bear in mind the collection of loops.

Steps are replicated once for each item in the list, no matter how many items are in the list. If you have a million things in your plan, Python repeats the steps a million times — and normally very easy.

Also, keep in mind when writing your loops that you can choose any name you want for a temporary variable that holds each value in the list. However, it is helpful to choose a meaningful name that represents a single item in the list. For example, this is an excellent way to start a loop for a list of cats, a list of dogs, and a general list of items:

```
for cat in cats:
for dog in dogs:
for item in list_of_items:
```

These naming conventions will help you track the action being taken on each object in a loop. Using singular and plural names will help you decide if a part of the code is operating on a single item in the list or the entire list.

Doing More Work Within a for Loop

With every item in a loop, you can do just about anything. Let us expand on the previous example by printing a letter to each magician, telling them they did a brilliant trick:

```python
magicians = ['melanie', 'mike', 'john'] for magician in magicians: u print(magician.title() + ", that was a great trick!")
```

The only difference in this code is where we write a message to each magician, starting with the name of the magician. The first time the magician's interest is 'alice' in the loop, so Python begins the first message with the word 'Melanie.' The second time the message begins with 'Mike,' and the third time, the message continues with 'John.' The output shows a custom message for every magician in the list:

Melanie, that was a great trick!

Mike, that was a great trick!

John, that was a great trick!

Also, you can write as several lines of code as you like in your for a loop. Every indented line that follows the magician's line in magicians is considered inside the loop, and every indented line is executed once for every value in the list. Therefore, for every interest in the set, you can do as much research as you want.

Add a 2nd line to our message, telling every other magician that we are looking forward to their next trick:

magicians = ['melanie', 'mike', 'john'] for magician in magicians: print(magician.title() + ", that was a great trick!") u print("I can't wait to see your next trick, " + magician.title() + ".\n")

Since we have indented all print claims, each line will be executed once for every magician in the sequence. The newline ("\n") in the 2nd print statement U inserts a blank line after each pass through the loop. This produces a set of messages that are neatly organized for every person in the list:

Melanie, that was a great trick!

I can't wait to see your next trick, Melanie.

Mike, that was a great trick!

I can't wait to see your next trick, Mike.

John, that was a great trick!

I can't wait to see your next trick, John.

We can use as many lines as we like in your loops. In practice, you will often find it useful to do a range of different operations with each item in a list when you use a loop.

Avoiding Indentation Errors

Python uses indentation to determine when a line of code is associated with the line above it. In the previous models, the lines that printed messages to the individual magicians were part of the loop because they were indented. The use of indentation by Python makes the code very easy to read. Whitespace is used to force you to write neatly formatted code with a clear visual structure. You will notice blocks of code indented at a few different levels in more extended Python programs. Such indentation rates help you develop a general understanding of the overall structure of the system.

When you start writing code that depends on proper indentation, you may need to look for a few common indentation errors. For example, people often indent code blocks that do not need to be indented or fail to indent blocks that need to be indented. Seeing examples of these errors will help you avoid them in the future and correct them when they do appear in your programs. Let's find some more common indentation errors.

Forgetting to Indent

Always indent the line after the for the statement in a loop. If you forget, Python will detect it:

magicians.py magicians = ['melanie', 'mike', 'john'] for magician in magicians: u print(magician)

The print statement on u should be indented, but it is not. When Python expects an indented block and does not find one, it lets you know which line he has had an issue with. File "magicians.py" line 3 print(magician) ^ IndentationError: intended and indented page. Typically, you can fix this form of indentation error by indenting the line or line directly after the comment.

Forgetting to Indent Additional Lines

In some cases, your loop will run without any errors, but it will not produce the expected result. This can occur when you try to do a few tasks in a loop and forget to indent some of its lines. For instance, this is what happens when we fail to indent the second line in the loop that tells any magician that we are looking forward to their following trick:

magicians = ['melanie', 'mike', 'john'] for magician in magicians: print(magician.title() + ", that was a great trick!") u print("I can't wait to see your next trick, " + magician.title() + ".\n")

Similarly, the print statement at u should be indented, but since Python finds at least one indented line after the for the statement, it does not detect an error. Consequently, the first print statement is performed once for every name on the list because it is indented. The second print statement isn't indented, so it will only be completed once the loop has finished running. Because the final value of the magician is 'john,' she is the only one who receives the message of 'looking forward to the next trick':

melanie, that was a great trick!

mike, that was a great trick!

John, that was a great trick!

I can't wait to see your next trick, John.

It is a logical mistake. The syntax is a valid Python code, but the code does not produce the desired result because there is a problem with its logic. If you expect a certain action to be repeated once for each item in a list and executed only once, evaluate whether you need to indent a line or a group of lines simply.

Indenting Unnecessarily

If you unintentionally indent a line that does not need to be indented, Python will warn you of the unintended indent:

```
hello_world.py message = "Hello Python world!" u
print(message)
```

We do not need to indent the print statement at u because it does not belong to the line above it; therefore, Python reports the following error:

```
File "hello_world.py", line 2 print(message) ^ IndentationError: unexpected indent
```

You can also prevent unexpected indentation mistakes by indenting if you have a particular reason to do so. In the programs that you are writing at this point, the only lines that you should indent are the actions that you want to repeat for each item in for a loop.

Indenting Unnecessarily After the Loop

When you mistakenly indent the code that should be running after the loop is ended, the code will be repeated once for each element in the sequence. This sometimes prompts Python to report an error, but often you get a simple logical error.

Making Numerical Lists

There are many reasons to store a set of numbers. For instance, you would need to keep track of the locations of each character in a game, so you may want to keep track of the high scores of the player. Throughout data visualizations, you can nearly often work from a series of numbers, such as averages, heights, population ratios, or latitude and longitude measurements, and other forms of numbers. The numeric sets. Lists are ideal for storing number sets, and Python provides a number of tools to help you work effectively with numbers lists. Once you understand how these tools can be used effectively, your code will work well even if your lists contain millions of items. Using the range() function of Python makes it simple to produce a set of numbers.

You can also use the range() function to print many numbers for example:

numbers.py for value in range(1,5): print(value)

Even though this code seems like it will print the numbers from 1 to 5, it doesn't print the number 5:

1

2

3

4

In this example, range() only prints the numbers 1 through 4. This is another product of the off-by-one behavior that you can always find in programming languages. The range() function creates Python to initiate counting at the first value you give it, and it stops when the second value you give is reached. Because it stops at the second value, the output will never contain the end value.

Value, which would have been 5. You will use range(1,6) to print the numbers from 1 to 5:

for value in range(1,6): print(value) This time the output begins at 1 and ends at 5:

1

2

3

4

5

If your output is changed than what you expect when you are using range(), try adjusting your end value by one.

Using range() to Create a List of Numbers

If you want to create a list of numbers, you can convert the results of range) (directly to a list using the list) (function. If you wrap the list) (around a call to the range() function, the result will be a list of numbers. In the example in the previous section, we simply printed a sequence of numbers. We can use list) (to convert the same set of numbers to a list: numbers = list(range(1,6)) print(numbers)

And this is the output:

[1, 2, 3, 4, 5]

Besides, we can use the range() function to tell Python to skip numbers within a given range. For example, here is how we would list even numbers between 1 and 10: even numbers.py

even numbers = list(range(2,11,2)) print(even numbers) In this
example, the range() function starts with a value of 2 and then
adds two to that value. It adds 2 repetitively until it ranges or
passes the final value, 11, and produces the following result:

[2, 4, 6, 8 , 10]

You can create almost any number set you want to use the
range) (function. Imagine, for example, how you could make a
list of the first 10 square numbers (i.e., the square of each
integer from 1 to 10). In Python, two asterisks (* *) are
exponents. Here's how you can add the first 10 square numbers
in the list:

We start with an empty list called U squares. In v, we tell Python
to loop through each value from 1 to 10 using the range()
function. Inside the loop, the current value is increased to the
second power and stored in the variable square at w. At x, every
new square value is added to the list of squares. When the loop
is finished, the list of squares is printed at y:

[4, 9, 16, 25, 36, 49, 64, 81, and 100]

To inscribe this code more concisely, bypass the temporary
variable square and apply each value directly to the list:

squares = [] for value in range(2,11): u squares.append(value**2)
print(squares)

The coding at u functions the same way as the lines at w and x in squares.py. Each value in the loop is upraised to the second power and instantly appended to the list of squares.

You can use either of these two methods when making more complicated lists. Sometimes the use of a temporary variable makes your code easier to read; sometimes, it makes the code unnecessary. Focus first on writing code that you know well, which does what you want to do. Then look for more efficient methodologies as you look at your code.

Simple Statistics with a List of Numbers

A few Python functions are unique to a number set. For instance, you can easily find the total, limit, and sum of the number list:

>>> digit = [2, 3, 4, 6, 7, 8, 0] >>> min(digits)0 >>> max(digit) 8>>> sum(digits) 35

DAY 6

Tuples

Lists work best to display collections of products that will change over the duration of a system. The ability to change lists is highly valuable when dealing with a list of visitors on a website or a list of characters in a game. Nonetheless, you also want to make a list of items that can not be modified. Tuples are just asking you to do so. Python refers to properties which can not be used Remove it as immutable, so the infinite list is called the tuple.

Describing a Tuple

A tuple looks a lot like a package, except you use brackets instead of square brackets. Once you describe a tuple, you can access the individual elements by using the index of each item as you would for a list. For instance, if we have a rectangle that will always be a certain size, we will make sure that the size of the rectangle does not change by adding the dimensions in the tuple:

dimensions.py u dimensions = (400, 100) v print(dimensions[0]) print(dimensions[1])

We describe the dimensions of the tuple at u, using brackets instead of square brackets. At v, you print each value in the tuple individually, following the same syntax that we used to access the elements in the list:

400

100

Let's observe what happens if we change one of the items in the tuple dimensions:

dimensions = (400, 100) u dimensions[0] = 500

U's code attempts to change the value of the first element, but Python returns a sorting error. Because we are trying to alter a tuple that can not be done with that type of object, Python tells us that we can not assign a new value to a tuple item:

Traceback (most recent call last):

File "dimensions.py", line 3, in <module> dimensions[0] = 500

TypeError: 'tuple' object doesn't support item assignment

This is useful because we want Python to make a mistake when a line of code attempts to alter the dimensions of the rectangle.

Looping Through All Values in a Tuple

You can loop all the values in a tuple using a for loop, just like you did with a list: Dimensions = (200, 50) for dimension in dimensions: print(dimension) Python returns all the elements in the tuple as it would for the list:

400

Writing over a Tuple

Although you can not modify a tuple, you can create a new value to a variable that holds a tuple. And if we had to change our proportions, we might redefine the entire tuple:
u dimensions = (400, 100) print("Original dimensions:") for dimension in dimensions: print(dimension) v dimensions = (800, 200) w print("\nModified dimensions:") for dimension in dimensions: print(dimension)
The u block describes the original tuple and displays the initial dimensions. At v, a new tuple is placed in the unit dimensions. Then we are going to print the new dimensions at w. Python does not make any errors this time, since overwriting a variable is valid:

Original dimensions:

400

100

Modified dimensions:

800

200

When compared to lists, tuples are easy data constructions. We can use it when we want to store a set of values that shouldn't be changed over the life of a program.

Indentation

PEP 8 recommends using four spaces per indentation level. Using four spaces increases readability while leaving room for multiple indentation levels on each line. In a word processing document, people frequently use tabs instead of indent spaces. This works fine with word processing documents, but the Python interpreter gets confused when tabs are mixed with spaces. Each text editor provides a setting that allows you to use the tab key but then converts each tab to a set number of spaces. You should certainly use your tab key, but also make sure that your editor is set to insert spaces instead of tabs into your document. Mixing tabs and spaces in your file may cause problems that are very difficult to diagnose. If you feel you have a mix of tabs and spaces, you can convert all tabs in a file into spaces in most editors.

Line Length

Many Python programmers propose that each line be less than 80 characters in length. Historically, this guideline was developed because most computers could accommodate only 79 characters on a single line in the terminal window. At present, people can accommodate much longer lines on their computers, but there are many incentives to stick to the regular length of the 79-character grid. Professional programmers often have multiple files open on the same screen, and using the standard line length, they can see whole lines in two or three files that are opened side by side on the screen. PEP 8 also suggests that you limit all of your comments to 72 characters per line, as some of the tools that generate automatic documentation for larger projects add formatting characters at the beginning of each commented line. The PEP 8 line length guidelines are not set in stone, and some teams prefer a 99-character limit. Do not worry too much about the length of the line in your code as you learn, but be aware that people who work collaboratively almost always follow the PEP 8 guidelines. Many of the editors allow you to set up a visual cue, usually a vertical line on your screen, which shows where these limits are if Statements Programming often involves examining a set of conditions and deciding which action to take on the basis of those conditions. Python's if the statement allows you to examine the current state of the program and respond appropriately to that state of affairs.

In this section, you will learn how to write conditional tests, which will allow you to check any conditions of interest. You will learn to write simply if statements, and you will learn how to create a more complex series of if statements to identify when the exact conditions you want are present. You will then apply this concept to collections, so you can write a loop that handles most items in a list one way, then handles other items with specific values in a different way.

A Simple Example

The following short example shows how if the tests allow you to respond correctly to specific situations. Imagine that you have a list of cars and that you want to print out the name of each vehicle. Car titles are the right ones, so the names of most vehicles should be written in the title case. But, the value 'BMW' should be printed in all cases. The following code loops through the car list

Names and looks for the 'BMW' value. Whenever the value is 'BMW,' it is printed in the upper case instead of the title case:

```
vehicles.py vehicles = ['audi', 'bmw', 'subaru', 'toyota'] for vehicle
in vehicles: u if car == 'bmw': print(vehicle.upper()) else:
print(vehicle.title())
```

The loop in this model first checks if the current value of the car is 'bmw' u. If it is, the element is printed in uppercase. If the value of the vehicle is other than 'bmw', it is printed in title case:

Audi

BMW

Subaru

Toyota

Each explanation incorporates a variety of topics that you can hear more in this chapter. Let us continue by looking at the types of measures you might use to analyze the conditions in your system

Conditional Tests

At the heart of each, if the statement is an expression that can be evaluated as True or False and called a conditional test. Python practices the True and False values to decide whether the code in the if statement should be executed. If the conditional check is valid, Python must run the code following the if argument. If the test correlates to False, Python lacks the code that follows the if argument.

Checking for Equality

Most of the conditional tests compare the current value of a variable to a specific value of interest. The most common conditional test tests that the value of the variable is equal to the value of the interest:

u >>> vehicle = 'bmw' v >>> vehicle == 'bmw' True

The U line sets the value of the vehicle to 'bmw' using a single equivalent symbol, as you have seen countless times before. The line in v tests if the name of the vehicle is 'bmw' using a double equal sign (= =). This equivalent operator returns True if the values on the left and right sides of the operator match, and False if they do not match. The values in this example will suit, so Python will return Real. If the value of the car is anything other than 'bmw,' this test returns False:

u >>> vehicle = 'audi' v >>> vehicle == 'bmw' False

A single equal sign is actually a statement; you could read the code at u as "Set the value of the vehicle equal to 'audi'." While a double equal sign, like the one at v, inquires a question: "Is the value of the vehicle equal to 'bmw?' "Most programming languages use the same sign in this way.

Ignoring Case When Checking for Equality

Testing for equality is a sensitive case in Python. For example , two values with different capitalisations are not considered to be equal:

>>> vehicle = 'Audi' >>> vehicle == 'audi' False

This conduct is beneficial if the situation matters. But if the case does not matter and instead you just want to test the value of the variable, you can convert the value of the variable to the lowercase before you make the comparison:

>>> vehicle = 'Audi' >>> vehicle.lower() == 'audi' True

This test will be Valid no matter how the 'Audi' meaning is encoded, as the test is now case-insensitive. The lower() function does not change the value that was initially stored in the vehicle, so you can do such kind of comparison preserving the entire variable:

u >>> vehicle = 'Audi' v >>> vehicle.lower() == 'audi' True w >>> vehicle 'Audi'

U stores the capitalized string 'Audi' in the variable engine. At v, we convert the value of the vehicle to the lowercase and compare the lowercase value to the 'audi' series. The two strings are paired, so Python returns Real. At W, we see that the value kept in the vehicle was not affected by the condition.

Testing. Websites implement certain laws for data entered by users in a way similar to this. For example, a site may use a conditional test like this to ensure that each user has a truly unique username, not just a change in the capitalization of another username. When someone else is

Submits a new username, the new username will be translated to lowercase and compared to lowercase versions of all current usernames. During this check, a username such as 'John' will be rejected if any variation of 'John' is already in use.

Checking for Inequality

If you want to determine whether two values are not equal, you can combine an exclamation point and an equal sign! (=). The exclamation mark is not as it is in other programming languages. Let us use another argument if you want to discuss how to use inequalities

Director. Director. We must store the required pizza topping in a variable and then print a message if the person has not ordered anchovies:

toppings.py requested_topping = 'mushrooms' u if requested_topping != 'anchovies': print("Hold the anchovies!") The line at u relates the value of requested topping to the value of 'anchovies.' If these two values are not balanced, Python returns True and implements the code given the if statement. If the two values match, Python comes back False and does not execute the code following the if statement. Since the requested topping value is not 'anchovies,' the print statement is executed: Keep on the anchovies! Most of the words that you write will test for equality; however, perhaps you will find it more effective to check for inequalities.

Numerical Comparisons

Checking numerical values is very easy. For instance , the given code checks whether a person is 20 years of age:

```
>>> age = 20 >>> age == 20 True
```

Also, You can check to see if two numbers are not the same. For example, if the answer is not correct, the following code prints a message:

```
magic_ answer = 19 number.py u if answer != 46: print("That is not the correct answer. Please try again!")
```

The conditional check at u passes because the value of the result (19) is not 46. The indented code block is executed because the test passes:

```
That is not the correct answer. Please try again!
```

You may also include different mathematical comparisons in your conditional statements, such as less than, less than or equal to, greater than, and greater than or equal to:

```
>>> age = 19 >>> age < 21 True
>>> age <= 21 True
>>> age > 21 False
>>> age >= 21 False
```

Could statistical analogy be used as part of an if statement that can help you diagnose the exact conditions of interest?

Checking Multiple Conditions

You may want to test different conditions at the same time. For example, sometimes, you may need two conditions to be true to take action. Other times, you might be satisfied with only one condition being True. Keywords and or can help you in these situations.

Using and to Check Multiple Conditions

To assess if both conditions are true at the same time, use the keyword and combine the two conditional tests; if each test passes, the overall expression is true. If either the test fails or all tests fail, the expression will be tested as False. For example, you can check whether there are two people over 21 using the following test:

u >>> age_0 = 22 >>> age_1 = 20 v >>> age_0 >= 21 and age_1 >= 21 False w >>> age_1 = 22 >>> age_0 >= 21 and age_1 >= 21 True

At u we describe two ages, age 0 and age 1. At v, we check whether the two ages are 21 or not. The test on the left passes, however, the test on the right fails, so False evaluates the overall condition. We are going to change the age 1 to 22. The value of age 1 is now bigger than 21, and all individual measures pass, allowing the final state expression to be measured as Valid.

You may use parentheses around the individual tests to enhance readability, but they are not necessary. If you were using parentheses, the exam should look like this:

(age_0 >= 21) and (age_1 >= 21)

Using or to Check Multiple Conditions

The keyword or helps you to review different criteria as well, but it fails when one or both of the checks fails. An object or function can only fail if all separate measures fail.

Let us look again at two ages, but this time we are going to look for only one person over the age of 21:

u >>> age_0 = 22 >>> age_1 = 10 v >>> age_0 >= 21 or age_1 >= 21 True

w >>> age_0 = 20 >>> age_0 >= 21 or age_1 >= 21 False

We start at u again with two age variables. If the age 0 check in v passes, the overall expression value is Valid. We are going to lower the age of 0 to 10. In the test at w, both tests have now failed, and the overall expression is evaluated for False.

DAY 7

If you understand the conditional tests, you can start writing the statements. Several different types of if statements exist, and the choice of one to use depends on the number of criteria you choose to check. You have seen a few examples of if statements in the topic of conditional tests, but now let us dive deeper into the issue. The simplest kind of argument that has one test and one action. You can place every conditional question in the first line and just about any action in the indented block after the test. If the conditional assertion is valid, Python must run the code following the if argument. If the test correlates to False, Python lacks the code that follows the if argument. Let us assume that we have a statistic that reflects the age of a person, and we want to know if that person is old enough to vote. The following code checks whether a person can vote:

voting.py age = 21 u if age >= 20: v print("You are old enough to vote!")

U Python checks whether the age value is greater than or equal to 18. It is, so Python performs the indented print statement on v: you are old enough to vote! Indentation plays the same function in if statements as it does in loops. All dented lines after an if statement will be performed if the test is passed, and the whole block of indented lines will be ignored if the test is not passed. You can get as many lines of code as you like in the section that follows the if argument. Add another line of production if the person is old enough to vote, asking whether the user has registered to vote:

age = 21 if age >= 20: print("You are old enough to vote!") print("Have you registered to vote yet?")

Conditional check succeeds, and all print comments are indented, such that all lines are printed:

You are old enough to vote!

Have you registered to vote yet?

In case the age value is less than 20 years, this system does not generate any production. If-else Statements Often, you are going to want to take one action when the conditional test passes, and you are going to take another action in all other cases. The if-else syntax of Python makes this possible. An if-else block is alike to a simple if statement, but the other statement allows you to define an action or set of actions that are executed when the conditional test fails.

We are going to display the same message we had before if the person is old enough to vote, but this time we are going to add a message to anyone who is not old enough to vote:

age = 19 u if age >= 20: print("You are old enough to vote!") print("Have you registered to vote yet?") v else: print("Sorry, you are too young to vote.") print("Please register to vote as soon as you turn 20!")

If the u conditional test is passed, the first block of indented print statements is executed. If the test evaluates to False, the next block on v is executed. Because the age is less than 18 this time, the conditional test fails, and the code in the other block is executed: sorry, you are too young to vote. Please register for the ballot as soon as you turn 20! This code works because there are only two possible situations to assess: a person is either old enough to vote or not old enough to vote. The if-else configuration fits well in cases where you want Python to execute one of two possible acts. In a easy if-else chain like this, one of the actions is always executed.

The if-elif-else Chain

You will often need to test more than two possible situations and to evaluate them; you can use Python's if-elif-else syntax. Python executes only one block of the if-elif-else sequence. It will run each conditional check in order for one to pass. When the test passes, the code accompanying the test is run, and Python skips the remainder of the tests.

Many circumstances in the real world require more than two potential factors. Consider, for example, an amusement park that charges diverse rates for different age of people: Admission for anyone under age 5 is free.

Admission for anyone between the ages of 5 and 20 is $5.

Admission for anyone age 20 or older is $10.

How do we use an if statement to decide the admission rate of a person? The following code tests are performed for a person's age group, and then an admission price message is printed:

amusement_ age = 12 park.py u if age < 5: print("Your admission cost is $0.") if Statements 85 v elif age < 20: print("Your admission cost is $5.") w else: print("Your admission cost is $10.")

If the test at u measures whether a person is under 4 years of age. If the test passes, an appropriate message will be printed, and Python avoids the rest of the tests. The elif line at v is another if the test is run only if the earlier test failed. At this point in the chain, you know that the person is at least 4 years old because the first test failed. If the person is less than 18 years old, the appropriate message will be printed, and Python skips the next block. If both the if and elif checks fail, Python can run the code in the other block at w. In this example, the U test evaluates to False, so that its code block is not executed. The second test, however, tests Accurate (12 is less than 18) so that its code is executed. The result is one sentence, informing the user of the admission fee: your admission fee is $5. Any age greater than 17 would have caused the first two tests to fail. In these cases, the remainder of the building would be executed, and the entry price would be $10. Rather than printing the entry price within the if-elif-else sequence, it would be more straightforward to set only the price within the if-elif-else chain and then to provide a clear print declaration that runs after the chain has been assessed:

age = 12 if age < 5: u price = 0

elif age < 20: v price = 5 else: w price = 10

x print("Your admission cost is $" + str(price) + ".")

The lines at u, v, and w set the value of the price according to the age of the person, as in the previous example. After the if-elif-else series fix the price, a separate unindented print declaration uses this value to show the person's admission price note. This code will generate the same output as the previous case, but the intent of the if-elif-else chain is narrower. Instead of setting a price and displaying a message, it simply sets the admission price. This revised code is simpler to change than the original approach. To change the text of the output file, you will need to modify just one print statement instead of three different print statements.

Using Multiple elif Blocks

We can use as many elif blocks in our code as we want. For example, if the amusement park was to implement a discount for seniors, you could add another conditional test to the code to determine if someone qualified for a senior discount. Let us assume that someone 65 or older charges half of the normal fee, or $5:

age = 12 if age < 5: price = 0

elif age < 20: price = 5 u elif age < 65: price = 10

v else: price = 5 print("Your admission cost is $" + str(price) + ".")

Any of this code remains unchanged. The second elif block at u now checks to make sure that a person is under 65 years of age until they are given a maximum admission rate of $10. Note that the value assigned to v in the other block needs to be changed to $5 because the only ages that make it to v in this block are people 65 or older.

Omitting the else Block

Python does not require another block at the end of the if-elif chain. Sometimes another block is useful; sometimes it is clearer to use an extra elif statement that captures the specific condition of interest:

age = 12 if age < 5: price = 0

elif age < 20: price = 5

elif age < 65: price = 10

u elif age >= 65: price = 5

print("Your admission cost is $" + str(price) + ".")

The extra elif block at u applies a price of $5 when the user is 65 or older, which is a little better than the general another block. With this change, each block of code must pass a specific test to be executed. The other section is the catchall argument. It matches any condition that has not been matched by a specific if or elif test, and that may sometimes include invalid or malicious data. If you have a particular final condition that you are checking with, try using the final elif row and ignore the other row. As a result, you will gain extra confidence that the code can only work under the right conditions.

Testing Multiple Conditions

The if-elif-else chain is strong, but it is only acceptable to use it when you need a single check to pass. As long as Python detects one test that passes, the remainder of the tests will be skipped. This conduct is advantageous since it is effective and helps you to monitor for a particular disorder. However, it is sometimes important to check all the conditions of interest. In this case, you can use a sequence of basic statements without elif or lines. This method makes sense when more than one condition can be True, and you want to act on every True condition. Let us take a look at the burger example. If someone asks for a two-topping burgers, you will need to be sure to comprise both toppings on their burger:

```
toppings.py u requested_toppings = [coconut, 'extra cream']
          v if 'coconut' in requested_toppings: print("Adding coconut.")
          w if ' sausage ' in requested_toppings: print("Adding sausage.")
          x if 'extra cream' in requested_toppings: print("Adding extra cream.")
          print("\nFinished making your burger!")
```

We start with a list of the requested toppings. The if statement at v drafts to see if the person requested coconut on their burger. If this is the case, a message confirming that topping is printed. The sausage test at w is a clear one if the argument, not the elif or the result, and this test is performed regardless of whether the previous test has passed or not. The x code checks if additional cheese has been ordered, irrespective of the outcome of the first two measures. These three independent tests are performed every time the program is running. Because each condition in this example is assessed, both coconut and extra cream are added to the burger:

```
Adding coconut.

Adding extra cream.

Finished making your burger!
```

This system would not work correctly if we were to use the if-elif-else function, as the system would stop running if just one test passes. Here's what it should feel like:

requested_toppings = ['coconut ', 'extra cream'] if 'coconut' in requested_toppings:

print("Adding coconut.") elif 'sausage' in requested_toppings:

print("Adding sausage.") elif 'extra cream in requested_toppings:

print("Adding extra cream.") print("\nFinished making your

burger!")

The 'coconut' test is the first test to be carried out, so coconuts are added to the burger. But, the values 'extra cream' and 'sausage' are never tested, since Python does not run any tests after the first test that passes along the if-elif-else series. The first topping of the customer will be added, but all of their other toppings will be missed:

Adding coconuts.

Finished making your burger!

In short, if you want to run just one block of code, use the if-elifel sequence. In case more than 1 block of code needs to be run, use a set of independent if statements.

A Simple Dictionary

Consider a game featuring aliens that may have different colors and point values. This basic dictionary stores details about an alien:

alien.py alien_0 = {'color': 'red', 'points': 5}

print(alien_0['colour']) print(alien_0['points'])

The alien 0 dictionary stores the color and meaning of the alien. The two print statements access and display the information as shown here:

red 3

Like most new programming concepts, dictionaries are used to practice. Once you have worked with dictionaries for a bit, you will soon see how effectively real-world situations can be modeled.

Working with Dictionaries

The Python dictionary is a list of key-value pairs. -- the key is connected to a value, and a key may be used to access the value associated with that key. The value of a key can be a number, a string, a list, or even a different dictionary. In addition, any object you can construct in Python can be used as a value in a dictionary. In Python, the dictionary is wrapped in bracelets,}, {with a sequence of key-value pairs within bracelets, as seen in the previous example:

alien_0 = {'colour': 'red', 'points': 3}

A key-value duo is a set of values that are connected. When you enter a key, Python returns the value associated with that key. Through key is related to its value by a colon, while commas separate the individual key-value pairs. You can save as many key-value pairs as you like in a dictionary. The easiest dictionary has exactly one key-value pair, as shown in the modified version of the alien_0_dictionary:

alien_0 = {'colour': 'red'}

This dictionary stores one piece of info about alien 0, the color of the alien. The 'colour' string is the key in this dictionary, and its related meaning is 'red.

Accessing Values in a Dictionary

To obtain the value connected with the key, enter the name of the dictionary and then place the key inside the square bracket set, as shown here:

alien_0 = {'color': 'red'} print(alien_0['colour'])

This reverts the value connected with the key 'colour' from the dictionary alien_0:

red

You can have an infinite amount of key-value pairs in your dictionary. For example, here is the original alien 0 dictionary with two key-value pairs:

alien_0 = {'colour': 'red', 'points': 3}

You can now access either the color or the point value of alien 0. If a player shoots this alien down, you can see how many points they are supposed to earn using code like this:

alien_0 = {'colour': 'red', 'points': 3} u new_points = alien_0['points']

v print("You just got " + str(new_points) + " points!")

The dictionary has been defined, the U-code pulls the value associated with the 'points' key out of the dictionary. This value is then stored in the new point variable. The v line transforms this integer value to a string and prints a declaration of how many points the player has just earned:

You just earned 3 points!

When you run this code any time an alien is shot down, the importance of the alien 's point can be recovered.

Adding New Key-Value Pairs

The dictionaries are dynamic structures, and you can add new key-value pairs to your dictionary at any time. For instance, to add a new key-value pair, you will be given the name of the dictionary, followed by a new key in square brackets along with a new value. Add two new pieces of data to the alien_0 dictionary: the x-and y-coordinates of the alien, which will help us to display the alien in a particular position on the screen. Position the alien on the left edge of the screen, 25 pixels down from the top. Since the screen coordinates normally start at the top left corner of the screen, we can position the alien at the left edge of the screen by setting the x-coordinate to 0 and 25 pixels from the top by setting the y-coordinate to positive 25, as seen here:

alien_0 = {'colour': 'red', 'points': 3} print(alien_0)

u alien_0['x_position'] = 0 v alien_0['y_position'] = 15

print(alien_0)

We define the same dictionary that we worked with. Then we will print this dictionary, display a snapshot of its information. U adds a new key-value pair to the dictionary: key 'x position' and value 0. We do the same for the 'y position' key in v. When we print the revised dictionary, we see 2 additional key-value pairs:

{'colour': 'red', 'points': 3}

{'colour': 'red', 'points': 3, 'y_position': 15, 'x_position': 0}

The final version of the dictionary consists of four key-value pairs. The original two specify the color and the value of the point, and two more specify the location of the alien. Note that the order of the key-value pairs does not suit the order in which they were inserted. Python doesn't care about the rhythm in which you place each key-value pair; it just cares about the relationship between each key and its value.

Starting with an Empty Dictionary

In most cases, it is useful, or even essential, to start with an empty dictionary and then add each new element to it. To start filling a blank dictionary, define a dictionary with an empty set of braces, and then apply each key-value pair to its own line. For example, below is how to construct the alien 0 dictionaries using the following approach:

alien_0 = {} alien_0['colour'] = 'red'

alien_0['points'] = 5 print(alien_0)

We define a blank alien_0 dictionary, and then add colour and value to it. The result is the dictionary that we used in previous examples:

{'colour': 'red', 'points': 3}

Typically, empty dictionaries are used when storing user-supplied data in a dictionary or when writing code that automatically generates a large number of key-value pairs.

Modifying Values in a Dictionary

To change the value in the dictionary, enter the name of the dictionary with the key in square brackets, and then the new value you want to associate with that key. Consider, for example, an alien who changes from green to yellow as the game progresses:

alien_0 = {'colour': 'red'} print("The alien is " + alien_0['colour'] + ".")

alien_0['colour'] = 'yellow' print("The alien is now " + alien_0['colour'] + ".")

First, we describe a dictionary for alien 0 that includes only the color of the alien; then, we change the meaning associated with the 'colour' key to 'black.' The performance reveals that the alien actually shifted from green to yellow:

The alien is red.

The alien is now yellow.

For a more interesting example, let us take a look at the position of an alien who can move at different speeds. We will store a value that represents the current speed of the alien and then use it to determine how far the alien should move to the right:

alien_0 = {'x_position': 0, 'y_position': 15, 'speed': 'medium'}

print("Original x-position: " + str(alien_0['x_position']))

Change the alien to your right.

#Identify how far to move the alien based on its current speed.

u if alien_0['speed'] == 'slow': x_increment = 1

elif alien_0['speed'] == 'medium': x_increment = 2 else:

```python
# This must be a fast alien. x_increment = 3
# The fresh position is the previous position plus the increment.
v alien_0['x_position'] = alien_0['x_position'] + x_increment
print("New x-position: " + str(alien_0['x_position']))
```

We begin by defining an alien with an initial position of x and y and a speed of 'medium.' We have omitted color and point values for simplicity, but this example would work the same way when you include those key-value pairs as well. We also print the real value of x position to see how far the alien is moving to the right. At u, the if-elif-else string determines how far the alien should move to the right and stores this value in the x increment variable. If the speed of the alien is 'slow,' it moves one unit to the right; if the speed is 'medium,' it moves two units to the right; and if it is 'fast,' it moves three units to the right. If the calculation has been calculated, the value of x position is added to v, and the sum is stored in the x position dictionary. Since this is a medium-speed alien, its position shifts two units to the right:

Original x-position: 0 New x-position: 2

This approach is pretty cool: by modifying one meaning in the alien's vocabulary, you can alter the alien 's overall actions. For example, to transform this medium-speed alien into a fast alien, you should add the following line:

```python
alien_0['speed'] = fast
```

The if-elif-else block will then add greater value to x increment the next time the code is running.

CONCLUSION

Python is one of the several open-source, object-oriented programming applications available on the market. Some of the other uses of Python are application development, the introduction of the automated testing process, multiple programming build, fully developed programming library, all major operating systems, and platforms, database system usability, quick and readable code, easy to add to complicated software development processes, test-driven software application support.

Python is a programming language that assists you to work easily and implement your programs more effectively. Python is a versatile programming language used in a wide variety of application domains. Python is also compared with Perl, Ruby, or Java. Some of the main features are as follows:

Python enthusiasts use the term "batteries included" to describe the main library, which includes anything from asynchronous processing to zip files. The language itself is a versatile engine that can manage nearly every issue area. Create your own web server with three lines of JavaScript.

Create modular data-driven code using Python's efficient, dynamic introspection capabilities, and advanced language functionality such as meta-classes, duck typing, and decorators. Python lets you easily write the code you need. And, due to a highly optimized byte compiler and library support, Python code is running more than fast enough for most programs. Python also comes with full documentation, both embedded into the language and as separate web pages. Online tutorials are targeted at both the experienced programmer and the beginner. They are all built to make you successful quickly. The inclusion of an excellent book complements the learning kit.

PYTHON FOR DATA SCIENCE

Guide to computer programming and web coding. Learn machine learning, artificial intelligence, NumPy and Pandas packages for data analysis. Step-by-step exercises included.

JASON TEST

Introduction

Data Science has been very popular over the last couple of years. The main focus of this sector is to incorporate significant data into business and marketing strategies that will help a business expand. And get to a logical solution, the data can be stored and explored. Originally only the leading IT corporations were engaged throughout this field, but today information technology is being used by companies operating in different sectors and fields such as e-commerce, medical care, financial services, and others. Software processing programs such as Hadoop, R code, SAS, SQL, and plenty more are available. Python is, however, the most famous and easiest to use data and analytics tools. It is recognized as the coding world's Swiss Army Knife since it promotes structured coding, object-oriented programming, the operational programming language, and many others. Python is the most widely used programming language in the world and is also recognized as the most high - level language for data science tools and techniques, according to the 2018 Stack Overflow study.

In the Hacker rank 2018 developer poll, which is seen in their love-hate ranking, Python has won the developer's hearts. Experts in data science expect to see an increase in the Python ecosystem, with growing popularity. And although your journey to study Python programming may just start, it's nice to know that there are also plentiful (and increasing) career options. Data analytics Python programming is extensively used and, along with being a flexible and open-source language, becomes one of the favorite programming languages. Its large libraries are used for data processing, and even for a beginner data analyst, they are very easy to understand. Besides being open-source, it also integrates easily with any infrastructure that can be used to fix the most complicated problems. It is used by most banks for data crunching, organizations for analysis and processing, and weather prediction firms such as Climate monitor analytics often use it. The annual wage for a Computer Scientist is $127,918, according to Indeed. So here's the good news, the figure is likely to increase. IBM's experts forecast a 28 percent increase in data scientists' demands by 2020. For data science, however, the future is bright, and Python is just one slice of the golden pie. Luckily mastering Python and other principles of programming are as practical as ever.

DATA SCIENCE AND ITS SIGNIFICANCE

Data Science has come a long way from the past few years, and thus, it becomes an important factor in understanding the workings of multiple companies. Below are several explanations that prove data science will still be an integral part of the global market.

1. The companies would be able to understand their client in a more efficient and high manner with the help of Data Science. Satisfied customers form the foundation of every company, and they play an important role in their successes or failures. Data Science allows companies to engage with customers in the advance way and thus proves the product's improved performance and strength.

2. Data Science enables brands to deliver powerful and engaging visuals. That's one of the reasons it's famous. When products and companies make inclusive use of this data, they can share their experiences with their audiences and thus create better relations with the item.

3. Perhaps one Data Science's significant characteristics are that its results can be generalized to almost all kinds of industries, such as travel, health care, and education. The companies can

quickly determine their problems with the help of Data Science, and can also adequately address them

4. Currently, data science is accessible in almost all industries, and nowadays, there is a huge amount of data existing in the world, and if used adequately, it can lead to victory or failure of any project. If data is used properly, it will be important in the future to achieve the product 's goals.

5. Big data is always on the rise and growing. Big data allows the enterprise to address complicated Business, human capital, and capital management problems effectively and quickly using different resources that are built routinely.

6. Data science is gaining rapid popularity in every other sector and therefore plays an important role in every product's functioning and performance. Thus, the data scientist's role is also enhanced as they will conduct an essential function of managing data and providing solutions to particular issues.

7. Computer technology has also affected the supermarket sectors. To understand this, let's take an example the older people had a fantastic interaction with the local seller. Also, the seller was able to meet the customers' requirements in a personalized way. But now this attention was lost due to the emergence and increase of supermarket chains. But the sellers are able to communicate with their customers with the help of data analytics.

8. Data Science helps companies build that customer connection. Companies and their goods will be able to have a better and deeper understanding of how clients can utilize their services with the help of data science.

Data Technology Future: Like other areas are continually evolving, the importance of data technology is increasingly growing as well. Data science impacted different fields. Its influence can be seen in many industries, such as retail, healthcare, and education. New treatments and technologies are being continually identified in the healthcare sector, and there is a need for quality patient care. The healthcare industry can find a solution with the help of data science techniques that helps the patients to take care with. Education is another field where one can clearly see the advantage of data science. Now the new innovations like phones and tablets have become an essential characteristic of the educational system. Also, with the help of data science, the students are creating greater chances, which leads to improving their knowledge.

Data Science Life Cycle:

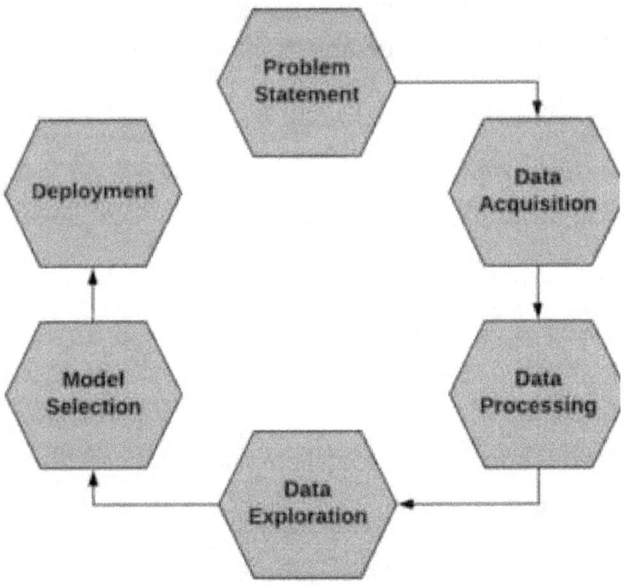

Data Structures

A data structure may be selected in computer programming or designed to store data for the purpose of working with different algorithms on it. Every other data structure includes the data values, data relationships, and functions between the data that can be applied to the data and information.

Features of data structures

Sometimes, data structures are categorized according to their characteristics. Possible functions are:

Linear or non-linear: This feature defines how the data objects are organized in a sequential series, like a list or in an unordered sequence, like a table.

Homogeneous or non-homogeneous: This function defines how all data objects in a collection are of the same type or of different kinds.

Static or dynamic: This technique determines to show to assemble the data structures. Static data structures at compilation time have fixed sizes, structures, and destinations in the memory. Dynamic data types have dimensions, mechanisms, and destinations of memory that may shrink or expand depending on the application.

Data structure Types

Types of the data structure are determined by what sorts of operations will be needed or what kinds of algorithms will be implemented. This includes:

Arrays: An array stores a list of memory items at adjacent locations. Components of the same category are located together since each element's position can be easily calculated or accessed. Arrays can be fixed in size or flexible in length.

Stacks: A stack holds a set of objects in linear order added to operations. This order may be past due in first out (LIFO) or first-out (FIFO).

Queues: A queue stores a stack-like selection of elements; however, the sequence of activity can only be first in the first out. Linked lists: In a linear order, a linked list stores a selection of items. In a linked list, every unit or node includes a data item as well as a reference or relation to the next element in the list.

Trees: A tree stocks an abstract, hierarchical collection of items. Each node is connected to other nodes and can have several sub-values, also known as a child.

Graphs: A graph stores a non-linear design group of items. Graphs consist of a limited set of nodes, also called vertices, and lines connecting them, also known as edges. They are useful for describing processes in real life, such as networked computers.

Tries: A tria or query tree is often a data structure that stores strings as data files, which can be arranged in a visual graph.

Hash tables: A hash table or hash chart is contained in a relational list that labels the keys to variables. A hash table uses a hashing algorithm to transform an index into an array of containers containing the desired item of data. These data systems are called complex because they can contain vast quantities of interconnected data. Examples of primal, or fundamental, data structures are integer, float, boolean, and character.

Utilization of data structures

Data structures are generally used to incorporate the data types in physical forms. This can be interpreted into a wide range of applications, including a binary tree showing a database table. Data structures are used in the programming languages to organize code and information in digital storage. Python databases and dictionaries, or JavaScript array and objects, are popular coding systems used to gather and analyze data. Also, data structures are a vital part of effective software design. Significance of Databases Data systems is necessary to effectively handle vast volumes of data, such as data stored in libraries, or indexing services.

Accurate data configuration management requires memory allocation identifier, data interconnections, and data processes, all of which support the data structures. In addition, it is important to not only use data structures but also to select the correct data structure for each assignment.

Choosing an unsatisfactory data structure could lead to slow running times or disoriented code. Any considerations that need to be noticed when choosing a data system include what type of

information should be processed, where new data will be put,
how data will be organized, and how much space will be
allocated for the data.

PYTHON BASICS

You can get all the knowledge about the Python programming language in 5 simple steps.

Step 1: Practice Basics in Python
It all starts somewhere. This first step is where the basics of programming Python will be learned. You are always going to want an introduction to data science. Jupyter Notebook, which comes pre-portioned with Python libraries to help you understand these two factors, which make it one of the essential resources which you can start using early on your journey.

Step 2: Try practicing Mini-Python Projects
We strongly believe in learning through shoulders-on. Try programming stuff like internet games, calculators, or software that gets Google weather in your area. Creating these mini-projects can help you understand Python. Projects like these are standard for any coding languages, and a fantastic way to strengthen your working knowledge. You will come up with better and advance API knowledge, and you will continue site scraping with advanced techniques. This will enable you to learn

Python programming more effectively, and the web scraping method will be useful to you later when collecting data.

Stage 3: Learn Scientific Libraries on Python

Python can do anything with data. Pandas, Matplotliband, and NumPyare are known to be the three best used and most important Python Libraries for data science. NumPy and Pandas are useful for data creation and development. Matplotlib is a library for analyzing the data, creating flow charts and diagrams as you would like to see in Excel or Google Sheets.

Stage 4: Create a portfolio

A portfolio is an absolute need for professional data scientists. These projects must include numerous data sets and leave important perspectives to readers that you have gleaned. Your portfolio does not have a specific theme; finding datasets that inspire you, and then finding a way to place them together. Showing projects like these provide some collaboration to fellow data scientists, and demonstrates future employers that you have really taken the chance to understand Python and other essential coding skills. Some of the good things about data science are that, while showcasing the skills you've learned, your portfolio serves as a resume, such as Python programming.

Step 5: Apply Advanced Data Science Techniques

Eventually, the target is to strengthen your programming skills. Your data science path will be full of continuous learning, but you can accomplish specialized tutorials to make sure you have specialized in the basic programming of Python. You need to get confident with clustering models of regression, grouping, and k-means. You can also leap into machine learning-using sci-kit lessons to bootstrap models and create neural network models. At this point, developer programming could include creating models using live data sources. This type of machine learning technique adjusts s its assumptions over time.

How significant is Python for Data Science?

Efficient and simple to use – Python is considered a tool for beginners, and any student or researcher with only basic understanding could start working on it. Time and money spent debugging codes and constraints on different project management are also minimized. The time for code implementation is less compared to other programming languages such as C, Java, and C #, which makes developers and software engineers spend far more time working on their algorithms.

Library Choice-Python offers a vast library and machine learning and artificial intelligence database. Scikit Learn, TensorFlow, Seaborn, Pytorch, Matplotlib, and many more are among the most popular libraries. There are many online tutorial

videos and resources on machine learning and data science, which can be easily obtained.

Scalability – Python has proven itself to be a highly scalable and faster language compared to other programming languages such as c++, Java, and R. It gives flexibility in solving problems that can't be solved with other computer languages. Many companies use it to develop all sorts of rapid techniques and systems.

#Visual Statistics and Graphics-Python provides a number of visualization tools. The Matplotlib library provides a reliable framework on which those libraries such as gg plot, pandas plotting, PyTorch, and others are developed. These services help create graphs, plot lines ready for the Web, visual layouts, etc.

How Python is used for Data Science

#First phase – First of all, we need to learn and understand what form a data takes. If we perceive data to be a huge Excel sheet with columns and crows lakhs, then perhaps you should know what to do about that? You need to gather information into each row as well as column by executing some operations and searching for a specific type of data. Completing this type of computational task can consume a lot of time and hard work. Thus, you can use Python's libraries, such as Pandas and Numpy, that can complete the tasks quickly by using parallel computation.

#Second phase – The next hurdle is to get the data needed. Since data is not always readily accessible to us, we need to dump data from the network as needed. Here the Python Scrap and brilliant Soup libraries can enable us to retrieve data from the internet.

#Third phase – We must get the simulation or visual presentation of the data at this step. Driving perspectives gets difficult when you have too many figures on the board. The correct way to do that is to represent the data in graph form, graphs, and other layouts. The Python Seaborn and Matplotlib libraries are used to execute this operation.

#Fourth phase – The next stage is machine-learning, which is massively complicated computing. It includes mathematical tools such as the probability, calculus, and matrix operations of columns and rows over lakhs. With Python's machine learning library Scikit-Learn, all of this will become very simple and effective.

Standard Library

The Python Standard library consists of Python's precise syntax, token, and semantic. It comes packaged with deployment core Python. When we started with an introduction, we referenced this. It is written in C and covers features such as I / O and other core components. Together all of the versatility renders makes Python the language it is. At the root of the basic library, there are more than 200 key modules. Python ships that library. But aside from this library, you can also obtain a massive collection of several thousand Python Package Index (PyPI) components.

1. Matplotlib

'Matplotlib' helps to analyze data, and is a library of numerical plots. For Data Science, we discussed in Python.

2. Pandas

'Pandas' is a must for data-science as we have said before. It provides easy, descriptive, and versatile data structures to deal with organized (tabulated, multilayered, presumably heterogeneous) and series data with ease (and fluidly).

3. Requests

'Requests' is a Python library that allows users to upload HTTP/1.1 requests, add headers, form data, multipart files, and simple Python dictionary parameters. In the same way, it also helps you to access the response data.

4. NumPy

It has basic arithmetic features and a rudimentary collection of scientific computing.

5. SQLAlchemy

It has sophisticated mathematical features, and SQLAlchemy is a basic mathematical programming library with well-known trends at a corporate level. It was created to make database availability efficient and high-performance.

6. BeautifulSoup

This may be a bit on the slow side. BeautifulSoup seems to have a superb library for beginner XML- and HTML- parsing.

7. Pyglet

Pyglet is an outstanding choice when designing games with an object-oriented programming language interface. It also sees use in the development of other visually rich programs for Mac OS X, Windows, and Linux in particular. In the 90s, they turned to play Minecraft on their PCs whenever people were bored. Pyglet is the mechanism powering Minecraft.

8. SciPy

Next available is SciPy, one of the libraries we spoke about so often. It does have a range of numerical routines that are user-friendly and effective. Those provide optimization routines and numerical integration procedures.

9. Scrapy

If your objective is quick, scraping at the high-level monitor and crawling the network, go for Scrapy. It can be used for data gathering activities for monitoring and test automation.

10. PyGame

PyGame offers an incredibly basic interface to the system-independent graphics, audio, and input libraries of the Popular Direct Media Library (SDL).

11. Python Twisted

Twisted is an event-driven networking library used in Python and authorized under the MIT open-source license.

12. Pillow

Pillow is a PIL (Python Imaging Library) friendly fork but is more user efficient. Pillow is your best friend when you're working with pictures.

13. pywin32

As the name suggests, this gives useful methods and classes for interacting with Windows.

14. wxPython

For Python, it's a wrapper around wxWidgets.

15. iPython

iPython Python Library provides a parallel distributed computing architecture. You will use it to create, run, test, and track parallel and distributed programming.

16. Nose

The nose provides alternate test exploration and test automation running processes. This intends to mimic the behavior of the py.test as much as possible.

17. Flask

Flask is a web framework, with a small core and several extensions.

18. SymPy

It is a library of open-source symbolic mathematics. SymPy is a full-fledged Computer Algebra System (CAS) with a very simple and easily understood code that is highly expandable. It is implemented in python, and therefore, external libraries are not required.

19. Fabric

As well as being a library, Fabric is a command-line tool to simplify the use of SSH for installation programs or network management activities. You can run local or remote command line, upload/download files, and even request input user going, or abort activity with it.

20. PyGTK

PyGTK allows you to create programs easily using a Python GUI (Graphical User Interface).

Operators and Expressions

Operators

In Python, operators are special symbols that perform mathematical operation computation. The value in which the operator is running on is called the operand.

Arithmetic operators

It is used by arithmetic operators to perform mathematical operations such as addition, subtraction, multiplying, etc.

Comparison operators

Comparison operators can be used for value comparisons. Depending on the condition, it returns either True or False.

Logical operators

Logical operators are and, or, not.

Operator	Meaning	Example
And	True if both operands are true	x and y
Or	True if either of the operands is true	x or y
Not	True if the operand is false (complements the operand)	not x

Bitwise operators

Bitwise operators operate as if they became binary-digit strings on operands. Bit by bit they work, and therefore the name. For example, in binary two is10, and in binary seven is 111.

Assignment operators

Python language's assignment operators are used to assign values to the variables. a = 5 is a simple task operator assigning 'a' value of 5 to the right of the variable 'a' to the left. In Python, there are various compound operators such as a + = 5, which adds to the variable as well as assigns the same later. This equals a= a + 5.

Special operators

Python language gives other different types of operators, such as the operator of the identity or the operator of membership. Examples of these are mentioned below.

Identity operators

'Is' and 'is not' are Python Identity Operators. They are used to test if there are two values or variables in the same memory section. Two equal variables do not mean they are equivalent.

Membership operator

The operators that are used to check whether or not there exists a value/variable in the sequence such as string, list, tuples, sets, and dictionary. These operators return either True or False if a variable is found in the list, it returns True, or else it returns False

Expressions

An expression is a mix of values, variables, operators, and function calls. There must be an evaluation of the expressions. When you ask Python to print a phrase, the interpreter will evaluate the expression and show the output.

Arithmetic conversions

Whenever an arithmetic operator interpretation below uses the phrase "the numeric arguments are converted to a common type," this means the execution of the operator for the built-in modes operates as follows
If one argument is a complex quantity, then the other is converted to a complex number; If another argument is a floating-point number, the other argument is transformed to a floating-point; Or else both will be integers with no need for conversion.

Atoms

Atoms are the most important expressional components. The smallest atoms are literals or abstract identities. Forms contained in parentheses, brackets, or braces are also syntactically known as atoms. Atoms syntax is:
atom ::= identifier | enclosure| literal

enclosure ::= list_display| parenth_form| dict_display |
set_display

Identifiers (Names)

A name is an identifier that occurs as an atom. See section
Lexical Description Identifiers and Keywords and group Naming
and binding for naming and binding documents. Whenever the
name is connected to an entity, it yields the entity by evaluating
the atom. When a name is not connected, an attempt to assess it
elevates the exception for NameError.

Literals

Python provides logical string and bytes and numerical literals of
different types:
literal::= string literal | bytes literal
        | integer | float number | image number
Assessment of a literal yield with the predicted set an object of
that type (bytes, integer, floating-point number, string, complex
number). In the scenario of floating-point and imaginary
(complex) literals, the value can be approximated.

Parenthesized forms

A parenthesized type is an available set of parentheses for the expression:

parenth_form ::= "(" [starred_expression] ")"

A list of parenthesized expressions yields whatever the list of expressions produces: if the list includes at least one comma, it produces a tuple. If not, it yields the sole expression that forms up the list of expressions. A null pair of parentheses generates an incomplete object of tuples. As all tuples are immutable, the same rules would apply as for literals (i.e., two empty tuple occurrences does or doesn't yield the same entity).

Displays for lists, sets, and dictionaries

For the construction of a list, Python uses a series or dictionary with a particular syntax called "displays," each in complementary strands:

The contents of the container are listed explicitly, or They are calculated using a series of instructions for looping and filtering, named a 'comprehension.' Common features of syntax for comprehensions are:

comprehension ::= assignment_expressioncomp_for

comp_for   ::= ["async"] "for" target_list "in" or_test [comp_iter]

comp_iter   ::= comp_for | comp_if

comp_if   ::= "if" expression_nocond [comp_iter]

A comprehension contains one single sentence ready for at least one expression for clause, and zero or more for or if clauses. Throughout this situation, the components of the container are those that will be generated by assuming each of the for or if clauses as a block, nesting from left to right, and determining the phase for creating an entity each time the inner core block is approached.

List displays

A list view is a probably empty sequence of square brackets including expressions:

list_display ::= "[" [starred_list | comprehension] "]"

A list display generates a new column object, with either a list of expressions or a comprehension specifying the items. When a comma-separated database of expressions is provided, its elements are assessed from left to right and positioned in that order in the category entity. When Comprehension is provided, the list shall be built from the comprehension components.

Set displays

Curly braces denote a set display and can be distinguished from dictionary displays by the lack of colons dividing data types:

set_display ::= "{" (starred_list | comprehension) "}"

A set show offers a new, mutable set entity, with either a series of expressions or a comprehension defining the contents. When supplied with a comma-separated list of expressions, its elements are evaluated from left to right and assigned to the set entity. Whenever a comprehension is provided, the set is formed from the comprehension-derived elements. Unable to build an empty set with this {}; literal forms a blank dictionary.

Dictionary displays

A dictionary view is a potentially empty sequence of key pairs limited to curly braces:

dict_display   ::= "{" [key_datum_list | dict_comprehension] "}"
key_datum_list   ::= key_datum ("," key_datum)* [","]
key_datum   ::= expression ":" expression | "**" or_expr
dict_comprehension ::= expression ":" expression comp_for

The dictionary view shows a new object in the dictionary. When a comma-separated series of key / datum pairs is provided, they are analyzed from left to right to identify dictionary entries: each key entity is often used as a key to hold the respective datum in the dictionary. This implies you can clearly state the very same key numerous times in the key /datum catalog, but the last one given will become the final dictionary's value for that key.

Generator expressions

A generator expression is the compressed syntax of a generator in the parenthesis :

generator_expression ::= "(" expression comp_for ")"

An expression generator produces an entity that is a new generator. Its syntax will be the same as for comprehensions, except for being enclosed in brackets or curly braces rather than parentheses. Variables being used generator expression are assessed sloppily when the generator object (in the same style as standard generators) is called by the __next__() method. Conversely, the iterate-able expression in the leftmost part of the clause is evaluated immediately, such that an error that it produces is transmitted at the level where the expression of the generator is characterized, rather than at the level where the first value is recovered.

For instance: (x*y for x in range(10) for y in range(x, x+10)).

Yield expressions

yield_atom   ::= "(" yield_expression ")"
yield_expression ::= "yield" [expression_list | "from" expression]

The produced expression is used to define a generator function or async generator function, and can therefore only be used in the function definition body. Using an expression of yield in the body of a function tends to cause that function to be a generator, and to use it in the body of an asynchronous def function induces that co-routine function to become an async generator. For example:

def gen(): # defines a generator function

yield 123

asyncdefagen(): # defines an asynchronous generator function

yield 123

Because of their adverse effects on the carrying scope, yield expressions are not allowed as part of the impliedly defined scopes used to enforce comprehensions and expressions of generators.

Input and Output of Data in Python

Python Output Using print() function

To display data into the standard display system (screen), we use the print() function. We may issue data to a server as well, but that will be addressed later. Below is an example of its use.

>>>>print('This sentence is output to the screen')

Output:

This sentence is output to the screen

Another example is given:

```
a = 5
print('The value of a is,' a)
```

Output:

The value of a is 5

Within the second declaration of print(), we will note that space has been inserted between the string and the variable value a. By default, it contains this syntax, but we can change it.

The actual syntax of the print() function will be:

```
print(*objects, sep=' ', end='\n', file=sys.stdout, flush=False)
```

Here, the object is the value(s) that will be printed. The sep separator between values is used. This switches into a character in space. Upon printing all the values, the finish is printed. It moves into a new section by design. The file is the object that prints the values, and its default value is sys.stdout (screen). Below is an example of this.

```
print(1, 2, 3, 4)
print(1, 2, 3, 4, sep='*')
print(1, 2, 3, 4, sep='#', end='&')
```

Run code

Output:

1 2 3 4

1*2*3*4

1#2#3#4&

Output formatting

Often we want to style our production, so it looks appealing. It can be done using the method str.format(). This technique is visible for any object with a string.

>>> x = 5; y = 10

>>>print('The value of x is {} and y is {}'.format(x,y))

Here the value of x is five and y is 10

Here, they use the curly braces{} as stand-ins. Using numbers (tuple index), we may specify the order in which they have been printed.

print('I love {0} and {1}'.format('bread','butter'))

print('I love {1} and {0}'.format('bread','butter'))

Run Code

Output:

I love bread and butter

I love butter and bread

People can also use arguments with keyword to format the string.

>>>print('Hello {name}, {greeting}'.format(greeting = 'Goodmorning', name = 'John'))

Hello John, Goodmorning

Unlike the old sprint() style used in the C programming language, we can also format strings. To accomplish this, we use the '%' operator.

```
>>> x = 12.3456789
>>>print('The value of x is %3.2f' %x)
The value of x is 12.35
>>>print('The value of x is %3.4f' %x)
The value of x is 12.3457
```

Python Indentation

Indentation applies to the spaces at the start of a line of the compiler. Whereas indentation in code is for readability only in other programming languages, but the indentation in Python is very important. Python supports the indent to denote a code block.

Example

```
if 5 > 2:
print("Five is greater than two!")
```

Python will generate an error message if you skip the indentation:

Example

Syntax Error:

```
if 5 > 2:
print("Five is greater than two!")
```

Python Input

Our programs have been static. Variables were described or hard-coded in the source code. We would want to take the feedback from the user to allow flexibility. We have the input() function in Python to enable this. input() is syntax as:

input([prompt])

While prompt is the string we want to show on the computer, this is optional.

```
>>>num = input('Enter a number: ')
Enter a number: 10
>>>num
'10'
```

Below, we can see how the value 10 entered is a string and not a number. To transform this to a number we may use the functions int() or float().

```
>>>int('10')
10
>>>float('10')
10.0
```

The same method can be done with the feature eval(). Although it takes eval much further. It can even quantify expressions, provided that the input is a string

```
>>>int('2+3')
Traceback (most recent call last):
  File "<string>", line 301, in runcode
  File "<interactive input>", line 1, in <module>
ValueError: int() base 10 invalid literal: '2+3'
>>>eval('2+3')
5
```

Python Import

As our software gets larger, splitting it up into separate modules is a smart idea. A module is a file that contains definitions and statements from Python. Python packages have a filename, and the .py extension begins with it. Definitions may be loaded into another module or to the integrated Python interpreter within a module. To do this, we use the keyword on import.

For instance, by writing the line below, we can import the math module:

```
import math
```

We will use the module as follows:

```
import math
print(math.pi)
```

Run Code

Output

3.141592653589793

So far, all concepts are included in our framework within the math module. Developers can also only import certain particular attributes and functions, using the keyword.

For instance:

```
>>>from math import pi
>>>pi
3.141592653589793
```

Python looks at multiple positions specified in sys.path during the import of a module. It is a list of positions in a directory.

```
>>> import sys
>>>sys.path
['',
 'C:\\Python33\\Lib\\idlelib',
 'C:\\Windows\\system32\\python33.zip',
 'C:\\Python33\\DLLs',
 'C:\\Python33\\lib',
 'C:\\Python33',
 'C:\\Python33\\lib\\site-packages']
```

We can insert our own destination to that list as well.

FUNCTIONS

You utilize programming functions to combine a list of instructions that you're constantly using or that are better self-contained in sub-program complexity and are called upon when required. Which means a function is a type of code written to accomplish a given purpose. The function may or may not need various inputs to accomplish that particular task. Whenever the task is executed, one or even more values can or could not be returned by the function. Basically there exist three types of functions in Python language:

Built-in functions, including help() to ask for help, min() to just get the minimum amount, print() to print an attribute to the terminal. More of these functions can be found here.

User-Defined Functions (UDFs) that are functions created by users to assist and support them out;

Anonymous functions, also labeled lambda functions since they are not defined with the default keyword.

Defining A Function: User Defined Functions (UDFs)

The following four steps are for defining a function in Python:

Keyword def can be used to declare the function and then use the function name to backtrack.

Add function parameters: They must be within the function parentheses. Finish off your line with a colon.

Add statements which should be implemented by the functions. When the function should output something, end your function with a return statement. Your task must return an object None without return declaration. Example:

```python
def hello():
print("Hello World")
return
```

It is obvious as you move forward, the functions will become more complex: you can include for loops, flow control, and more to make things more fine-grained:

```python
def hello():
name = str(input("Enter your name: "))
if name:
print ("Hello " + str(name))
else:
print("Hello World")
return
hello()
```

In the feature above, you are asking the user to give a name. When no name is provided, the 'Hello World' function will be printed. Otherwise, the user will receive a custom "Hello" phrase. Also, consider you can specify one or more parameters for your UDFs function. When you discuss the segment Feature Statements, you will hear more about this. Consequently, as a result of your function, you may or may not return one or more values.

The return Statement

Note that since you're going to print something like that in your hello) (UDF, you don't really have to return it. There'll be no distinction between the above function and this one:

Example:

1. defhello_noreturn():
2. print("Hello World")

Even so, if you'd like to keep working with the result of your function and try a few other functions on it, you'll need to use the return statement to simply return a value, like a string, an integer. Check out the following scenario in which hello() returns a "hello" string while the hello_noreturn() function returns None:

1.   def hello():

2.   print("Hello World")

3.   return("hello")

4.   defhello_noreturn():

5.   print("Hello World")

6.   # Multiply the output of `hello()` with 2

7.   hello() * 2

8.   # (Try to) multiply the output of `hello_noreturn()` with 2

9.   hello_noreturn() * 2

The secondary part gives you an error because, with a None, you cannot perform any operations. You will get a TypeError that appears to say that NoneType (the None, which is the outcome of hello_noreturn()) and int (2) cannot do the multiplication operation. Tip functions leave instantly when a return statement is found, even though that means they will not return any result:

1. def run():

2. for x in range(10):

3. if x == 2:

4. return

5. print("Run!")

6.   run()

Another factor worth noting when dealing with the 'return expression' is many values can be returned using it. You consider making use of tuples for this. Recall that this data structure is very comparable to a list's: it can contain different values. Even so, tuples are immutable, meaning you can't alter any amounts stored in it! You build it with the aid of dual parentheses). With the assistance of the comma and the assignment operator, you can disassemble tuples into different variables.

Read the example below to understand how multiple values can be returned by your function:

1.   # Define `plus()`

2.   def plus(a,b):

3.sum = a + b

4.return (sum, a)

5.   # Call `plus()` and unpack variables

6.   sum, a = plus(3,4)

7.   # Print `sum()`

8.   print(sum)

Notice that the return statement sum, 'a' will result in just the same as the return (sum, a): the earlier simply packs total and an in a tuple it under hood!

How To Call A Function

You've already seen a lot of examples in previous sections of how one can call a function. Trying to call a function means executing the function you have described-either directly from the Python prompt, or by a different function (as you have seen in the "Nested Functions" portion). Call your new added hello() function essentially by implementing hello() as in the DataCamp Light chunk as follows:

1.   hello()

Adding Docstrings to Python Functions

Further valuable points of Python's writing functions: docstrings. Docstrings define what your function does, like the algorithms it conducts or the values it returns. These definitions act as metadata for your function such that anybody who reads the docstring of your feature can understand what your feature is doing, without having to follow all the code in the function specification. Task docstrings are placed right after the feature header in the subsequent line and are set in triple quote marks. For your hello() function, a suitable docstring is 'Hello World prints.'

```
def hello():
"""Prints "Hello World".

Returns:
  None
```

    """

print("Hello World")

return

Notice that you can extend docstrings more than the one provided here as an example. If you want to study docstrings in more depth information, you should try checking out some Python library Github repositories like scikit-learn or pandas, in which you'll find lots of good examples!

Function Arguments in Python

You probably learned the distinction between definitions and statements earlier. In simple terms, arguments are the aspects that are given to any function or method call, while their parameter identities respond to the arguments in the function or method code. Python UDFs can take up four types of arguments:

Default arguments

Required arguments

Keyword arguments

Variable number of arguments

Default Arguments

Default arguments would be those who take default data if no value of the argument is delivered during the call function. With the assignment operator =, as in the following case, you may assign this default value:

1.   #Define `plus()` function
2. def plus(a,b = 2):
3.return a + b
4. # Call `plus()` with only `a` parameter
5. plus(a=1)
6. # Call `plus()` with `a` and `b` parameters
7.   plus(a=1, b=3)

Required Arguments

Because the name sort of brings out, the claims a UDF needs are those that will be in there. Such statements must be transferred during the function call and are absolutely the right order, such as in the example below:

1. # Define `plus()` with required arguments
2. def plus(a,b):
3. return a + b

Calling the functions without getting any additional errors, you need arguments that map to 'a' as well as the 'b' parameters. The result will not be unique if you swap round the 'a' and 'b,' but it could be if you modify plus() to the following:

1. # Define `plus()` with required arguments

2. def plus(a,b):

3.return a/b

Keyword Arguments

You will use keyword arguments in your function call if you'd like

to make sure you list all the parameters in the correct order. You

use this to define the statements by the name of the function.

Let's take an example above to make it a little simpler:

1. # Define `plus()` function

2. def plus(a,b):

3.return a + b

4. # Call `plus()` function with parameters

5. plus(2,3)

6. # Call `plus()` function with keyword arguments

7.   plus(a=1, b=2)

Notice that you can also alter the sequence of the parameters

utilizing keywords arguments and still get the same outcome

when executing the function:

1. # Define `plus()` function

2. def plus(a,b):

3.return a + b

4. # Call `plus()` function with keyword arguments

5.   plus(b=2, a=1)

Global vs. Local Variables

Variables identified within a function structure usually have a local scope, and those specified outside have a global scope. This shows that the local variables are specified within a function block and can only be retrieved through that function, while global variables can be retrieved from all the functions in the coding:

1. # Global variable `init`
2. init = 1
3. # Define `plus()` function to accept a variable number of arguments
4. def plus(*args):
5. # Local variable `sum()`
6.total = 0
7.fori in args:
8.total += i
9.return total
10.# Access the global variable
11.print("this is the initialized value " + str(init))
12.# (Try to) access the local variable
13.print("this is the sum " + str(total))

You will find that you can get a NameError that means the name 'total' is not specified as you attempt to print out the total local variable that was specified within the body of the feature. In comparison, the init attribute can be written out without any complications.

Anonymous Functions in Python

Anonymous functions are often termed lambda functions in Python since you are using the lambda keyword rather than naming it with the standard-def keyword.

1. double = lambda x: x*2
2. double(5)

The anonymous or lambda feature in the DataCamp Light chunk above is lambda x: x*2. X is the argument, and x*2 is the interpretation or instruction that is analyzed and given back. What is unique about this function, and it has no tag, like the examples you saw in the first section of the lecture for this function. When you had to write the above function in a UDF, you would get the following result:

def double(x):

return x*2

Let us see another example of a lambda function where two arguments are used:

1. # `sum()` lambda function

2. sum = lambda x, y: x + y;

3. # Call the `sum()` anonymous function

4. sum(4,5)

5. # "Translate" to a UDF

6. def sum(x, y):

7. returnx+y

When you need a function with no name for a short interval of time, you utilize anonymous functions and this is generated at runtime. Special contexts where this is important are when operating with filter(), map() and redu():

1. from functools import reduce

2. my_list = [1,2,3,4,5,6,7,8,9,10]

3. # Use lambda function with `filter()`

4. filtered_list = list(filter(lambda x: (x*2 > 10), my_list))

5. # Use lambda function with `map()`

6. mapped_list = list(map(lambda x: x*2, my_list))

7. # Use lambda function with `reduce()`

8. reduced_list = reduce(lambda x, y: x+y, my_list)

9. print(filtered_list)

10. print(mapped_list)

11. print(reduced_list)

As the name states the filter() function it help filters the original list of inputs my_list based on a criterion > 10.By contrast, with

map(), you implement a function to every components in the
my_listlist. You multiply all of the components with two in this
scenario. Remember that the function reduce() is a portion of
the functools library. You cumulatively are using this function to
the components in the my_list() list, from left to right, and in this
situation decrease the sequence to a single value 55.

Using main() as a Function

If you have got any knowledge with other programming
languages like java, you'll notice that executing functions
requires the main feature. As you've known in the above
examples, Python doesn't really require this. However, it can be
helpful to logically organize your code along with a main()
function in your python code- - all of the most important
components are contained within this main() function.
You could even simply achieve and call a main() function the
same as you did with all of those above functions:
1. # Define `main()` function
2. def main():
3. hello()
4. print("This is the main function")
5. main()

After all, as it now appears, when you load it as a module, the script of your main ( ) function will indeed be called. You invoke the main() function whenever name == ' main ' to ensure this does not happen.

That implies the source above code script becomes:

1.# Define `main()` function

2.def main():

3.hello()

4.print("This is a main function")

5.# Execute `main()` function

6. if __name__ == '__main__':

7. main()

Remember that in addition to the main function, you too have a init function, which validates a class or object instance. Plainly defined, it operates as a constructor or initializer, and is termed automatically when you start a new class instance. With such a function, the freshly formed object is assigned to the self-parameter that you've seen in this guide earlier.

Consider the following example:

class Dog:

    """

    Requires:

legs – legs for a dog to walk.

color – Fur color.

```python
    """
    def __init__(self, legs, color):
        self.legs = legs
        self.color = color

    def bark(self):
        bark = "bark" * 2
        return bark

if __name__ == "__main__":
    dog = Dog(4, "brown")
    bark = dog.bark()
    print(bark)
```

LISTS AND LOOPS

Lists

A list is often a data structure in Python, which is an ordered list of elements that is mutable or modifiable. An item is named for each element or value inside a list. Just like strings are defined like characters between quotations, lists are specified by square brackets '[ ]' having values.

Lists are nice to have because you have other similar principles to deal with. They help you to hold data that are relevant intact, compress the code, and run the same numerous-value methods and processes at once.

It could be helpful to get all the several lists you have on your computer when beginning to think about Python lists as well as other data structures that are types of collections: Your assemblage of files, song playlists, browser bookmarks, emails, video collections that you can access through a streaming platform and much more.

We must function with this data table, taken from data collection of the Mobile App Store (RamanathanPerumal):

Name	price	currency	rating_count	rating
Instagram	0.0	USD	2161558	4.5

Clash of Clans	0.0	USD	2130805	4.5
Temple Run	0.0	USD	1724546	4.5
Pandora – Music & Radio	0.0	USD	1126879	4.0
Facebook	0.0	USD	2974676	3.5

Every value is a data point in the table. The first row (just after titles of the columns) for example has 5 data points:

Facebook

0.0

USD

2974676

3.5

Dataset consists of a collection of data points. We can consider the above table as a list of data points. Therefore we consider the entire list a dataset. We can see there are five rows and five columns to our data set.

Utilizing our insight of the Python types, we could perhaps consider we can store each data point in their own variable — for example, here's how we can store the data points of the first row:

```python
# script.py
track_name_row1 = 'Facebook'
price_row1 = 0.0
currency_row1 = 'USD'
rating_count_tot_row1 = 2974676
user_rating_row1 = 3.5
```

Above, we stored:

Text for the string as "Facebook."

Float 0.0 as a price

Text for the string as "USD."

Integer 2,974,676 as a rating count

Float 3.5 for user rating

A complicated process would be to create a variable for every data point in our data set. Luckily we can use lists to store data more effectively. So in the first row, we can draw up a list of data points:

```python
# script.py
row_1 = ['Facebook', 0.0, 'USD', 2974676, 3.5]
print(row_1)
type(row_1)
```

```
Output
['Facebook', 0.0, 'USD', 2974676, 3.5]
list
```

For list creation, we:

Separating each with a comma while typing out a sequence of data points: 'Facebook,' 0.0, 'USD,' 2974676, 3.5

Closing the list with square brackets: ['Facebook', 0.0, 'USD', 2974676, 3.5]

After the list is created, we assign it to a variable named row_1and the list is stored in the computer's memory.

For creating data points list, we only need to:

Add comma to the data points for separation.

Closing the list with brackets.

See below as we create five lists, in the dataset each row with one list:

```
row_1 =]['FACEBOOK', 0.0, 'usd', 2974676, 3.5]

row_2 = ['INSTAGRAM', 0.0, 'usd', 2161558, 4.5

row_3 = ['CLASH OF CLANS', 0.0, 'usd', 2130805, 4.5]

row_4 = ['TEMPLE RUN', 0.0, 'usd', 1724546, 4.5]

row_5 =['PANDORA', 0.0, 'usd', 1126879, 4.0]
```

Index of Python Lists

A list could include a broader array of data types. A list containing [4, 5, 6] includes the same types of data (only integers), while the list ['Facebook', 0.0, 'USD,' 2974676, 3.5]

contains many types of data:

Consisting Two types of floats (0.0, 3.5)

Consisting One type of integer (2974676)

Consisting two types of strings ('Facebook,' 'USD')

`['FACEBOOK', 0.0, 'usd', 2974676, 3.5]` list got 5 data

points. For the length of a list, len() command can be used:

```
script.py
row_1 = ['Facebook', 0.0, 'USD', 2974676, 3.5]
print(len(row_1))

list_1 = [1, 6, 0]
print(len(list_1))

list_2 = []
print(len(list_2))
```

```
Output
5
3
0
```

For smaller lists, we can simply count the data points on our

displays to figure the length, but perhaps the len() command will

claim to be very useful anytime you function with lists containing

many components, or just need to compose data code where

you really don't know the length in advance.

Every other component (data point) in a list is linked to a

particular number, termed the index number. The indexing also begins at 0, which means that the first element should have the index number 0, the 2nd element the index number 1, etc.

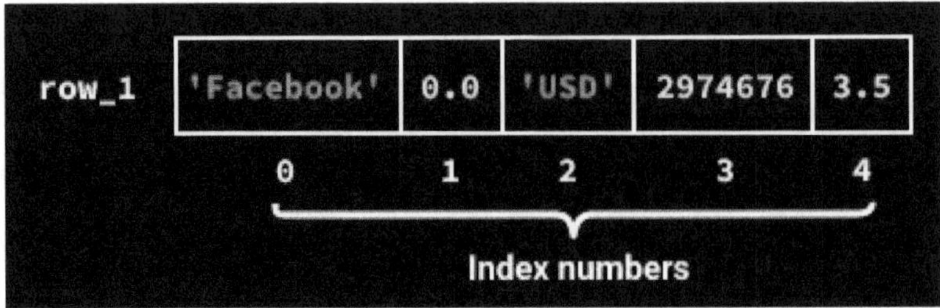

To locate a list element index rapidly, determine its location number in the list and then subtract it by 1. The string 'USD,' for instance, is the third item in the list (stance number 3), well its index number must be two because 3 − 1 = 2.

The index numbers enable us to locate a single item from a list. Going backward through the list row 1 from the example above, by executing code row 1[0], we can obtain the first node (the string 'Facebook') of index number 0.

```
script.py

row_1 = ['Facebook', 0.0, 'USD', 2974676, 3.5]
row_1[0]

Output
'Facebook'
```

The Model list_name[index number] follows the syntax for locating specific list components. For example, the title of our list above is row_1 and the index number of a first element is 0, we get row_1[0] continuing to follow the list_name[index number] model, in which the index number 0 is in square brackets just after the name of the variable row_1.

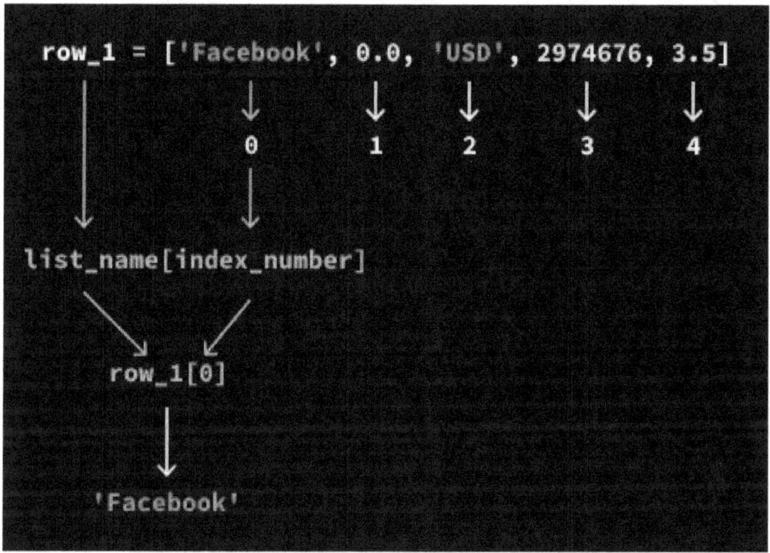

The method to retrieve each element in row_1:

```
script.py

row_1 = ['Facebook', 0.0, 'USD', 2974676, 3.5]
            0            1       2        3       4
```



```
print(row_1[0])
print(row_1[1])
print(row_1[2])
print(row_1[3])
print(row_1[4])

Output
Facebook
0.0
USD
2974676
3.5
```

Retrieval of list elements makes processes easier to execute. For example, Facebook and Instagram ratings can be selected, and the aggregate or distinction between the two can be found:

```
script.py

row_1 = ['Facebook', 0.0, 'USD', 2974676, 3.5]
row_2 = ['Instagram', 0.0, 'USD', 2161558, 4.5]

difference = row_2[4] - row_1[4]
average_rating = (row_1[4] + row_2[4]) / 2

print(difference)
print(average_rating)

Output
1.0
4.0
```

Try Using list indexing to retrieve and then average the number of ratings with the first 3 rows:

ratings_1 = row_1[3]

ratings_2 = row_2[3]

ratings_3 = row_3[3]

total = ratings_1 + ratings_2 + ratings_3

average = total / 3

print(average)

2422346.3333333335

Using Negative Indexing with Lists

There are two indexing systems for lists in Python:

Positive indexing: The index number of the first element is 0; the index number of the second element is 1 and furthermore.

Negative indexing: The index number of the last element is -1; the index number of the second element is -2 and furthermore.

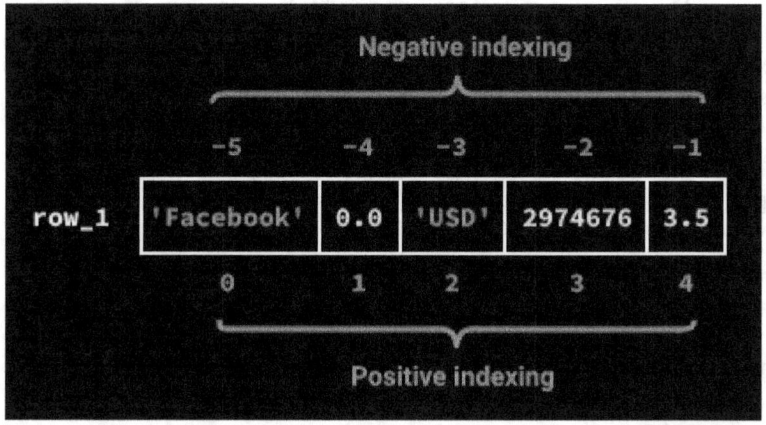

In exercise, we mostly use positive indexing to obtain elements of the list. Negative indexing is helpful whenever we want to pick the last element in such a list, mostly if the list is lengthy, and by calculating, we cannot figure out the length.

```
script.py
row_1 = ['Facebook', 0.0, 'USD', 2974676, 3.5]

print(row_1[-1])
print(row_1[4])
```

```
Output
3.5
3.5
```

Note that when we use an index number just outside of the
scope of the two indexing schemes, we are going to have an
IndexError.

```
script.py
row_1 = ['Facebook', 0.0, 'USD', 2974676, 3.5]
row_1[6]
```

```
Output
IndexError: list index out of range
```

```
script.py
row_1 = ['Facebook', 0.0, 'USD', 2974676, 3.5]
row_1[-7]
```

```
Output
IndexError: list index out of range
```

How about using negative indexing to remove from each of the top 3 rows the user rating (the very last value) and afterwards average it.

row_1 [-1]=rating_1

row_2[-1]=rating_2

row_3[-1]=rating_3

rating_1 + rating_2 + rating_3=total_rating

total_rating / 3= average_rating

print(average)

2422346.33333

Slice Python Lists

Rather than selecting the list elements separately, we can pick two consecutive elements using a syntax shortcut:

```
script.py
row_3 = ['Clash of Clans', 0.0, 'USD', 2130805, 4.5]

cc_pricing_data = row_3[0:3]  ⟵ syntax shortcut
print(cc_pricing_data)

Output
['Clash of Clans', 0.0, 'USD']
```

While selecting the first n elements from a list called a list (n stands for a number), we can use the list syntax shortcut [0: n].

In the above example, we had to choose from the list row 3 the first three elements, so we will use row 3[0:3].

When the first three items were chosen, we sliced a portion of the set. For this function, the collection method for a section of a list is known as list slicing.

List slice can be done in many ways:

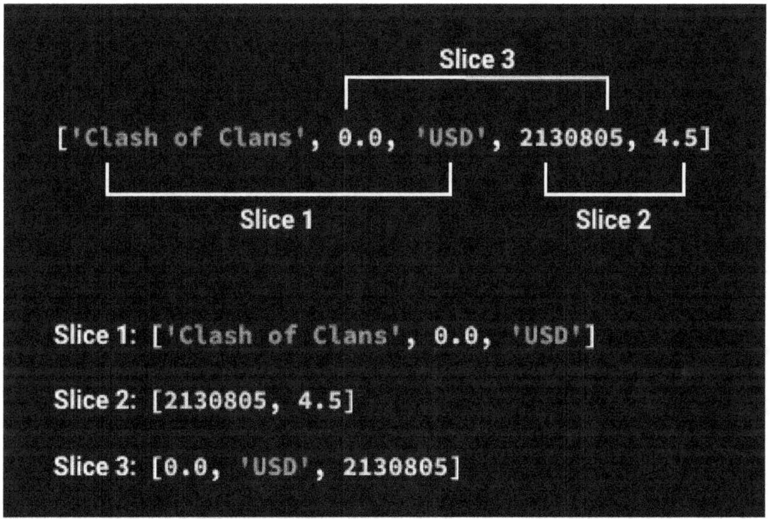

Retrieving any list slice we need:

Firstly identify the first and last elements of the slice.

The index numbers of the first and last element of the slice must then be defined.

Lastly, we can use the syntax a list[m: n] to extract the list slice we require, while:

'm' means the index number of both the slice's 1st element; and

'n' symbolizes the index number of the slice's last element in addition to one (if the last element seems to have index number 2, after which n is 3, if the last element seems to have index number 4, after which n is 5, and so on).


```
row_3 = ['Clash of Clans', 0.0, 'USD', 2130805, 4.5]
```

When we want to choose the 1st or last 'x' elements (x represents a number), we may use even less complex shortcuts for syntax:

a_list[:x] when we need to choose the first x elements.

a_list[-x:] when we need to choose the last x elements.

```
script.py

row_3 = ['Clash of Clans', 0.0, 'USD', 2130805, 4.5]

first_3 = row_3[:3]
last_3 = row_3[-3:]

print(first_3)
print(last_3)
```

```
Output
['Clash of Clans', 0.0, 'USD']
['USD', 2130805, 4.5]
```

See how we retrieve from the first row the first four elements (with Facebook data):

first_4_fb = row_1[:4]

print(first_4_fb)

['Facebook', 0.0, 'USD', 2974676]

From the same row, the last three elements are:

last_3_fb = row_1[-3:]

print(last_3_fb)

['USD', 2974676, 3.5]

In the fifth row (data in the row for Pandora) with elements third and fourth are:

pandora_3_4 = row_5[2:4]

print(pandora_3_4)

['USD', 1126879]

Python List of Lists

Lists were previously introduced as a viable approach to using one variable per data point. Rather than having a different variable for any of the five 'Facebook' data points, 0.0, 'USD,' 2974676, 3.5, we can connect the data points into a list together and then save the list in a variable.

We have worked with a data set of five rows since then and have stored each row as a collection in each different variable (row 1, row 2, row 3, row 4, and row 5 variables). Even so, if we had a data set of 5,000 rows, we would probably have ended up with 5,000 variables that will create our code messy and nearly difficult to work with.

To fix this issue, we may store our five variables in a unified list:

```python
row_1 = ['Facebook', 0.0, 'USD', 2974676, 3.5]
row_2 = ['Instagram', 0.0, 'USD', 2161558, 4.5]
row_3 = ['Clash of Clans', 0.0, 'USD', 2130805, 4.5]
row_4 = ['Temple Run', 0.0, 'USD', 1724546, 4.5]
row_5 = ['Pandora - Music & Radio', 0.0, 'USD', 1126879, 4.0]

data_set = [row_1, row_2, row_3, row_4, row_5]
data_set
```

Output ──── Notice the double brackets

```
[['Facebook', 0.0, 'USD', 2974676, 3.5],     ──── Notice the commas
['Instagram', 0.0, 'USD', 2161558, 4.5],
['Clash of Clans', 0.0, 'USD', 2130805, 4.5],
['Temple Run', 0.0, 'USD', 1724546, 4.5],
['Pandora - Music & Radio', 0.0, 'USD', 1126879, 4.0]]
```

As we're seeing, the data set is a list of five additional columns (row 1, row 2, row 3, row 4, and row 5). A list containing other lists is termed a set of lists.

The data set variable is already a list, which indicates that we can use the syntax we have learned to retrieve individual list elements and execute list slicing. Under, we have:

Use datset[0] to locate the first list element (row 1).

Use datset[-1] to locate the last list element (row 5).

Obtain the first two list elements (row 1 and row 2) utilizing data set[:2] to execute a list slicing.

```
script.py

data_set = [row_1, row_2, row_3, row_4, row_5]
print(data_set[0])
print(data_set[-1])
print(data_set[:2])
```

```
Output

['Facebook', 0.0, 'USD', 2974676, 3.5]
['Pandora - Music & Radio', 0.0, 'USD', 1126879, 4.0]
[['Facebook', 0.0, 'USD', 2974676, 3.5],
['Instagram', 0.0, 'USD', 2161558, 4.5]]
```

Often, we will need to obtain individual elements from a list that is a portion of a list of lists — for example; we might need to obtain the rating of 3.5 from the data row ['FACEBOOK', 0.0, 'USD', 2974676, 3.5], which is a portion of the list of data sets. We retrieve 3.5 from data set below utilizing what we have learnt:

Using data set[0], we locate row_1, and allocate the output to a variable named fb_row.

fb_row ['Facebook', 0.0, 'USD', 2974676, 3.5] outputs, which we printed.

Using fb_row[-1], we locate the final element from fb_row (because fb row is a list), and appoint the output to a variable called fb_rating.

Print fb_rating, outputting 3.5

```
script.py

data_set = [row_1, row_2, row_3, row_4, row_5]
fb_row = data_set[0]
print(fb_row)

fb_rating = fb_row[-1]
print(fb_rating)

Output
['Facebook', 0.0, 'USD', 2974676, 3.5]
3.5
```

Earlier in this example, we obtained 3.5 in two steps: data_set[0] was first retrieved, and fb_row[-1] was then retrieved. There is also an easy way to get the same 3.5 output by attaching the two indices ([0] and [-1]); the code data_set[0][-1] gets 3.5.:

```
script.py

data_set = [row_1, row_2, row_3, row_4, row_5]
print(data_set[0][-1])
              ‾‾‾‾‾‾‾‾‾‾‾‾‾
                  row_1
                   ‾‾‾
   ['Facebook', 0.0, 'USD', 2974676, 3.5]

Output
3.5
```

Earlier in this example, we have seen two ways to get the 3.5 value back. Both methods lead to the same performance (3.5), but the second approach requires fewer coding, as the steps we see from the example are elegantly integrated. As you can select an alternative, people generally prefer the latter.

Let's turn our five independent lists in to the list of lists:

app_data_set = [row_1, row_2, row_3, row_4, row_5]

then use:

print(app_data_set)

```
[
  ['FACEBOOK', 0.0, 'usd', 2974676, 3.5]

  ['INSTAGRAM', 0.0, 'usd', 2161558, 4.5

  ['CLASH OF CLANS', 0.0, 'usd', 2130805, 4.5]

  ['TEMPLE RUN', 0.0, 'usd', 1724546, 4.5]

  ['PANDORA', 0.0, 'usd', 1126879, 4.0]                    ]
[
```

List Processes by Repetitive method

Earlier, we had an interest in measuring an app's average ranking in this project. It was a feasible task while we were attempting to work only for three rows, but the tougher it becomes, the further rows we add. Utilizing our tactic from the beginning, we will:

Obtain each individual rating.

Take the sum of the ratings.

Dividing by the total number of ratings.

```
script.py

row_1 = ['Facebook', 0.0, 'USD', 2974676, 3.5]
row_2 = ['Instagram', 0.0, 'USD', 2161558, 4.5]
row_3 = ['Clash of Clans', 0.0, 'USD', 2130805, 4.5]
row_4 = ['Temple Run', 0.0, 'USD', 1724546, 4.5]
row_5 = ['Pandora - Music & Radio', 0.0, 'USD', 1126879, 4.0]


app_data_set = [row_1, row_2, row_3, row_4, row_5]
avg_rating = (app_data_set[0][-1] + app_data_set[1][-1] +
              app_data_set[2][-1] + app_data_set[3][-1] +
              app_data_set[4][-1]) / 5

avg_rating

Output
4.2
```

As you have seen that it becomes complicated with five ratings.
Unless we were dealing with data that includes thousands of
rows, an unimaginable amount of code would be needed! We
ought to find a quick way to get lots of ratings back.

Taking a look at the code example earlier in this thread, we see
that a procedure continues to reiterate: within app_data_set, we
select the last list element for every list. What if we can just
directly ask Python we would like to repeat this process in
app_data_set for every list?

Luckily we can use it — Python gives us a simple route to repeat a plan that helps us tremendously when we have to reiterate a process tens of thousands or even millions of times.

Let's assume we have a list [3, 5, 1, 2] allocated to a variable rating, and we need to replicate the following procedure: display the element for each element in the ratings. And this is how we can turn it into syntax with Python:

```
script.py

ratings = [3, 5, 1, 2]

for element in ratings:
    print(element)
```

```
Output
3
5
1
2
```

The procedure that we decided to replicate in our first example above was "generate the last item for each list in the app_data_set." Here's how we can transform that operation into syntax with Python:

```
script.py

app_data_set = [row_1, row_2, row_3, row_4, row_5]

for each_list in app_data_set:
    rating = each_list[-1]
    print(rating)
```

```
Output
3.5
4.5
4.5
4.5
4.0
```

Let's attempt and then get a good idea of what's going on above. Python differentiates each list item from app_data_set, each at a time, and assign it to each_list (which essentially becomes a vector that holds a list — we'll address this further):

```
script.py

app_data_set = [row_1, row_2, row_3, row_4, row_5]

for each_list in app_data_set:
    print(each_list)
```

```
Output

['Facebook', 0.0, 'USD', 2974676, 3.5]
['Instagram', 0.0, 'USD', 2161558, 4.5]
['Clash of Clans', 0.0, 'USD', 2130805, 4.5]
['Temple Run', 0.0, 'USD', 1724546, 4.5]
['Pandora - Music & Radio', 0.0, 'USD', 1126879, 4.0]
```

In the last figure earlier in this thread, the code is a much simpler

and much more conceptual edition of the code below:

```
script.py

app_data_set = [row_1, row_2, row_3, row_4, row_5]

print(app_data_set[0])  ⎤
print(app_data_set[1])  ⎥
print(app_data_set[2])  ⎥   for each_list in app_data_set:
print(app_data_set[3])  ⎥       print(each_list)
print(app_data_set[4])  ⎦
```

```
Output

['Facebook', 0.0, 'USD', 2974676, 3.5]
['Instagram', 0.0, 'USD', 2161558, 4.5]
['Clash of Clans', 0.0, 'USD', 2130805, 4.5]
['Temple Run', 0.0, 'USD', 1724546, 4.5]
['Pandora - Music & Radio', 0.0, 'USD', 1126879, 4.0]
```

Utilizing the above technique requires that we consider writing a line of code for each row in the data set. But by using the app_data_set methodology for each list involves that we write only two lines of code irrespective of the number of rows in the data set — the data set may have five rows or a hundred thousand.

Our transitional goal is to use this special method to calculate the average rating of our five rows above, in which our ultimate goal is to calculate the average rating of 7,197 rows for our data set. We 're going to get exactly that within the next few displays of this task, but we're going to concentrate for now on practicing this method to get a strong grasp of it.

We ought to indent the space characters four times to the right before we want to write the code:

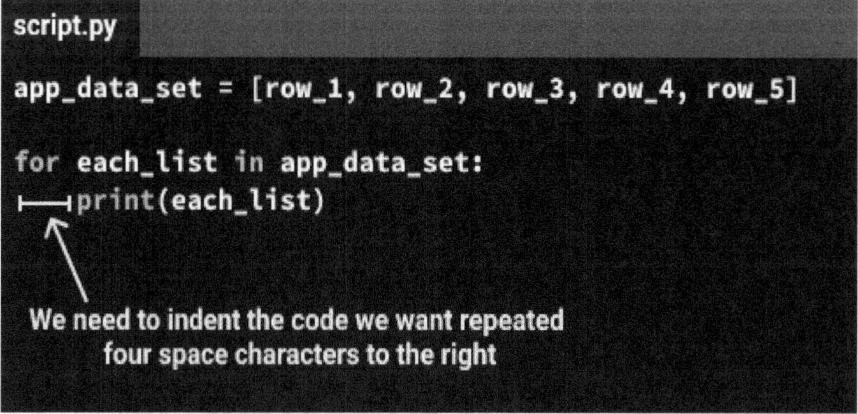

Theoretically, we would only have to indent the code to the right with at least one space character, but in the Python language, the declaration is to use four space characters. This assists with readability — reading your code will be fairly easy for other individuals who watch this convention, and you will find it easier to follow theirs.

Now use this technique to print each app's name and rating:

foreach_list in app_data_set:

name = each_list[0]

rating = each_list[-1]

print(name, rating)

Facebook 3.5

Instagram 4.5

Clash of Clans 4.5

Temple Run 4.5

Pandora - Music & Radio 4.0

Loops

A loop is frequently used to iterate over a series of statements. We have two kinds of loops, 'for loop' and 'while loop' in Python. We will study 'for loop' and 'while loop' in the following scenario.

For Loop

Python's for loop is used to iterate over a sequence (list, tuple, string) or just about any iterate-able object. It is called traversal to iterate over a sequence.

Syntax of For loop in Python

for<variable> in <sequence>:

   # body_of_loop that has set of statements

   # which requires repeated execution

In this case < variable > is often a variable used to iterate over a < sequence >. Around each iteration the next value is taken from < sequence > to approach the end of the sequence.

Python – For loop example

The example below illustrates the use of a loop to iterate over a list array. We calculate the square of each number present in the list and show the same with the body of for loop.

#Printing squares of all numbers program

List of integer numbers

numbers = [1, 2, 4, 6, 11, 20]

#variable to store each number's square temporary

sq = 0

#iterating over the given list

forval in numbers:

   # calculating square of each number

sq = val * val

    # displaying the squares

print(sq)

Output:

1

4

16

36

121

400

For loop with else block

Excluding Java, we can have the loop linked with an optional 'else' block in Python. The 'else' block only runs after all the iterations are finished by the loop. Let's see one example:

For val in range(5):

        print(val)

else:

        print("The loop has completed execution")

Output:

0

1

2

3

4

The loop has completed execution

Note: else block is executed when the loop is completed.

Nested For loop in Python

If there is a loop within another for loop, then it will be termed a nested for loop. Let's take a nested for loop example.

```python
for num1 in range(3):
        for num2 in range(10, 14):
                print(num1, ",", num2)
```

Output:

0 , 10

0 , 11

0 , 12

0 , 13

1 , 10

1 , 11

1 , 12

1 , 13

2 , 10

2 , 11

2 , 12

2 , 13

While Loop

While loop is also used to continuously iterate over a block of code until a specified statement returns false, we have seen in many for loop in Python in the last guide, which is used for a similar intent. The biggest distinction is that we use for looping when we are not sure how many times the loop needs execution, yet on the other side when we realize exactly how many times we have to execute the loop, we need for a loop. Syntax of while loop

while conditioning:

    #body_of_while

The body of the while is a series of statements from Python which require repetitive implementation. These claims are consistently executed until the specified condition returns false.

while loop flow

1. Firstly given condition is inspected, the loop is canceled if the condition returns false, and also the control moves towards the next statement in the compiler after the loop.

2. When the condition returns true, the set of statements within the loop will be performed, and the power will then switch to the loop start for the next execution.

Those two measures continuously occur as long as the condition defined in the loop stands true.

While loop example

This is an example of a while loop. We have a variable number in this case, and we show the value of the number in a loop, the loop will have an incremental operation where we increase the number value. It is a very crucial component, while the loop should have an operation of increase or decrease. Otherwise, the loop will operate indefinitely.

num = 1

#loop will repeat itself as long as it can

#num< 10 remains true

whilenum< 10:`

print(num)

   #incrementing the value of num

num = num + 3

Output:

1

4

Infinite while loop

Example 1:

This will endlessly print the word 'hello' since this situation will always be true.

while True:

print("hello")

Example 2:

num = 1

whilenum<5:

print(num)

This will endlessly print '1' since we do not update the number value inside the loop, so the number value would always remain one, and the condition number<5 would always give back true.

Nested while loop in Python

While inside another while loop a while loop is present, then it will be considered nested while loop. To understand this concept, let us take an example.

i = 1

j = 5

while i< 4:

```python
    while j < 8:
        print(i, ",", j)
        j = j + 1
    i = i + 1
```

Output:

1 , 5

2 , 6

3 , 7

Python – while loop with else block

We may add an 'else' block to a while loop. The section 'else' is possible. It executes only when the processing of the loop has ended.

```python
num = 10
whilenum> 6:
    print(num)
    num = num-1
else:
    print("loop is finished")
```

Output:

10

9

8

Loop is finished

ADDING MULTIPLE VALUED DATA IN PYTHON

Often the creator wants users to input multiple values or inputs in a line. In Python, users could use two techniques to take multiple values or inputs in one line.

Use of split() method

Use of List comprehension

Use of split() method :

This feature helps to receive many user inputs. It splits the defined separator to the given input. If no separator is given, then a separator is blank space. Users generally use a split() method to separate a Python string, but it can be used when multiple inputs are taken.

Syntax:

input().split(separator, maxsplit)

Example:

```
filter_none
edit
play_arrow
brightness_4
#Python program showing how to add
#multiple input using split
#taking two inputs each time
x, y = input("Enter a two value: ").split()
print("Number of boys: ", x)
print("Number of girls: ", y)
print()
# taking three inputs at a time
x, y, z = input("Enter a three value: ").split()
print("Total number of students: ", x)
print("Number of boys is : ", y)
print("Number of girls is : ", z)
print()
# taking two inputs at a time
a, b = input("Enter a two value: ").split()
print("First number is {} and second number is {}".format(a, b))
print()
# taking multiple inputs at a time
# and type casting using list() function
x = list(map(int, input("Enter a multiple value: ").split()))
print("List of students: ", x)
```

Output:

```
Enter a two value: 5 10
Number of boys:   5
Number of girls:  10


Enter a three value: 30 10 20
Total number of students:  30
Number of boys is :  10
Number of girls is :  20


Enter a four value: 20 30
First number is 20 and second number is 30


Enter a multiple value: 20 30 10 22 23 26
List of students:  [20, 30, 10, 22, 23, 26]
```

Using List comprehension:

Comprehension of lists is an easy way of describing and building a list in Python. Just like mathematical statements, we can generate lists within each line only. It is often used when collecting multiple device inputs.

Example:

```python
filter_none
edit
play_arrow
brightness_4
# Python program showing
# how to take multiple input
# using List comprehension
# taking two input at a time
x, y = [int(x) for x in input("Enter two value: ").split()]
print("First Number is: ", x)
print("Second Number is: ", y)
print()
# taking three input at a time
x, y, z = [int(x) for x in input("Enter three value: ").split()]
print("First Number is: ", x)
print("Second Number is: ", y)
print("Third Number is: ", z)
print()
# taking two inputs at a time
x, y = [int(x) for x in input("Enter two value: ").split()]
print("First number is {} and second number is {}".format(x, y))
print()
# taking multiple inputs at a time
x = [int(x) for x in input("Enter multiple value: ").split()]
print("Number of list is: ", x)
```

Output:

```
Enter two value: 2 5
First Number is:   2
Second Number is:   5

Enter three value: 2 4 5
First Number is:   2
Second Number is:   4
Third Number is:   5

Enter two value: 2 10
First number is 2 and second number is 10

Enter multiple value: 1 2 3 4 5
Number of list is:   [1, 2, 3, 4, 5]
```

Note: The definitions above take inputs divided by spaces. If we prefer to pursue different input by comma (","), we can just use the below:

```
# taking multiple inputs divided by comma at a time
x = [int(x) for x in input("Enter multiple value: ").split(",")]
print("Number of list is: ", x)
```

Assign multiple values to multiple variables

By separating the variables and values with commas, you can allocate multiple values to different variables.

```
a, b = 100, 200

print(a)

# 100

print(b)

# 200
```

You have more than three variables to delegate. In addition, various types can be assigned, as well.

```
a, b, c = 0.1, 100, 'string'

print(a)

# 0.1

print(b)

# 100

print(c)

#string
```

Assign the same value to multiple variables

Using = consecutively, you could even appoint multiple variables with the same value. For instance, this is helpful when you initialize multiple variables to almost the same value.

```
a = b = 100

print(a)

# 100

print(b)

# 100
```

Upon defining the same value, another value may also be converted into one. As explained later, when allocating mutable objects such as lists or dictionaries, care should be taken.

```
a = 200

print(a)
```

200

```python
print(b)
# 100
```

It can be written three or more in the same way.

```python
a = b = c = 'string'
print(a)
# string

print(b)
# string

print(c)
# string
```

Instead of immutable objects like int, float, and str, be careful when appointing mutable objects like list and dict.

When you use = consecutively, all variables are assigned the same object, so if you modify the element value or create a new element, then the other object will also modify.

```python
a = b = [0, 1, 2]
print(a is b)
# True

a[0] = 100
print(a)
# [100, 1, 2]

print(b)
# [100, 1, 2]
```

Same as below.

```python
b = [0, 1, 2]
a = b
print(a is b)
# True
a[0] = 100
print(a)
# [100, 1, 2]
print(b)
# [100, 1, 2]
```

If you would like to independently manage them you need to allocate them separately.

after c = []; d = [], c and d are guaranteed to link to two unique, newly created empty,different lists. (Note that c = d = [] assigns the same object to both c and d.)

Here is another example:

```python
a = [0, 1, 2]
b = [0, 1, 2]
print(a is b)
# False
a[0] = 100
print(a)
# [100, 1, 2]
print(b)
```

```
# [0, 1, 2]
```

Adding string data in Python

What is String in Python?

A string is a Character set. A character is just a symbol. The English language, for instance, has 26 characters. Operating systems do not handle characters they handle the (binary) numbers. And if you may see characters on your computer, it is represented internally as a mixture of 0s and 1s and is manipulated. The transformation of character to a number is known as encoding, and probably decoding is the reverse process. ASCII and Unicode are two of the widely used encodings. A string in Python is a series of characters in Unicode. Unicode was incorporated to provide all characters in all languages and to carry encoding uniformity. Python Unicode allows you to learn regarding Unicode.

How to create a string in Python?

Strings may be formed by encapsulating characters or even double quotes inside a single quotation. In Python, even triple quotes may be used but commonly used to portray multiline strings and docstrings.

```python
# defining strings in Python

# all of the following are equivalent

my_string = 'Hello'

print(my_string)

my_string = "Hello"

print(my_string)

my_string = '''Hello'''

print(my_string)

# triple quotes string can extend multiple lines

my_string = """Hello, welcome to the world of Python"""

print(my_string)
```

When the program is executed, the output becomes:

```
Hello

Hello

Hello

Hello, welcome to the world of Python
```

Accessing the characters in a string?

By indexing and using slicing, we can obtain individual characters and scope of characters. The index commences at 0. Attempting to obtain a character from index range will cause an IndexError to increase. The index has to be integral. We cannot use floats or other types, and this will lead to TypeError. Python lets its sequences be indexed negatively. The -1 index corresponds to the last object, -2 to the second object, and so forth. Using the slicing operator '(colon),' we can access a range of items within a string.

#Python string characters access:

```python
str = 'programiz'
print('str = ', str)
#first character
print('str[0] = ', str[0])
#last character
print('str[-1] = ', str[-1])
#slicing 2nd to 5th character
print('str[1:5] = ', str[1:5])
#slicing 6th to 2nd last character
print('str[5:-2] = ', str[5:-2])
```

If we execute the code above we have the following results:

```
str =  programiz
str[0] =  p
str[-1] =  z
str[1:5] =  rogr
str[5:-2] =  am
```

When we attempt to access an index out of the range, or if we are using numbers other than an integer, errors will arise.

```python
# index must be in the range
```

```
>>>my_string[15]

...

IndexError: string index out of range

# index must be an integer

>>>my_string[1.5]

...
```

TypeError: Define string indices as integers only

By analyzing the index between the elements as seen below, slicing can best be visualized. Whenever we want to obtain a range, we need the index that slices the part of the string from it.

How to change or delete a string?

Strings are unchangeable. This means elements of a list cannot be modified until allocated. We will easily reassign various strings of the same term.

```
>>>my_string = 'programiz'
>>>my_string[5] = 'a'
...
TypeError: 'str' object does not support item assignment
>>>my_string = 'Python'
>>>my_string
'Python'
```

We cannot erase characters from a string, or remove them. But it's easy to erase the string completely by using del keyword.

```
>>>delmy_string[1]
...
TypeError: 'str' object doesn't support item deletion
>>>delmy_string
>>>my_string
...
NameError: name 'my_string' is not defined
```

Python String Operations

There are many methods that can be used with string making it one of the most commonly used Python data types. See Python Data Types for more information on the types of data used in Python coding

Concatenation of Two or More Strings

The combination of two or even more strings into one is termed concatenation. In Python, the + operator does that. They are likewise concatenated by actually typing two string literals together. For a specified number of times, the * operator could be used to reiterate the string.

```python
# Python String Operations

str1 = 'Hello'

str2 ='World!'

# using +

print('str1 + str2 = ', str1 + str2)

# using *

print('str1 * 3 =', str1 * 3)
```

Once we execute the program above we get the following results:

```
str1 + str2 =  HelloWorld!

str1 * 3 = HelloHelloHello
```

Using two literal strings together would therefore concatenate them like + operator.

We might use parentheses if we wish to concatenate strings in various lines.

```
>>> # two string literals together

>>> 'Hello ''World!'

'Hello World!'

>>> # using parentheses

>>> s = ('Hello '

...      'World')

>>>s

'Hello World'
```

Iterating Through a string

With a for loop, we can iterate through a string. This is an example of counting the number of 'l's in a string function.

```python
#Iterating through a string
count = 0
for letter in 'Hello World':
if(letter == 'l'):
count += 1
print(count,'letters found')
```

If we execute the code above, we have the following results:
'3 letters found.'

String Membership Test

We can check whether or not there is a substring within a string by using keyword in.

```
>>> 'a' in 'program'
True
>>> 'at' not in 'battle'
False
```

Built-in functions to Work with Python

Different built-in functions which can also be work with strings in series. A few other commonly used types are len() and enumerate(). The function enumerate() returns an enumerate object. It includes the index and value as combinations of all elements in the string. This may be of use to iteration.

Comparably, len() returns the string length (characters number).

```python
str = 'cold'

# enumerate()

list_enumerate = list(enumerate(str))

print('list(enumerate(str) = ', list_enumerate)

#character count

print('len(str) = ', len(str))
```

Once we execute the code above we have the following results:

```
list(enumerate(str) =  [(0, 'c'), (1, 'o'), (2, 'l'), (3, 'd')]

len(str) =  4
```

Formats for Python String

Sequence for escaping

We can't use single quotes or double quotes if we want to print a text like He said, "What's there?" This would result in a SyntaxError because there are single and double quotations in the text alone.

```python
>>>print("He said, "What's there?"")
...
SyntaxError: invalid syntax
>>>print('He said, "What's there?"')
...
```

SyntaxError: invalid syntax

Triple quotes are one way to get round the problem. We might use escape sequences as a solution. A series of escape starts with a backslash, which is represented differently. If we are using a single quote to describe a string, it is important to escape all single quotes within the string. The case with double quotes is closely related. This is how the above text can be represented.

```python
# using triple quotes
print('''He said, "What's there?"''')
# escaping single quotes
print('He said, "What\'s there?"')
# escaping double quotes
print("He said, \"What's there?\"")
```

Once we execute the code above, we have the following results:

```
He said, "What's there?"
He said, "What's there?"
He said, "What's there?"
```

Raw String to ignore escape sequence

Quite often inside a string, we might want to reject the escape sequences. To use it, we can set r or R before the string. Which means it's a raw string, and it will neglect any escape sequence inside.

>>>print("This is \x61 \ngood example")

This is a

good example

>>> print(r"This is \x61 \ngood example")

This is \x61 \ngood example

The format() Method for Formatting Strings

The format() sources available and make with the string object is very flexible and potent in string formatting. Style strings contain curly braces{} as placeholders or fields of substitution, which are substituted.

To specify the sequence, we may use positional arguments or keyword arguments.

```python
# Python string format() method
# default(implicit) order
default_order = "{}, {} and {}".format('John','Bill','Sean')
print('\n--- Default Order ---')
print(default_order)
# order using positional argument
positional_order = "{1}, {0} and {2}".format('John','Bill','Sean')
print('\n--- Positional Order ---')
print(positional_order)
# order using keyword argument
keyword_order = "{s}, {b} and {j}".format(j='John',b='Bill',s='Sean')
print('\n--- Keyword Order ---')
print(keyword_order)
Once we execute the code above we have the following results:
--- Default Order ---
John, Bill and Sean
--- Positional Order ---
Bill, John and Sean
--- Keyword Order ---
Sean, Bill and John
```

The format() technique can have requirements in optional format. Using colon, they are divided from the name of the field. For example, a string in the given space may be left-justified <, right-justified >, or based ^.

Even we can format integers as binary, hexadecimal, etc. and floats can be rounded or shown in the style of the exponent. You can use tons of compiling there. For all string formatting available using the format() method, see below example:

```
>>> # formatting integers
>>> "Binary representation of {0} is {0:b}".format(12)
'Binary representation of 12 is 1100'
>>> # formatting floats
>>> "Exponent representation: {0:e}".format(1566.345)
'Exponent representation: 1.566345e+03'
>>> # round off
>>> "One third is: {0:.3f}".format(1/3)
'One third is: 0.333'
>>> # string alignment
>>> "|{:<10}|{:^10}|{:>10}|".format('butter','bread','ham')
'|butter    |  bread   |       ham|'
```

Old style formatting

We even can code strings such as the old sprint() style in the programming language used in C. To accomplish this; we use the '%' operator.

```
>>> x = 12.3456789

>>>print('The value of x is %3.2f' %x)

The value of x is 12.35

>>>print('The value of x is %3.4f' %x)

The value of x is 12.3457
```

String common Methods for Python

The string object comes with various methods. One of them is the format() method we described above. A few other frequently used technique include lower(), upper(), join(), split(), find(), substitute() etc. Here is a wide-range list of several of the built-in methodologies in Python for working with strings.

```
>>> "PrOgRaMiZ".lower()
'programiz'
>>> "PrOgRaMiZ".upper()
'PROGRAMIZ'
>>> "This will split all words into a list".split()
['This', 'will', 'split', 'all', 'words', 'into', 'a', 'list']
>>> ' '.join(['This', 'will', 'join', 'all', 'words', 'into', 'a', 'string'])
'This will join all words into a string'
>>> 'Happy New Year'.find('ew')
7
>>> 'Happy New Year'.replace('Happy','Brilliant')
'Brilliant New Year'
```

Inserting values into strings

Method 1 - the string format method

The string method format method can be used to create new strings with the values inserted. That method works for all of Python's recent releases. That is where we put a string in another string:

```
>>>shepherd = "Mary"
>>>string_in_string = "Shepherd {} is on duty.".format(shepherd)
>>>print(string_in_string)
```

Shepherd Mary is on duty.

The curved braces indicate where the inserted value will be going.

You can insert a value greater than one. The values should not have to be strings; numbers and other Python entities may be strings.

```
>>>shepherd = "Mary"

>>>age = 32

>>>stuff_in_string = "Shepherd {} is {} years old.".format(shepherd, age)

>>>print(stuff_in_string)

Shepherd Mary is 32 years old.

>>> 'Here is a {} floating point number'.format(3.33333)

'Here is a 3.33333 floating point number'
```

Using the formatting options within curly brackets, you can do more complex formatting of numbers and strings — see the information on curly brace string layout.

This process allows us to give instructions for formatting things such as numbers, using either: inside the curly braces, led by guidance for formatting. Here we request you to print in integer (d) in which the number is 0 to cover the field size of 3:

```
>>>print("Number {:03d} is here.".format(11))

Number 011 is here.

This prints a floating point value (f) with exactly 4 digits after the decimal point:

>>> 'A formatted number - {:.4f}'.format(.2)

'A formatted number - 0.2000'
```

Method 2 - f-strings in Python >= 3.6

When you can rely on having Python > = version 3.6, you will have another appealing place to use the new literal (f-string) formatted string to input variable values. Just at the start of the string, an f informs Python to permit any presently valid variable names inside the string as column names. So here's an example such as the one above, for instance using the f-string syntax:

```
>>>shepherd = "Martha"

>>>age = 34

>>> # Note f before first quote of string

>>>stuff_in_string = f"Shepherd {shepherd} is {age} years old."

>>>print(stuff_in_string)
```

Shepherd Martha is 34 years old.

Method 3 - old school % formatting

There seems to be an older string formatting tool, which uses the percent operator. It is a touch less versatile than the other two choices, but you can still see it in use in older coding, where it is more straightforward to use '%' formatting. For formatting the '%' operator, you demonstrate where the encoded values should go using a '%' character preceded by a format identifier to tell how to add the value.

So here's the example earlier in this thread, using formatting by '%.' Note that '%s' marker for a string to be inserted, and the '%d' marker for an integer.

```
>>>stuff_in_string = "Shepherd %s is %d years old." % (shepherd, age
>>>print(stuff_in_string)
```

Shepherd Martha is 34 years old.

MODULE DATA

What are the modules in Python?

Whenever you leave and re-enter the Python interpreter, the definitions you have created (functions and variables) will get lost. Consequently, if you'd like to develop a code a little longer, it's better to use a text editor to plan the input for the interpreter and execute it with that file as input conversely. This is defined as script formation. As the software gets bigger, you may want to break it into different files to make maintenance simpler. You might also like to use a handy function that you wrote in many other programs without having to replicate its definition inside each program. To assist this, Python has the option of putting definitions into a file and using them in the interpreter's code or interactive instances. This very file is considered a module; module descriptions can be loaded into certain modules or into the main module (the list of variables you have exposure to in a high-level script and in converter mode).

A module is a file that contains definitions and statements from Python. The name of the file is the name of the module with the .py suffix attached. The name of the module (only as string) inside a module is available as the value, including its global

variable __name__. For example, use your preferred text editor
to build a file named fibo.py with the following contents in the
current working directory:

```python
# Python Module example

def add(a, b):
    """This program adds two

numbers and return the result"""

result = a + b

return result
```

In this, we defined an add() function within an example titled "
module." The function requires two numbers and returns a total
of them.

How to import modules in Python?

Within a module, we can import the definitions to some other
module or even to the interactive Python interpreter. To do
something like this, we use the keyword import. To load our
recently specified example module, please enter in the Python
prompt.

>>> import example

This should not import the identities of the functions directly in the existing symbol table, as defined in the example. It just imports an example of the module name there.

Using the name of the module, we can use the dot(.) operator to access the function. For instance:

>>>example.add(4,5.5)

9.5

Python comes with lots of regular modules. Check out the complete list of regular Python modules and their usage scenarios. These directories are within the destination where you've installed Python in the Lib directory. Normal modules could be imported just the same as our user-defined modules are imported.

There are different ways of importing the modules. You'll find them below:

Python import statement

Using the import statement, we can extract a module by using the dot operator, as explained in the previous section and access the definitions within it. Here is another example.

```python
# import statement example

# to import standard module math

import math

print("The value of pi is", math.pi)
```

Once we execute the code above, we have the following results:
The value of pi is 3.141592653589793

Import with renaming

We can load a module in the following way by changing the
name of it:

```python
# import module by renaming it

import math as m

print("The value of pi is", m.pi)
```

We called the module Math as m. In certain instances, this will
save us time to type. Remember that in our scope, the name
math is not identified. Therefore math.pi is incorrect, and m.pi is
correctly implemented.

Python from...import statement

We can import individual names from such a module without having to import the entire module. Here is another example.

```
# import only pi from math module

from math import pi

print("The value of pi is", pi)
```

In this, only the pi parameter was imported from the math module. We don't utilize the dot operator in certain cases. We can likewise import different modules:

```
>>>from math import pi, e
>>>pi
3.141592653589793
>>>e
2.718281828459045
```

Import all names

With the following form, we can import all terms (definitions) from a module:

```
# import all names from standard module math
from math import *
print("The value of pi is," pi)
```

Above, we have added all of the math module descriptions. This covers all names that are available in our scope except those that start with an underscore. It is not a good programming technique to import something with the asterisk (*) key. This will lead to a replication of an attribute's meaning. This also restricts our code's readability.

Python Module Search Path

Python looks at many locations when importing a module. Interpreter searches for a built-in module instead. So if not included in the built-in module, Python searches at a collection of directories specified in sys.path. The exploration is in this sequence:

PYTHONPATH (list of directories environment variable)

The installation-dependent default directory

```
>>> import sys

>>>sys.path

['',

'C:\\Python33\\Lib\\idlelib',

'C:\\Windows\\system32\\python33.zip',

'C:\\Python33\\DLLs',

'C:\\Python33\\lib',

'C:\\Python33',

'C:\\Python33\\lib\\site-packages']
```

We can insert that list and customize it to insert our own location.

Reloading a module

During a session, the Python interpreter needs to import one module only once. This makes matters more productive. Here is an example showing how that operates.

Assume we get the code below in a module called my_module:

```
# This module shows the effect of

#  multiple imports and reload

print("This code got executed")
```

Now we suspect that multiple imports have an impact.

>>> import my_module

This code was executed:

>>> import my_module

>>> import my_module

We have seen our code was only executed once. This means that our module has only been imported once.

Also, if during the process of the test our module modified, we will have to restart it. The way to do so is to reload the interpreter. But that doesn't massively help. Python offers an effective way to do so. Within the imp module, we may use the reload() function to restart a module. Here are some ways to do it:

```
>>> import imp
>>> import my_module
```

This code executes

```
>>> import my_module
>>>imp.reload(my_module)
```

This code executes

```
<module 'my_module' from '.\\my_module.py'>
```

The dir() built-in function

We may use the dir() function to locate names specified within a module. For such cases, in the example of the module that we had in the early part, we described a function add().

In example module, we can use dir in the following scenario:

```
>>>dir(example)

['__builtins__',

'__cached__',

'__doc__',

'__file__',

'__initializing__',

'__loader__',

'__name__',

'__package__',

'add']
```

Now we'll see a list of the names sorted (alongside add). Many
other names that start with an underscore are module-
associated (not user-defined) default Python attributes. For
instance, the attribute name contains module __name__.

```
>>> import example
>>>example.__name__
'example'
```

You can find out all names identified in our existing namespace
by using dir() function with no arguments.

```
>>> a = 1
>>> b = "hello"
>>> import math
>>>dir()
['__name__', '__doc__','__builtins__ ', 'a', 'b', 'math', 'pyscripter']
```

Executing modules as scripts

Python module running with python fibo.py <arguments>the program will be running in such a way, just like it was being imported, but including the __name__ set to "__main__." That implies this program is inserted at the end of the module:

If __name__ == "__main__": import sys fib(int(sys.argv[1]))

You could even create the file usable both as a script and as an importable module since this code parsing the command - line interface runs only when the module is performed as the "main" file:

$ python fibo.py 50

0 1 1 2 3 5 8 13

When the module is imported, the code will not be executed:

```
>>>
>>> import fibo
>>>
```

It is most often used whether to get an efficient user interface to a module or for test purposes (the module runs a test suite as a script).

"Compiled" Python files

To speed up loading modules, Python caches the compiled version of each module in the __pycache__ directory with the name module.version.pyc, in which the version encapsulates the assembled file format; it normally includes the firmware version of Python. For instance, the compiled edition of spam.py in CPython launch 3.3 will be cached as __pycache__/spam.cpython-33.pyc. This naming convention enables the coexistence of compiled modules from various updates and separate versions of Python.

Python tests the source change schedule against the compiled edition to see if it is out-of-date and needs recompilation. That's a fully automated system. Even the assembled modules become platform-independent, so different algorithms will use the same library between systems. In two situations Pythoniswill not check the cache:

First, it often recompiles the output for the module, which is loaded explicitly from the command line but does not store it. Second, when there is no root module, it will not search the cache. The compiled module must be in the source directory to facilitate a non-source (compiled only) release, and a source module should not be installed.

Some tips for users:

To minimize the size of a compiled file, you can use the -O or -OO switches in the Python order. The -O switch erases statements of assert, the -OO switch removes statements of assert as well as strings of doc. Although some codes may support getting these options available, this method should only be used if you are aware of what you are doing. "Optimized" modules usually have such an opt-tag and are tinier. Future releases may modify the optimal control implications.

A project run no faster once it is read from a.pyc file than how it was read from a.py file; just one thing about.pyc files that are faster in the speed with which they will be loaded.

A compile all modules can generate .pyc files in a directory for all of the other modules.

More details on this process are given in PEP 3147, along with a flow chart of the decision making.

Standard Modules

Python has a standard modules library, mentioned in a separate section, the Python Library allusion (hereafter "Library Reference"). A few modules are incorporated into the interpreter; that provide direct exposure to processes that are not component of the language's base but are nonetheless built-in, whether for effectiveness or to supply access to primitive operating systems such as source code calls. The collection of these modules is an alternative to customize and also relies on the framework underlying it. The winreg module, for instance, is only available on Microsoft windows. One particular module is worthy of certain interest: sys, which is integrated into every Python interpreter. The sys.ps1 and sys.ps2 variables classify strings which are used as primary and secondary instructions:

```
>>>
>>> import sys
>>> sys.ps1
'>>> '
>>> sys.ps2
'... '
>>> sys.ps1 = 'C> '
C>print('Yuck!')
Yuck!
```

C>

Only when the interpreter is in interactive mode are those two variables defined. The sys.path variable is a collection of strings that defines the search path for modules used by the interpreter. When PYTHONPATH is not a part of the set, then it will be defined to a predefined path taken from either the PYTHONPATH environment variable or through a built-in default. You can change it with regular list procedures:

```
>>>
>>> import sys
>>>sys.path.append('/python/ufs/guido/lib/')
```

Packages

Packages are indeed a way to construct the namespace of the Python module by using "pointed names of the module." For instance, in a package called A., the module title A.B specifies a submodule named B. Even as the use of modules prevents the writers of various modules from stopping to know about the global variable names of one another, any use of dotted module names prevents the developers of multi-module bundles like NumPy or Pillow from needing to worry more about module names of one another. Consider making a series of lists of modules (a "package") to handle sound files and sound data in an even manner.

There are several various programs of sound files usually familiar with their extension, for example: 'wav,.aiff,.au,' though you'll need to build and maintain a massive collection of modules to convert between some of the multiple formats of files. There are several other different operations that you may like to run on sound data (such as blending, adding echo, implementing an equalizer function, producing an optical stereo effect), and you'll just be writing an infinite series of modules to execute those interventions. Here is another feasible package layout (described in terms of a hierarchical file system):

```
sound/                          Top level package
        __init__.py             sound package initialization
    formats/                    Subpackage for conversions of file format
                __init__.py
                wavread.py
                wavwrite.py
                aiffread.py
                aiffwrite.py
                auread.py
                auwrite.py
                ...
    effects/                    Sound effectssubpackage
                __init__.py
                echo.py
                surround.py
                reverse.py
                ...
    filters/                    Filterssubpackage
                __init__.py
                equalizer.py
                vocoder.py
                karaoke.py
                ...
```

While loading the bundle, Python checks for the packet subdirectory via the folders on sys.path. To allow Python view directories that hold the file as packages, the __init__.py files are needed. This protects directories with a common name, including string, from accidentally hiding valid modules, which later appear mostly on the search path of the module. In the correct order; __init__.py can only be a blank file, but it could also implement the package preprocessing code or establish the variable __all__ described below

Package users could even upload individual modules from the package, such as: 'import sound.effects.echo'

This loads the 'sound.effects.echo' sub-module. Its full name must be mentioned: 'sound.effects.echo.echofilter(input, output, atten=4, delay=0.7)'

Another way to import the submodule is: 'fromsound.effects import echo'

It, therefore, launches the sub-module echo and provides access but without package prefix: 'echo.echofilter(input, output, atten=4, delay=0.7)'

And just another option is to explicitly import the desired function or attribute: 'fromsound.effects.echo import echofilter'

This again activates the echo sub-module however this enables its echofilter() feature explicitly accessible: 'echofilter(input, output, delay=0.7, atten=4)'

So it heaps the sub-module echo; however this tends to make its function; remember that the object will either be a sub-module (or sub-package)of the package or any other name described in the package, such as a function, class or variable while using from package import object. Initially, the import statement analyses if the object is characterized in the package; otherwise, it supposes that it is a module and makes an attempt to load it. Once it fails to reach it, an exception to 'ImportError' will be promoted.

Referring to this, while using syntax such as import 'item.subitem.subsubitem', each item has to be a package, but the last one; the last item could be a module or package, but this cannot be a class or function or variable identified in the previous item.

CONCLUSION

Research across almost all fields has become more data-oriented, impacting both the job opportunities and the required skills. While more data and methods of evaluating them are becoming obtainable, more data-dependent aspects of the economy, society, and daily life are becoming. Whenever it comes to data science, Python is a tool necessary with all sorts of advantages. It is flexible and continually improving because it is open-source. Python already has a number of valuable libraries, and it cannot be ignored that it can be combined with other languages (like Java) and current frameworks. Long story short - Python is an amazing method for data science.

QUANTUM PHYSICS FOR BEGINNERS

The new comprehensive guide to master the 7 hidden secrets of the law of attraction and relativity.

Learn the origin of universe with step by step process

Jason Test

CHAPTER 1: INTRODUCTION

Quantum Physics VS. Rocket Science

 In modern years, rocket science has become a byword for something genuinely challenging. Rocket specialists need a thorough understanding of the properties of the materials used in spacecraft construction; they need to understand the ability and risk of the fuels used to power the rockets, and they need a thorough understanding of how planets and satellites are moving under the influence of gravity.

Quantum physics has a similar reputation for complexity, and, even for many highly educated physicists, a thorough understanding of the behaviour of many quantum phenomena definitely poses a significant challenge. Perhaps the best minds in physics are those working on the unsolved issue of how quantum physics can be applied to the incredibly strong gravitational forces that are supposed to exist inside black holes, which played a crucial role in our universe's early evolution.

The basic ideas of quantum physics, however, are not rocket science: their problem is more to do with their unfamiliarity than with their inherent difficulty. We have to abandon some of the ideas we all learned from our observation and knowledge of how the world functions, but once we have done so, it is more an exercise for the

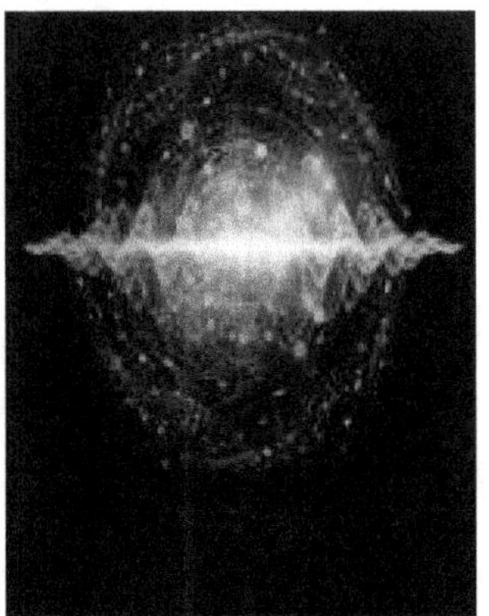

imagination than the intellect to replace them with the new concepts needed to understand quantum physics.
 It is also very easy to understand how many everyday phenomena underlie the concepts of quantum physics without using the complex mathematical research required for full clinical care.

Chapters Overview

The philosophical foundation of quantum physics is peculiar and unfamiliar, and it is still controversial in its interpretation. We will, however, postpone much of our discussion of this to the last chapter since the main purpose of this book is to understand how quantum physics explain many natural phenomena; these include the behavior of matter on the very small scale of atoms and the like, but also many of the phenomena we in the modern world are familiar with.

We shall establish the basic concepts of quantum physics in Chapter 2, where we will find that the fundamental particles of matter are not like ordinary objects, such as footballs or grains of sand, but can, in certain cases, behave as if they were waves. We will find that in deciding the structure and properties of atoms and the 'subatomic' environment beyond them, this 'wave-particle duality' plays an important role.

Chapter 3 starts our discussion of how important and common aspects of everyday life underlie the concepts of quantum physics. This chapter describes how quantum physics is central to many of the techniques used to produce power for modern society, called 'Power from the Quantum.' We can also find that the 'greenhouse effect' is essentially quantum, which plays an important role in regulating the temperature and, thus, our world's climate. Much of our industrial technology contributes to the greenhouse effect, contributing to global warming issues, but quantum physics also plays a role in combating the physics of some of the 'green' technologies being developed.

In Chapter 4, we can see how in some large-scale phenomena, wave-particle duality features; for instance; quantum physics explains why some materials are metals that can conduct electricity, while others are 'insulators' that fully block such current flow.

The physics of 'semi-conductors' whose properties lie between metals and insulators are discussed in Chapter 5. In these materials, which were used to build the silicon chip, we will find out how quantum physics plays an important role. This system forms the basis of modern electronics, which, in turn, underlies the technology of information and communication, which plays such a huge role in the modern world.

We shall turn to the 'superconductivity' phenomenon in Chapter 6, where quantum properties are manifested in a particularly dramatic way: in this case, the large-scale existence of the quantum phenomena creates materials whose resistance to electric current flow disappears entirely. Another intrinsically quantum phenomenon relates to newly established information processing techniques, and some of these will be discussed in Chapter 7.

There, we can discover that it is possible to use quantum physics to relay information in a way that no unauthorized individual can interpret. We can also learn how to construct 'quantum computers' one day to perform certain calculations several millions of times faster than any current machine would. Chapter 8 tries to bring everything together and make some guesses about where the topic might be going. Most of this book, as we see, relates to the influence of quantum physics on our daily world: by this, we mean phenomena where the quantum component is seen at the level of the phenomenon we are addressing and not just concealed in the quantum substructure of objects. For instance, while quantum physics is important to understand the internal structure of atoms, the atoms themselves follow the same physical laws in many circumstances as those governing the behavior of ordinary objects.

Thus, the atoms move around in gas and clash with the container walls and with each other as if they were very tiny balls. On the other hand, their internal structure is determined by quantum laws when a few atoms come together to form molecules, and these directly control essential properties such as their ability to absorb and re-emit greenhouse effect radiation (Chapter 3). The context needed to understand the ideas I will build in later chapters is set out in the current chapter. I begin by defining some basic ideas that were established before the quantum era in mathematics and physics; I then offer an account of some of the discoveries of the nineteenth century, especially about the nature of atoms, that revealed the need for a revolution in our thought that became known as 'quantum physics.'

Mathematics

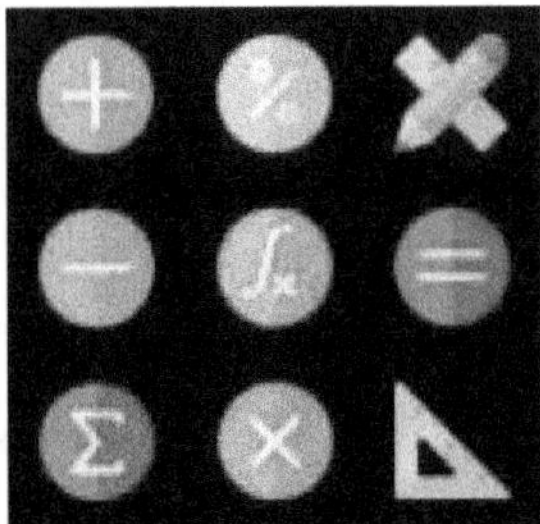

Mathematics poses a major hurdle to their comprehension of science for many individuals. Certainly, for four hundred years or more, mathematics has been the language of physics, and without it, it is impossible to make progress in understanding the physical universe. Why will this be the case? The physical universe seems to be primarily governed by the laws of cause and effect, for one explanation (although these break down to some extent in the quantum context, as we shall see). Mathematics is widely used to evaluate such causal relationships: the mathematical statement two plus two equals four 'implies as a very simple example that if we take any two physical objects and combine them with any two others, we will end up with four objects.

If an apple falls from a tree, to be a little more sophisticated, it will fall to the ground, and we can use mathematics to measure the time it will take, given we know the initial height of the apple and the strength of the gravity force acting on it. This shows the relevance of mathematics to science since the latter attempts to predict and compare the behavior of a physical system with the outcomes of 4 Quantum Physics: measurement.

Classical Physics

If quantum physics is not rocket science, we can also assume that quantum physics is not 'rocket science.' This is because it is possible to measure the motion of the sun and the planets as well as that of rockets and artificial satellites with total precision using pre-quantum physics developed by Newton and others between two and three hundred years ago.
The need for quantum physics was not understood until the end of the nineteenth century because in many familiar situation's quantum effects are far too small to be important. We refer to this earlier body of information as 'classical' when we address quantum physics.

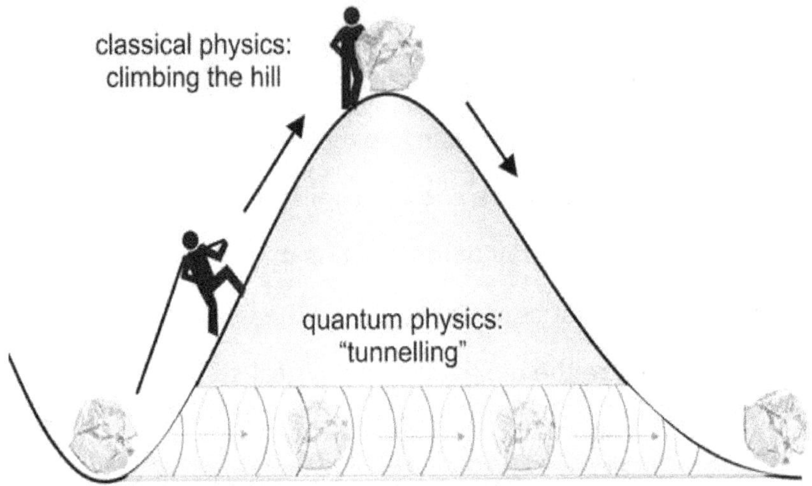

In some scientific fields, the term 'classical' is used to mean anything like 'what was understood before the subject we are addressing became important,' so it refers to the body of scientific information that preceded the quantum revolution in our sense. The early quantum physicists were acquainted with the notions of classical physics and used them to generate new ideas where they could. We will follow in their footsteps and will soon answer the key ideas of classical physics that will be needed in our subsequent debate.

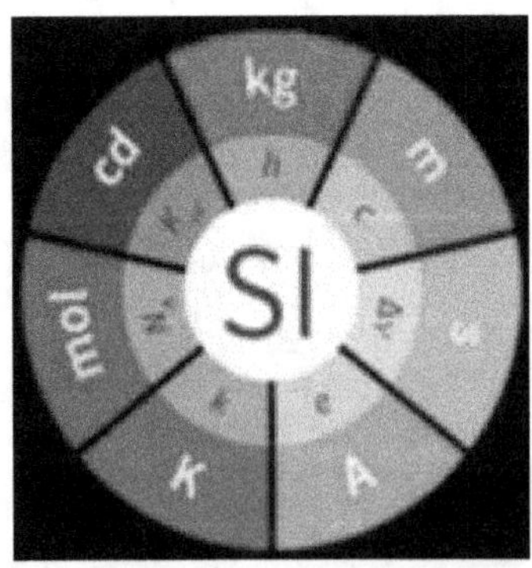

Units

We have to use a scheme of 'units' when physical quantities are represented by numbers. For instance, we could calculate the distance in miles, in which case the mile would be the unit of distance, and time in hours, where the hour would be the unit of time, and so on. By the French name 'Systeme Internationale' or 'SI' for short, the system of units used in all scientific work is known. The distance unit is the meter (abbreviation 'm') in this system, the time unit is the second ('s'), mass is calculated in kilogram units ('kg'), and the electrical charge is measured in coulomb units ('C').

Unit	Symbol	Quantity
kilogram	kg	mass
metre	m	length
second	s	time
ampere	A	electric current
kelvin	K	temperature
mole	mol	amount of substance
candela	cd	luminous intensity

When the metric system was developed in the late eighteenth and early nineteenth centuries, the dimensions of the fundamental units of mass, length, and time were originally specified. The meter was originally specified as one ten-millionth of the distance from the pole to the equator along the meridian that passes through Paris; the second as 1/86,400 of the average solar day; and the kilogram as one-thousandth of the mass of pure water per cubic meter. These concepts gave rise to problems because our ability to more precisely calculate the dimensions of the Earth and motion meant minor improvements in these standard values.

The meter and kilogram were redefined towards the end of the nineteenth century as, respectively, the distance between two marks on a standard platinum alloy rod and the mass of another particular piece of platinum; both of these standards were kept firmly in a standard laboratory near Paris, and 'secondary standards' were manufactured to be as identical as possible to the originals. In 1960, the definition of the second was updated and expressed in terms of the year's average duration.

As atomic measurements became more precise, the basic units were again redefined: the second is now known as 9,192,631,770 radiation oscillation cycles emitted during the change between the specific energy levels of the cesium atom, while the meter is defined as the distance traveled by light in a time equal to 1/299,792,458 of a second. The value of these concepts is that, everywhere on Earth, the standards can be replicated independently. However, no similar definition of a kilogram has yet been accepted, and this is still referred to as the primary standard kept by the Bureau of Standards of France. In our labs, kitchens, and elsewhere, the values of the standard masses we use were all obtained by comparing their weights with standard weights, which were compared with others in turn, and so on until we finally reached the Paris standard. The standard unit of charge is measured by means of the ampere, which is the current standard unit and is equal to one coulomb per second. The ampere itself is defined as the current needed between two parallel wires kept one meter apart to generate a magnetic force of a specific size. Other physical quantities are determined in units derived from these four: thus, by dividing the distance traveled by the time taken, the speed of a moving object is estimated, so the unit speed corresponds to one meter divided by one second, which is written as 'ms-1'.

Motion

A large part of physics concerns objects in motion, both classical and quantum, and the simplest definition used here is that of speed. For an object traveling at a steady speed, this is the distance it moves in one second (measured in meters). If the speed of an object changes, then its value is defined at any given time as the distance it would have traveled in one second had its speed remained constant.

For someone who has driven in a motorcar, this concept should be familiar, although the units are usually kilometers (or miles) per hour in this case. That of 'velocity' is closely linked to the idea of speed. Both words are interchangeable in everyday speech, but in physics, they are differentiated by the fact that velocity is a quantity of 'vector,' which means it has both direction and magnitude.

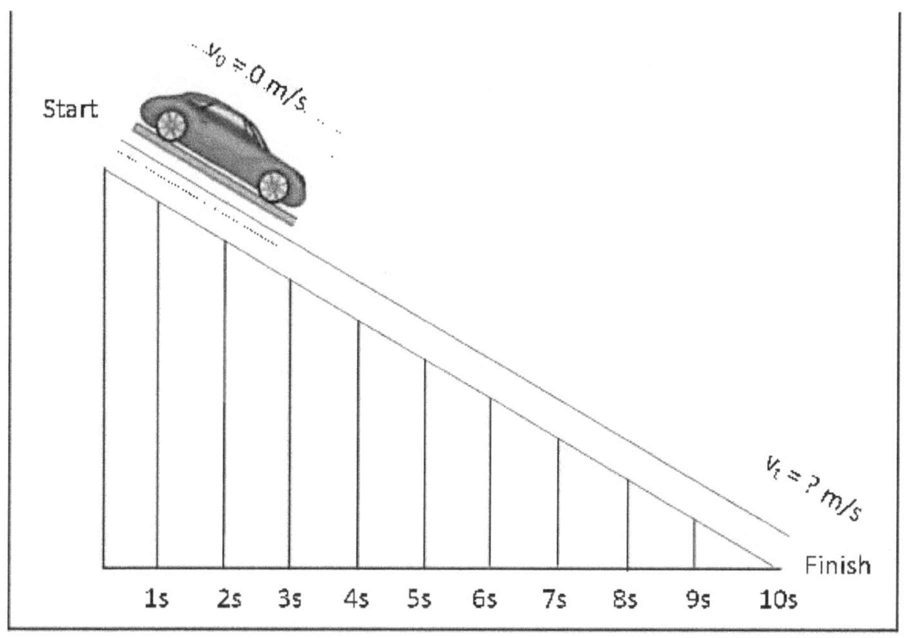

Therefore, an object traveling from left to right at a speed of 5 ms-1 has a five ms-1 positive velocity, but one moving from right to left at the same speed has a five ms-1 negative velocity. The rate at which it does so is known as acceleration, when the velocity of an object is changing. For example, if the speed of an object varies from 10 ms-1 to 11 ms-1 over a span of one second,

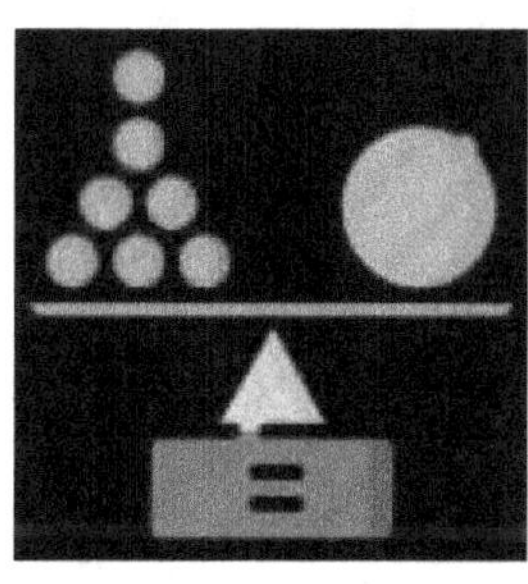

the velocity shift is 1 ms-1, so its acceleration is '1 meter per second squared' or 1 ms-2.

Mass

The mass of a body was defined by Isaac Newton as 'the amount of matter' it contains, which raises the question of what matter is or how its 'quantity' can be calculated. The problem is that while certain quantities can be described in terms of more simple quantities (e.g., speed in terms of distance and time), some definitions are so important that any such attempt leads to a circular description such as that just stated.

To escape from this, we should 'operationally' identify certain quantities, implying that we explain what they do rather than what they are, i.e., how they function. In the case of mass, when subjected to gravity, this can be achieved by force encountered by an object.

Thus, when positioned at the same point on Earth's surface, two bodies with the same mass can feel the same force, and the masses of two bodies can be measured using a balance.

Energy

In our later discussions, this is an idea we would always refer to. An example is energy possessed by a moving body, defined as 'kinetic energy'; this is measured by the square of its velocity as one-half of the body's mass-so its units are joules, equal to kgm2s-2.

Potential energy, which is related to the force acting on the body, is another essential source of energy. An example is gravity-related potential energy, which increases in proportion to the distance that an object is lifted from the floor. By multiplying the mass of the object by its height and then by the acceleration due to gravity, its weight is determined.

The units of these three quantities are kg, m, and ms-2, respectively, so the potential energy unit is kgm2s2, which is the same as the kinetic energy unit, which is to be expected since it is possible to transfer various sources of energy from one to another.

In both quantum and classical physics, an extremely significant concept is that of 'energy conservation,' which means that it is never possible to produce or destroy energy. It is possible to transform energy from one form to another, but the total quantity of energy is still the same. By considering one of the simplest examples of a physical operation, we can demonstrate this,

An object falls under gravity. If we take some object and drop it, we find that it travels faster and faster when it drops to the ground. As it moves, it decreases its potential energy, increasing its speed and thus its kinetic energy. The total energy is the same at any point.

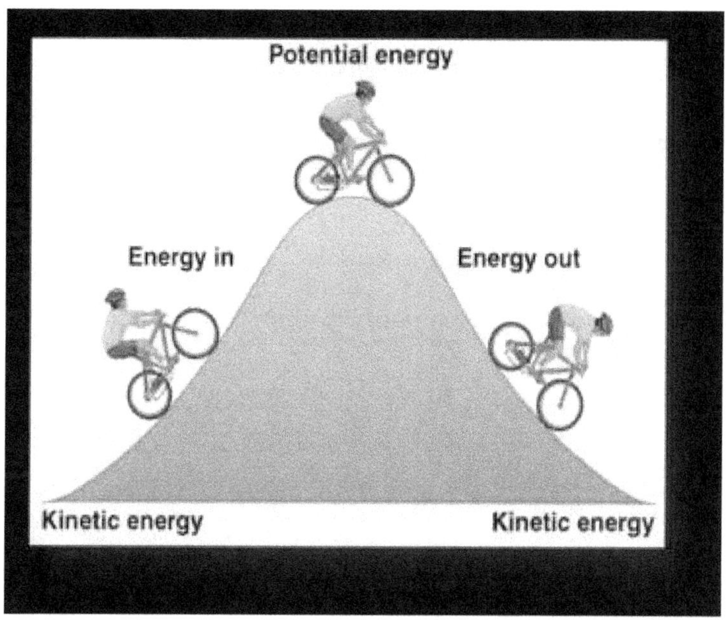

Now imagine what occurs on Earth after the dropping object falls. Assuming it doesn't bounce, both its kinetic and potential energies have diminished to zero, so where has the energy gone?

The reason is that it was turned into heat that warmed up the World around it.

In the case of ordinary objects, this is just a small impact, but the release of energy can be immense when large bodies fall: for instance, the collision of a meteorite with the Earth several million years ago is thought to have contributed to the extinction of dinosaurs. Electrical energy (to which we shall return shortly), chemical energy, and mass-energy are other examples of types of energy as expressed in Einstein's famous equation, $E = mc^2$.

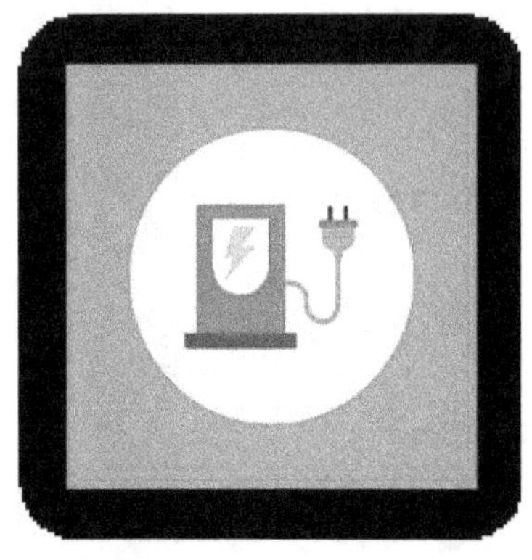

Electric Charge

In classical physics, there are two major sources of potential energy. One is gravity, which we alluded to above, and the other is energy, also called 'electromagnetism' and synonymous with magnetism. Electricity is a fundamental concept of electricity, and, as a mass, it is a quantity that is not readily described in terms of other more fundamental concepts, so we use an operational description again. A force is exerted on each other by two bodies bearing electric charges.

If the charges have the same signal, this force is repulsive and drives the bodies away from each other, while it is enticing and draws them together if the signals are opposite.

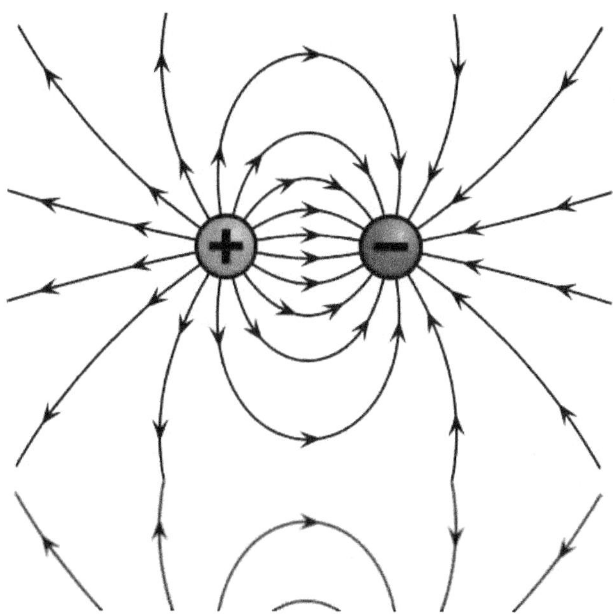

In both situations, they would gain kinetic energy if the bodies were released, flying apart in the like-charge case or together if the charges are opposite. There must be potential energy associated with the interaction between the charges to ensure the energy is conserved, one that gets larger as the related charges come together or as the different charges split.

Not only does the electric field shift as charges pass, but another field, the 'magnetic field,' is formed. Familiar examples of this field are those formed by a magnet or, indeed, by the Earth, which controls the direction of a compass's needle. In the form of 'electromagnetic waves,' one example of which is light waves, the coupled electrical and magnetic fields generated by moving charges propagate through space. In Chapter 2, we shall return to this in more detail.

Momentum

A moving body's momentum is defined as the product of its mass and its velocity, so a slow-moving heavy object may have the same momentum as a fast-moving light body. The cumulative momentum of both remains the same when two bodies collide, so the momentum is 'preserved' just as in the case of previously mentioned energy. In an important respect, however, momentum is different from energy: it is a vector quantity (like velocity) with both direction and magnitude. When we drop the ball on the ground, and it bounces upward at around the same speed, the sign of its momentum changes such that the cumulative change in momentum equals its initial value twice.

This transition must have come from somewhere, provided that momentum is retained, and the answer to this is that it has been absorbed into the Planet, the momentum of which shifts in the opposite direction by the same amount. However, the velocity change associated with this momentum shift is incredibly small and undetectable in nature since the Planet is enormously more massive than the ball. A collision between two balls, such as on a snooker table, is another example of momentum conservation, where we see how direction, as well as magnitude, are involved in the conservation of momentum.

Temperature

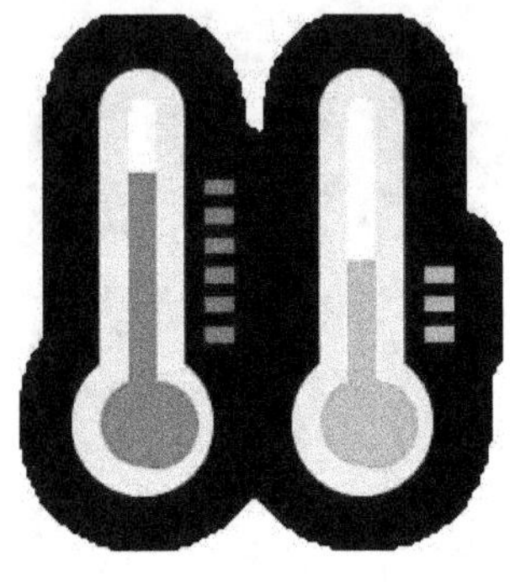

The value of temperature to physics is that it is a measure of heat-related energy. All matter is composed of atoms, as we shall discuss shortly. They are constantly in motion in a gas such as the air in a room and therefore possess kinetic energy. The higher the gas temperature, the higher the average kinetic energy of the gas, and if the gas is cooled to a lower temperature, the molecules will move slower, and the kinetic energy will be lower. We should finally reach a point where the molecules have stopped moving so that the kinetic energy and hence the temperature is zero if we were to continue this process.

This point is recognized as the 'absolute temperature zero' and on the Celsius scale corresponds to-273 degrees. In solids and liquids, atoms and molecules are both in thermal motion, but the specifics are somewhat

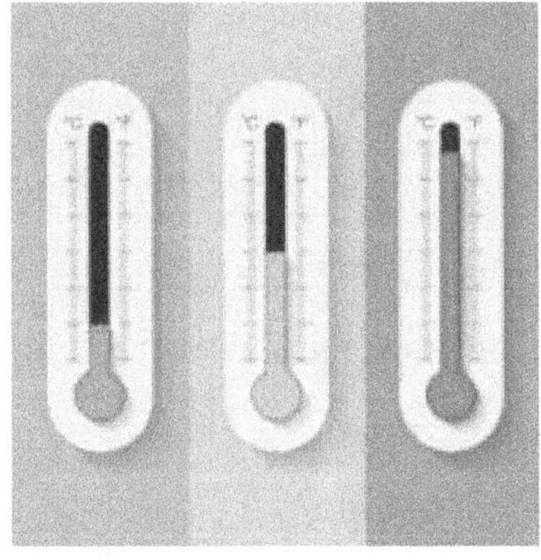

different: in solids, for example, the atoms are kept close to and vibrate around specific points. In any case, however, as the temperature is lowered and stops as absolute zero is reached, this thermal motion decreases.

In order to describe an 'absolute degree' of temperature, we use the definition of absolute zero. The degree of this scale's temperature is the same as that of the Celsius scale, except the zero is equal to absolute zero. Temperatures on this scale are known as 'absolute temperatures' or 'kelvins' (abbreviated as 'K'). Thus, absolute zero degrees (i.e., 0 K) corresponds to-273 ° C, while a room temperature of 20 ° C equals 293 K, the water boiling point (100 ° C) is 373 K, and so on.

The Quantum Objects

In the latter half of the nineteenth century, the need for radically new physical theories arose as scientists found themselves being unable to account for some of the manifestations that had recently been discovered. Some of these were linked to a thorough analysis of light and similar radiation, to which we will return in the next chapter, whilst others emerged from the study of matter and the discovery that 'atoms' are made of.

Atom

Since the time of the ancient Greek philosophers, there has been speculation that if the matter were divided into smaller and smaller sections, a point would be reached where it was impossible to subdivide further. In the nineteenth century, these theories were established when it was recognized that the characteristics of various chemical elements could be attributed to the fact that they were composed of atoms that were similar but varied from element to element in the case of a particular element.

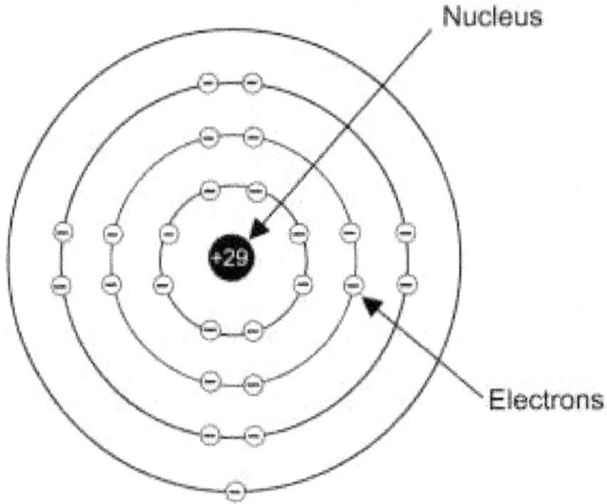

Thus, a hydrogen gas container consists of only one type of atom (known as a hydrogen atom), only another type of carbon lump (i.e., carbon atoms), and so on. It has become possible to measure the size and mass of atoms by various methods, such as studies of the precise properties of gases.

These are very small on the scale of everyday objects, as expected: the size of an atom is about 10-10 m and, in the case of hydrogen, it weighs between about 10-27 kg and, in the case of uranium, 10-24 kg (the heaviest naturally occurring element). While atoms are the smallest objects that bear the identity of a particular element, they are made from a 'nucleus' and many 'electrons' and have an internal structure.

Electron

Electrons are matter particles that weigh much less than the atoms that contain them, with an electron's mass being a little less than 10-30 kg. They are 'point particles,' which suggests that their size is zero or at least too small to have been determined by any experiments carried out to date. All electrons bear an equal negative electric charge.

Nucleus

Almost all of the atom's mass is contained in a 'nucleus' that is much smaller than the whole atom, usually 1015 m in diameter or around 105 times the atom's diameter. In order to make the atom uncharged or 'neutral' overall, the nucleus bears a positive charge equal and opposite to the total charge borne by the electrons. It is understood that the nucleus, along with some uncharged particles known as 'neutrons, can be further divided into some positively charged particles known as' protons '; the charge on the proton is positive, equal, and opposite to that on the electron.

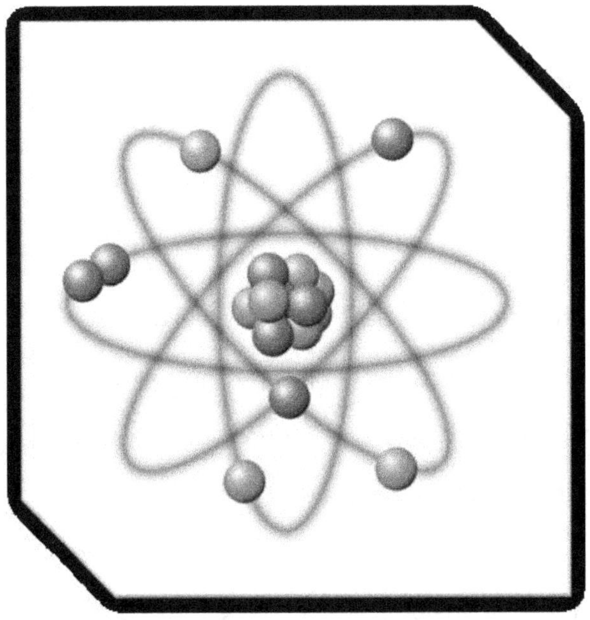

The neutron and proton masses are somewhat similar (though not identical) to each other, both being about two thousand times the mass of the electron. The hydrogen nucleus containing one proton and no neutrons are examples of nuclei; the carbon nucleus containing six protons and six neutrons; and the uranium nucleus containing ninety-two protons and between 142 and 146 neutrons-see 'isotopes' below.

We call it a 'nucleon' when we want to refer to one of the particles making up the nucleus without knowing whether it's a proton or a neutron. Nucleons, like the electron, are not pointed particles but have a structure of their own. They are each made from three-point particles referred to as 'quarks.' In the nucleus, two kinds of quarks are present, and these are known as the 'up' quark and the 'down' quark, but these names should not be correlated with any physical meaning. Up and down quarks bear positive value charges, 2/3 and 1/3 of the overall charge on a proton, which comprises two up and one down quarks, respectively.

The neutron is built from one quark up and two quarks down, which is consistent with its absolute zero charges. In almost all cases, the quarks inside a neutron or proton are bound together very closely so that the nucleons can be viewed as single particles. The neutrons and protons interact less strongly but also interact much more strongly than the electrons, which means that a nucleus can also be viewed as a single particle to a very good approximation, and its internal structure is overlooked when we consider the atom's structure.

Isotopes

The majority of atomic properties are derived from electrons, and the number of electrons charged negatively is equal to the number of protons charged positively in the nucleus. The nucleus, however, also contains several uncharged neutrons, as mentioned above, which contribute to the mass of the nucleus but otherwise do not significantly affect the atom's properties.

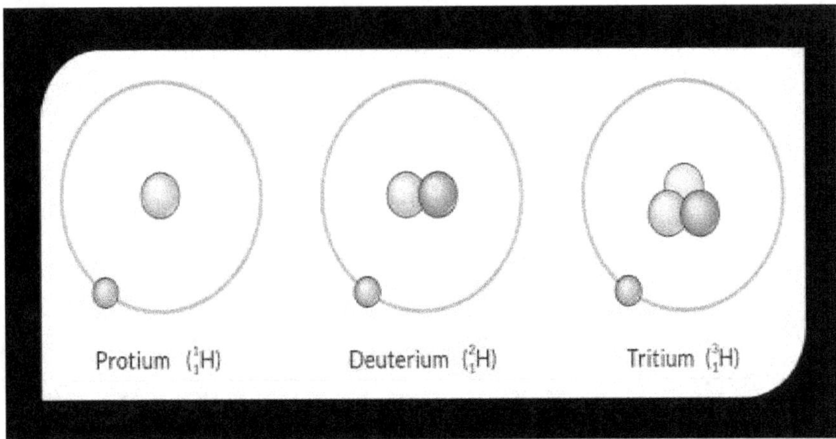

They are classified as 'isotopes' if two or more atoms have the same number of electrons (and hence protons) but different numbers of neutrons. An example is 'deuterium,' whose nucleus comprises one proton and one neutron, and which is thus an isotope of hydrogen; approximately one atom in every ten thousand is deuterium in naturally occurring hydrogen.

The number of isotopes, i.e., those with a higher number of nucleons, varies from element to element and is greater for heavier elements. Uranium, which has nineteen isotopes, all of which has 92 protons, is the strongest naturally occurring element. U238, which comprises 146 neutrons, is the most common of these, while the isotope included in nuclear fission (see Chapter 3) is U235 with 143 neutrons. Note the notation where the total number of nucleons is the superscript number.

Atomic Structure

We have shown so far that an atom consists of a very small nucleus that is positively charged, surrounded by many electrons. The simplest atom is hydrogen, with one electron, and uranium, which comprises ninety-two electrons, is the largest naturally occurring atom. It is obvious that a large part of the volume filled by the atom must be a vacuum, realizing that the nucleus is very small and that the electron's dimensions are essentially zero. This means that, even though there is an electrical attraction between each negatively charged electron and the positively charged nucleus, the electrons must remain some distance from the nucleus.

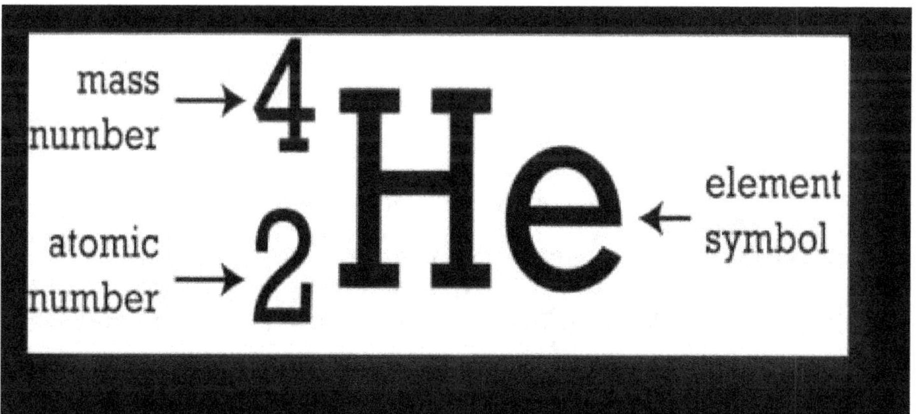

Why doesn't an electron fall into the nucleus, then? One theory proposed early in the subject's development is that the electrons are in orbit around the nucleus, much like the planets in the solar system orbiting the sun. However, a significant difference is that orbital charges are known to lose energy by emitting electromagnetic radiation such as light between satellite orbits in a gravitational field and those where the orbiting particles are charged.

They should travel closer to the nucleus to save energy, where the potential energy is lower, and calculations indicate that this should lead to a small fraction of a second of the electron falling into the nucleus. However, this does not and must not occur in order for the atom to have its known size. This observed property of atoms cannot be accounted for by any model based on classical physics, and a new physics, quantum physics, is needed.

Atomic Properties

A basic atomic property that is incomprehensible from a classical point of view is that all the atoms associated with a specific element are identical. The atom would have all the properties associated with the product, provided it contains the correct number of electrons and a nucleus bearing a compensating positive charge. Thus, one electron is found in a hydrogen atom, and all hydrogen atoms are equal. Think again about a traditional orbiting dilemma to see if this is classically shocking.

If we place a
satellite in orbit
around the Earth,
then it can be at
any distance from
the Earth that we
want, provided we
do rocket science
properly. But all
hydrogen atoms

are the same size, which not only means that their electrons

must be kept at a certain distance from the nucleus but also

implies that this distance is the same at all times for all hydrogen

atoms (unless an atom is intentionally 'excited' as we discuss

below). Once again, we see that the atom has properties that are

not explainable.

Consider what we would do to an atom to alter its size to explore

this argument further. We will have to inject energy into the

atom as pushing the electron away from the nucleus increases

its electrical potential energy, which has to come from

somewhere. This can be done without getting too deep into the

functional specifics by moving an electric discharge through a gas

consisting of atoms. We notice the energy is naturally absorbed and then re-emitted in the form of light or other sources of electromagnetic radiation.

 If we do this: we see this happening if a fluorescent light is turned on. It seems that it returns to its initial state by releasing radiation when we excite the atom in this manner, rather than as we expected in the case of a charge in a classical orbit.

Atomic Radiation

There are, however, two major variations in the case of atoms. The first, discussed above, is that for all atoms of the same form, the final configuration of the atom corresponds to the electron being some distance from the nucleus, and this state is always the same. The second distinction has to do with the existence of the released radiation.

Radiation is in the form of electromagnetic waves, which will be explored in more detail in the next chapter; we only need to know for the moment that such a wave has a characteristic wavelength corresponding

to the light color. Classically, the light of all colors should be produced by a spiraling charge, but when the light emitted by an atomic discharge is analyzed, it is found to contain only certain colors matching unique wavelengths.

These form a fairly simple pattern in the case of hydrogen, and it was one of the key early triumphs of quantum physics that it was able to predict this quite accurately. The principle that the potential values of an atom's energy are limited to such 'quantized' values, which include the lowest value or 'ground state' in which the electron stays some distance from the nucleus, is one of the latest ideas on which this is based. As the atom consumes energy, it will only do so if one of the other permitted values ends up with the energy. The atom is said to be in an 'excited state' with the electron further from the nucleus than it is in the ground state. It then returns to its ground state, releasing radiation, the wavelength of which is determined by the energy difference between the initial and final states.

CHAPTER 2: WAVES AND PARTICLES

Many people have heard that a major aspect of quantum mechanics is 'wave-particle duality.' We will try to explain what this means in this chapter and how it allows us to understand a number of physical phenomena, including the atomic structure issue that I presented at the end of the previous chapter. We can find that the effects of certain physical processes are not precisely calculated at the quantum level, and the most we can do is estimate the likelihood of 'probability' of different future events. In evaluating these probabilities, we will find that something called the 'wave function' plays an important role: its power, or intensity, for instance, at any point, represents the likelihood that we will detect a particle at or near that point.

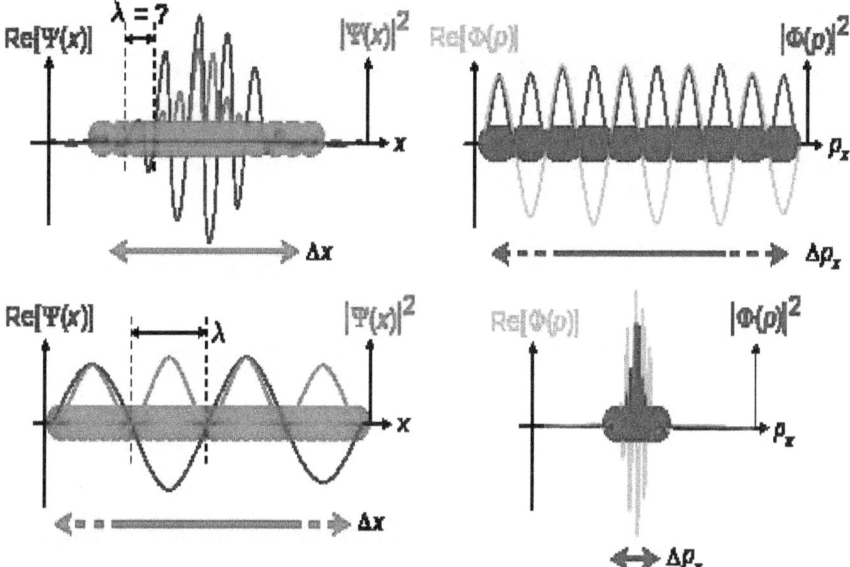

We have to know more about the wave function relevant to the
physical situation we are considering in order to make progress.
By solving a very complex mathematical equation, known as the
Schrödinger equation (after the Austrian physicist Erwin
Schrödinger, who discovered this equation in the 1920s), trained
quantum physicists calculate it; but without doing this, we can
find that we can get quite a long way. Instead, we're going to
build up an image based on some of the fundamental
characteristics of waves, and we're going to start with a
discussion of them as they appear in classical physics. We all
have a certain experience with waves.

Ocean waves would be known to those who have lived near or
visited the seacoast or have traveled on a ship. They can be very

big, impacting ships with violent results, and when they roll on a beach, they provide surfers with entertainment. However, it would be more helpful for our purposes to think of the more gentle waves or ripples that occur when an object is dropped into a calm pond, such as a stone.

That shows a profile of such a wave, showing how it shifts at various locations in time. The water surface oscillates up and down in a normal way at every specific point in space. The ripple height is known as the 'amplitude' of the wave, and the 'period' is known as the time taken for a complete oscillation. It is also beneficial to refer to the wave's 'frequency,' which is the number of times a second it passes over a full oscillation period. The form of the wave repeats in space at any point in time, and the repeat distance is known as the 'wavelength.' The pattern travels over a distance equal to the wavelength during a time corresponding to one duration, which implies that the wave moves at a speed corresponding to one wavelength per period.

Traveling Waves and Standing Waves

Since they 'travel' in space, waves are what are called 'traveling waves.' The motion is from left to right in the illustration shown, but it could also have been from right to left indeed that the ripples spread out in all directions from a stone dropped in water. We will have to hear about 'standing waves' as well as moving waves.

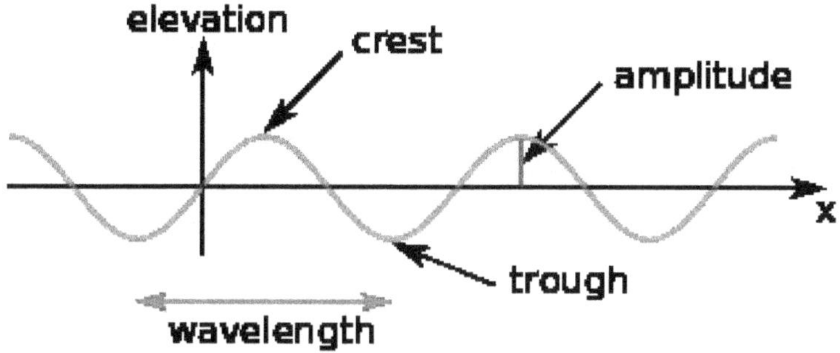

An example, we see that the wave has a shape similar to that previously mentioned, and the water oscillates up and down again, except now the wave does not travel along but remains in the same position, hence its name. When it is confined to a 'cavity' surrounded by two borders, a standing wave usually occurs. It is mirrored at one of the boundaries and travels back in the opposite direction if a moving wave is set up. The net effect is the standing wave when the waves moving in the two directions are combined. In certain cases, the cavity walls are such that they can not be penetrated by the wave, and this results in the amplitude of the wave being equal to zero at the borders of the cavity.

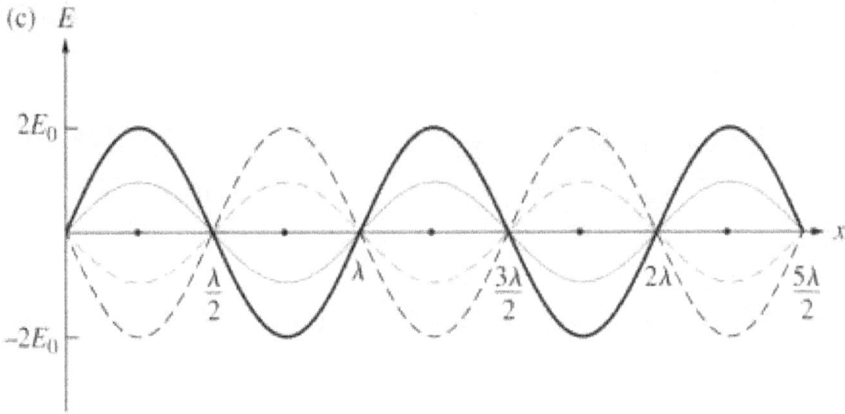

This means that only standing waves of unique wavelengths will fit into the cavity, so for the wave to be zero at both borders, for a whole range of peaks or troughs to fit into the cavity, the wavelength must be just the right length.

However, the sound would never hit our ears if the standing waves were the whole story. The instrument's vibrations must produce moving waves in the air, which bring the sound to the listener for the sound to be transmitted to the listener. The body of the instrument oscillates in sympathy with the string in a violin, for example, and creates a moving wave that radiates out to the audience.

Most of the science (or art) of designing musical instruments consists of ensuring that in the emitted moving waves, the frequencies of the notes identified by the permissible wavelengths of the standing waves are reproduced.

A complete understanding of the actions of musical instruments and how they convey sound to an audience is a significant subject in itself, which we do not need to go deeper into here. A book on the physics of music should be consulted by interested readers.

Electromagnetic radiation, exemplified in the electromagnetic waves that carry signals to our radios and televisions and in light, is another widely observed wave-like phenomenon. These waves have different frequencies and wavelengths: standard FM radio signals, for example, have a wavelength of 3 m, while the wavelength of the light depends on the color, with blue light being approximately 4 x 108 m and red light being approximately 7 x 10-8 m; other colors have wavelengths between those values.

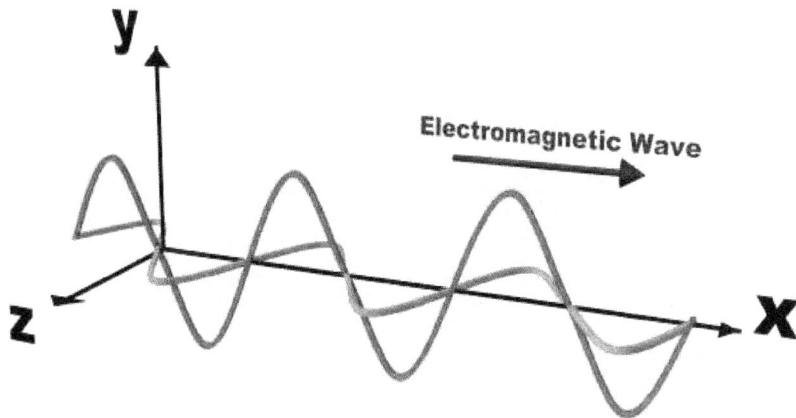

Light waves differ from water waves and sound waves in that, in the examples discussed earlier, nothing corresponds to the vibrating medium (i.e., water, string, or air). Indeed, as is evident from the fact that we can see the light produced by the sun and stars, light waves are capable of traveling across space. In the eighteenth and nineteenth centuries, this property of light waves posed a major issue to scientists.

Some concluded that space is not empty but filled with an otherwise undetectable material known as 'aether' that was believed to support lightwave oscillation. However, when it was discovered that the properties needed to accommodate the very high frequencies typical of light could not be reconciled with the fact that the aether does not provide any resistance to the passage of objects (such as the Earth in its orbit) through it, this theory ran into trouble.

Interference

Direct proof is derived by studying 'interference' that a phenomenon, such as light, is a wave. When two waves of the same wavelength are added together, interference is usually observed. We see that if the two waves are in step ('in phase' is the technical term), they join together to create a combined wave twice the amplitude of each of the originals. If, on the other hand, they are precisely out of step, they cancel each

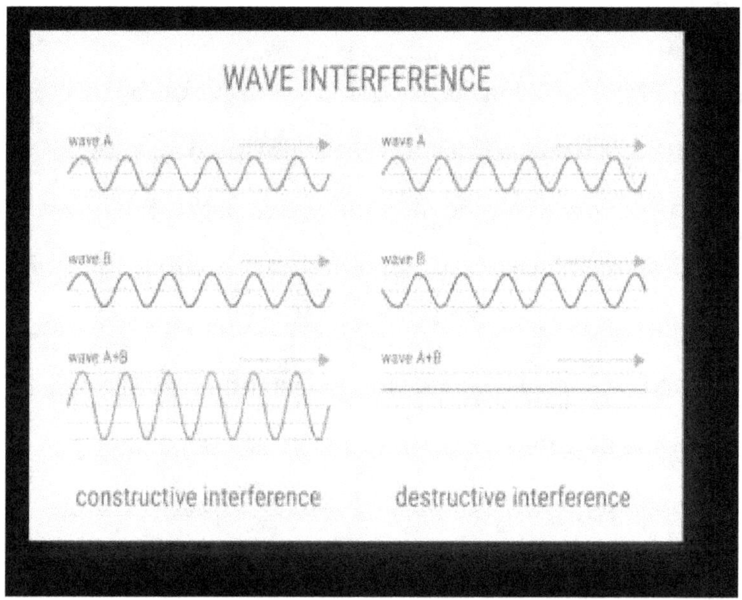

other out (in 'antiphase'). The waves partly cancel in intermediate situations, and there is a value between these extremes of the combined amplitude. Interference is an important proof of the wave properties of light, and this effect can not be accounted for by any other classical model. For instance, suppose we had two classical particle streams instead: the total number of particles would always be equal to the sum of the numbers in the two beams, and they would never be able to cancel each other out in the way waves do.

Thomas Young, who experimented around 1800, was the first person to observe and describe interference (c). Light passes through an O-labeled narrow slit, after which it meets a two-slit screen, A and B, and eventually enters the third screen, S, where it is observed. Either of two routes could have traveled by the light hitting the last panel, either by A or by B. The distances traveled by the light waves following these two paths, however, are not identical, so they normally do not arrive in step with each other on the frame. It follows from the discussion in the previous paragraph that the weaves will reinforce each other at certain points on S, while at others, they will cancel; as a result, a pattern is observed on the screen consisting of a sequence of light and dark bands.

In some cases, it exhibits particle properties, and a fuller understanding of the quantum essence of light will introduce us to 'wave-particle duality.'

Light Quanta

Evidence started to appear towards the end of the nineteenth century and the beginning of the twentieth, indicating that it is not sufficient to classify light as a wave to account for all of its observed properties. Two separate research areas were central to this. This heat radiation becomes noticeable at relatively high temperatures, and we identify the object as 'red hot' or, at even higher temperatures,' gives off a white heat.'

We note that red corresponds to the longest wavelength in the optical spectrum, so it appears that it is easier to produce long-wavelength light (i.e., at a lower temperature) than shorter wavelength light; indeed, long-wavelength heat radiation is generally referred to as 'infrasound.'

Physicists sought to understand the properties of heat radiation following the advent of Maxwell's theory of electromagnetic radiation and improvement in the understanding of heat (a field to which Maxwell himself made significant contributions).

It was then understood that temperature is energy-related: the hotter an object is, the more energy it contains from heat.

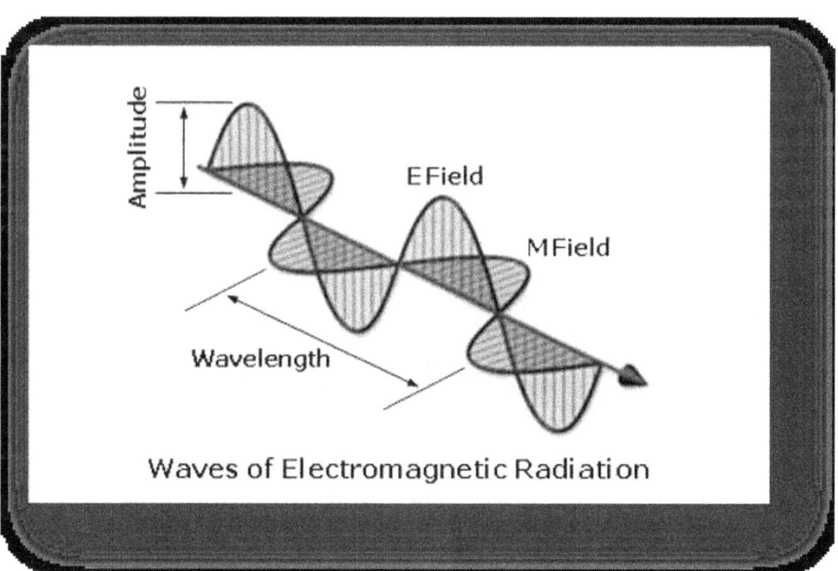

Also, Maxwell's theory predicted that an electromagnetic wave's energy should depend only on its amplitude and should be independent of its wavelength in particular. Therefore, as the temperature increases, one would imagine that a hot body will radiate at all wavelengths, the radiation being brighter but not changing color.

Detailed calculations showed that since the number of potential waves of a given wavelength increases as the wavelength decreases, the heat radiation of the shorter wavelength should actually be brighter than that of long wavelengths, but at all temperatures, it should be the same again. All objects could appear violet in color if this were valid, their average brightness being low at low temperatures and high at high temperatures, which is not what we observe, of course. This disparity was known as the 'ultraviolet catastrophe' between theory and observation.

Matter Waves

The fact that light has particle properties, and is conventionally called a wave, led the French physicist Louis de Broglie to speculate that other artifacts that we normally think of as particles may have wave properties. Thus, in certain cases, a beam of electrons, which is most naturally conceived as a stream of very small bullet-like particles, will act as if it were a wave. Davidson and Germer first explicitly confirmed this radical concept in the 1920s: they passed an electron beam through a graphite crystal and found a pattern of interference that was similar in principle to that created when light passes through a series of slits.

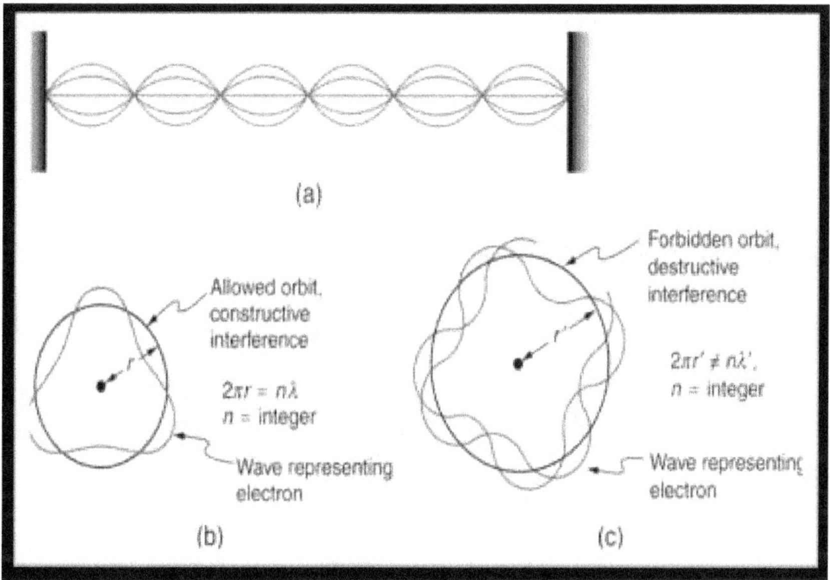

As we have shown, this property is fundamental to the proof that a wave is light, so this experiment is a clear confirmation that electrons can also be added to this model. Similar evidence was later found for the wave properties of heavier particles, such as neutrons, and wave-particle duality is now assumed to be a universal property of all particle forms. Even ordinary objects such as grains of sand, footballs, or motorcars have wave properties, but in these cases, the waves are totally unobservable in nature – partially because the appropriate wavelength is far too small to be visible, but also because classical objects are composed of atoms, each of which has its associated wave and all these waves are constantly chopping and shifting.

We have shown above that in the case of light, the wave vibration frequency is directly proportional to the quantum energy.

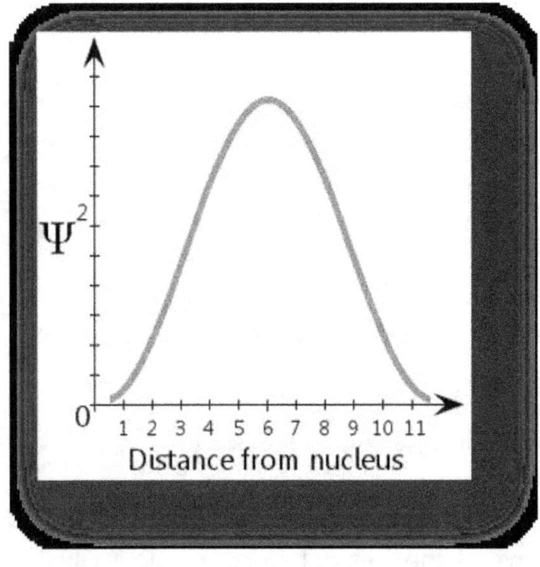

The frequency turns out to be hard to describe in the case of matter waves and difficult to calculate directly. There is, instead, a relation between the wavelength of the wave and the momentum of the object, so that the higher the momentum of the particle, the shorter the wavelength of the wave of matter. The surface of the water goes up and down, the air pressure oscillates in sound waves, and in electromagnetic waves, electric and magnetic fields differ.

What is the corresponding number in the case of waves of matter? The conventional answer to this question is that this corresponds to no physical quantity. We can do the wave estimation,

Using quantum mechanics principles and equations, we can use our results to estimate the values of quantities that can be experimentally tested, but we can not detect the wave itself directly, so we do not need to describe it physically and do not attempt to do so. We use the term 'wave function' rather than wave to emphasize this, which illustrates the fact that it is a mathematical function rather than a physical entity.

Another important technical distinction between wave functions and the classical waves we discussed earlier is that, while the classical wave oscillates at the wave frequency, the wave function stays constant in time in the matter-wave case. However, while not physical in itself, the wave function plays an integral role in the application of quantum mechanics to the understanding of waves.

First, if the electron is confined to a given area, the wave function forms standing waves similar to those described earlier; as a consequence, one of a collection of discrete quantized values is taken up by the wavelength and thus the momentum of the particle. Second, if we conduct experiments to detect the presence of the electron near a specific point, we are more likely to find it in regions where the function of the wave is high than in those where it is small.

Max Born, whose rule states that the likelihood of finding the particle near a certain point is proportional to the square of the magnitude of the wave function at that point. Atoms contain electrons that are restricted to a small region of space through the electrical force attracting them to the nucleus. We may expect the related wave functions to form a standing-wave pattern from what we said earlier, and we can soon see how this leads to an understanding of essential atomic properties. We start this debate by looking at a simpler framework in which we imagine that an electron is contained inside a small box.

Electron in a Box

We consider the case of a particle in this instance, which we will assume to be an electron stuck inside a box. By this, we say that if there is an electron in the box, there is a constant value of its potential energy, which can be taken to be zero. The electron is confined to the box since it is surrounded by a region of very high potential energy, which, without violating the principle of conservation of energy, the electron will not reach.

A ball inside a square box sitting on the floor would be a classical analogy: if the sides of the box are high enough, the ball will not escape from the box, so it would need to overcome gravity to do so. We will soon consider the material waves suitable to this situation, and we might compare them with the case of a pond or swimming pool, where the water is surrounded by a solid border: the solid shore is unable to vibrate, so the water must be confined to any waves produced.

We regard the issue as 'one-dimensional' as a further simplification, meaning that the electron is limited to moving in space in a specific direction such that motion in the other directions can be ignored. On a line, we can then make an analogy with waves, which are actually one-dimensional since they can only travel down the string. Now we are considering the shape of the function of the electron wave. Since the electron does not escape from the box, there is zero possibility of finding it outside.

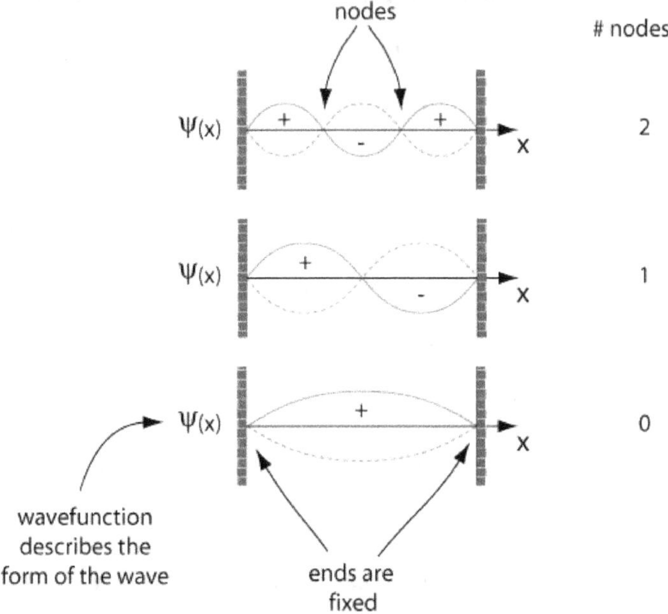

The chance of finding the particle at that point can only have one value if we consider the very edge of the box, so the fact that it is zero outside the box means that just inside it must also be zero. This situation is very close to that of a violin or guitar string, and we saw earlier that this means that the wave must be a standing wave with a wavelength that fits into the available space.

This is seen in the above example, and we see that one of the values corresponding to a whole number of half wavelengths fitting into the box is limited to the wavelength of the wave. This means that only these unique wavelength values are permitted, and since the electron momentum is determined by the wavelength via the de Broglie relationship, the momentum is therefore limited to a specific set of values.

Therefore, if we had several similar electron-containing boxes, their soil states would also be identical. One of the characteristics of atoms that we could not classically describe was that all atoms of a given form have the same characteristics, and that they all have the same lowest energy state, in particular. Quantum physics has demonstrated, by wave-particle duality, why such a condition occurs in the case of an electron in a box, and we shall soon see how the same concepts apply to an electron in an atom.

Varying Potential Energy

The matter waves associated with particles propagating in free space or captured in a one-dimensional box have been considered so far. The particle travels in an area where the potential energy is constant in all these situations because if we remember that the total energy is conserved, the kinetic energy and thus the momentum and speed of the particle would be the same everywhere it goes. In comparison, for example, a ball rolling up a hill absorbs potential energy, loses kinetic energy, and as it climbs, it slows down. We also know that the de Broglie relationship relates the velocity of the particle to the wavelength of the wave, so if the velocity remains constant, this number will also be the same everywhere, which is what we have implicitly assumed.

However, the wavelength must also differ if the speed is not constant, and the wave will not have the reasonably simple form we have considered so far. Therefore, as a particle travels through a region where the potential energy changes, it will also change its speed and therefore, the wave function's wavelength.

Quantum Tunneling

The case of a particle reaching a 'potential phase' we first consider. By this, we mean that at a given stage, the potential increases unexpectedly. In particular, we are interested in the case where the energy of the approaching particle is smaller than the height of the step, so we can expect the particle to bounce back from a classical point of view as soon as it hits the step and then travel backward at the same speed. When we apply quantum mechanics, almost the same thing occurs, but as we shall see, there are significant variations.

Second, we consider the shape of the wave-matter. Based on our earlier discussion, we expect particles entering the phase to be represented by traveling waves moving from left to right, while after they bounce back, the wave will be traveling from right to left. In general, at any given moment, we do not know what the particle is doing, so the wave function to the left of the phase would be a mixture of these, and this is proven when mathematically solving the Schrödinger equation.

In the form of the wave to the right of a phase, what is of real interest? There is no chance of finding the particle there classically, so we would expect the wave function in this area to be zero. However, when we solve the Schrödinger equation, we find that the measured wave function does not become zero until some way to the right of the phase.

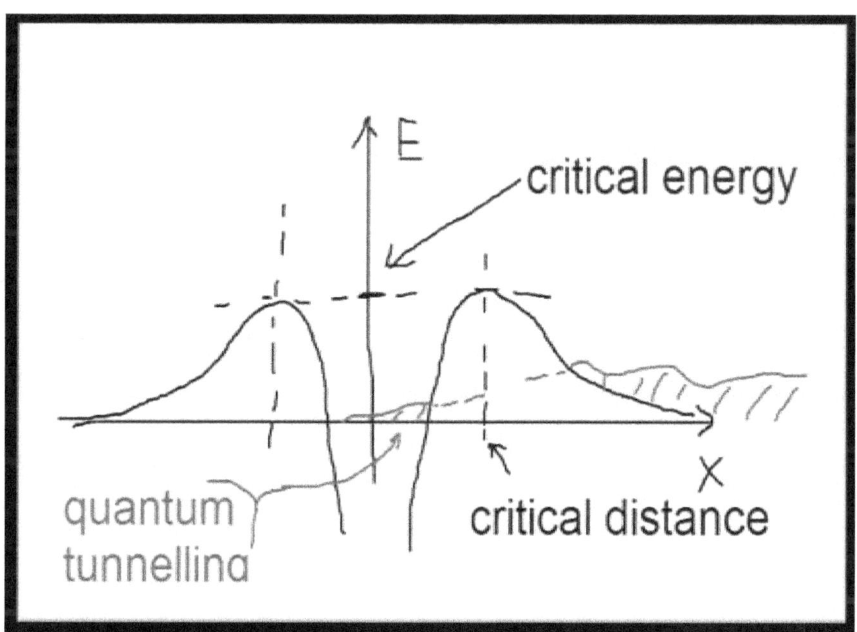

We see that quantum physics predicts that there is a finite probability of finding it in a region where it could never be if classical physics were the entire story, realizing that the amplitude of the wave function at any point reflects the possibility of finding a particle at that point.

A Quantum Oscillator

The second example we consider is the movement of a particle in a parabolic potential. In the classical case, the particle will oscillate periodically from one side of the potential well to the other with a frequency dictated by its mass and shape. The size of the oscillation, or 'amplitude,' is determined by the energy of the particle: all of this energy is kinetic at the foot of the well, while the particle comes to rest at the limits of its motion, where all of the energy is potential. By solving the Schrödinger equation, the wave functions are obtained, and it is found that standing-wave solutions are only possible for unique values of energy.

The Hydrogen Atom

 The simplest atom is that of the hydrogen element, which consists of a single negatively charged electron bound by the electrostatic (or 'Coulomb') force to a positively charged nucleus, which is heavy when the electron is close to the nucleus and decreases in intensity gradually when the electron is farther away. As a consequence, the potential energy near the nucleus is high and negative and gets closer to zero as we step away from it.

All the examples discussed so far have been onedimensional, which implies that we have implicitly concluded that the particle is forced to travel in a certain direction (from left to right or vice versa in our diagrams). However, atoms are three-dimensional objects, and before we can grasp them entirely, we will have to take this into account. A significant simplifying characteristic of the hydrogen atom is that 'spherically symmetric' is the Coulomb potential, i.e., it relies only on the distance between the electron and the nucleus, regardless of the direction of this separation. As a result, many of the wave functions associated with the energy levels permitted have the same symmetry; we will first discuss these and then return to the others.

Other Atoms

More than one electron is found in atoms other than hydrogen, creating further complications. Before we can answer these, after its inventor Wolfgang Pauli, we have to consider another quantum theory, known as the 'Pauli exclusion principle.' This states that any specific quantum state, such as an electron, does not contain more than one particle of a given kind. While easily stated, this theory can only be proven through the use of very advanced quantum analysis, and we will definitely not attempt to do this here.

However, we have to know about a further property possessed by quantum particles and known as 'spin' before we can correctly apply the exclusion principle. We know that the planet spins on its axis as it travels around the sun in orbit, so we would well expect the electron to spin similarly if the atom were a classical entity. To some extent, this analogy holds, but once again, there are major variations between classical and quantum circumstances. The spin properties are governed by two quantum rules: first, the rate of spin is always the same for any given form of the particle (electron, proton, neutron); and, second, the direction of spin around any axis is either clockwise or anticlockwise.

This suggests that an electron can have one of only two spin states in an atom. Thus, when they spin in opposite directions, any quantum state represented by a standing wave can contain two electrons. Consider what happens if we put several electrons in the box discussed earlier as an example of the application of the Pauli exclusion principle. All the electrons must occupy the lowest possible energy levels to form the state with the lowest total energy.

Therefore, if we think of adding them one at a time to the box, the first goes into the ground state, as does the second with the opposite spin to the first. This level is now complete, so the third electron, along with the fourth and the spins of adding up to two electrons to each energy state before all are accommodated, must go into the next highest energy level. We are now applying this approach to atoms, considering helium first, which has two electrons. Suppose the fact that electrons exert a repulsive electrostatic force on each other is initially overlooked. In that case, we can measure the quantum states in the same way as we did for hydrogen but allowing the nuclear charge to be doubled. This doubling means that all energy levels are considerably decreased (i.e., made more negative), but otherwise, the collection of standing waves is very close to those in hydrogen, and when the interactions between the electrons are included, it turns out that this pattern is not greatly altered. Therefore, with an opposite spin in the lowest, the lowest energy state has both electrons. Two of these would be in the lowest state in the case of lithium with three electrons, while the third would be in the next higher energy state.

A total of six electrons can be found in the above configuration: two of these occupy a spherical symmetry state, while the others fill three different non-spherical states. A group of states with the same value of n is known as a 'shell,' and it is called a 'closed-shell' if electrons occupy all these states. Therefore, lithium, like sodium with eleven electrons, has one electron outside a closed shell, i.e., two in the n = 1 closed shell, eight in the n = 2 closed shell, and one electron in the n = 3 shell. It is understood that many of the properties of sodium are similar to those of lithium, and what is known as the 'periodic table' of the elements is based on similar correspondences between the properties of other elements.

In terms of the atomic shell configuration, which in turn is a result of the properties of the quantum waves associated with the electrons, the entire structure of the periodic table can be understood.

CHAPTER 3: THE POWER OF QUANTUM

In this chapter, we will discover how quantum ideas play an essential role in the physics of energy production. Quantum physics was actively interested in energy production as soon as humans discovered fire and how to use it. This is still true for many of the types of energy generation that play a central role in modern life. In our cars, we burn fuel and use gas or oil to heat our houses. In the form of electricity, much of the power we use enter our houses, but it is important to note that this is not a source of power in itself but rather a means of moving energy from one location to another.

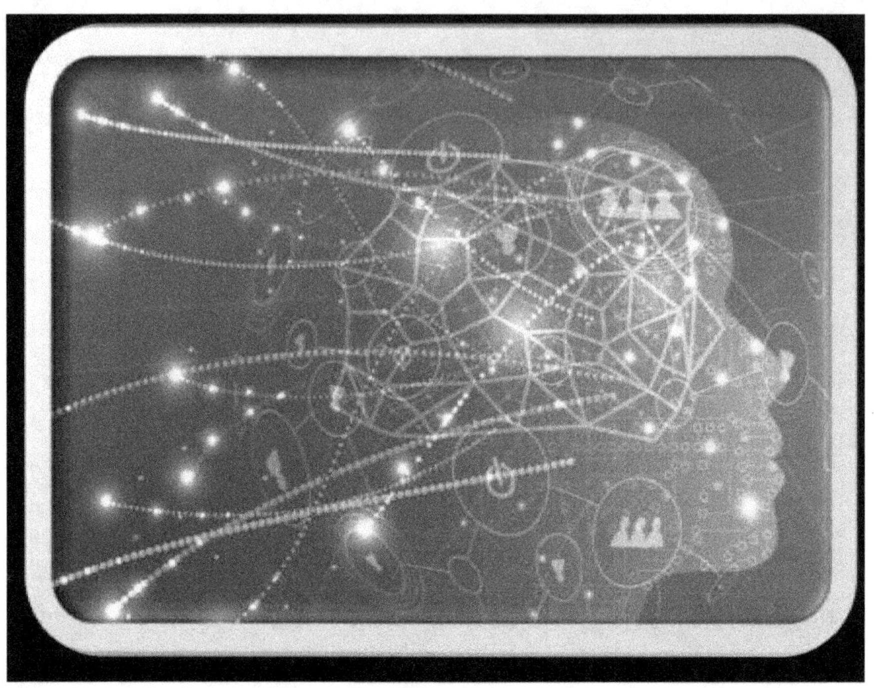

At a power station, electricity is produced from the energy contained in its fuel, which can be a 'fossil fuel' such as coal, oil, or gas; a nuclear fuel such as uranium or plutonium; or a 'sustainable' energy source such as solar, wind or wave energy. Of all of these, only wind and wave power do not depend on quantum physics directly.

Chemical Fuels

Many hydrocarbons contain a fuel such as wood, paper, oil, or coal, which are compounds composed primarily of hydrogen and carbon atoms. As they are heated in the air, hydrogen, and carbon combine to create water and carbon dioxide with oxygen from the air. Energy is produced in the process in the form of heat, which can then be used, for example, to generate electricity in a power station or to power a motor vehicle. We begin with the simplest instance of chemical combination, which is two hydrogen atoms coming together to form a hydrogen molecule, to see how this depends on quantum physics.

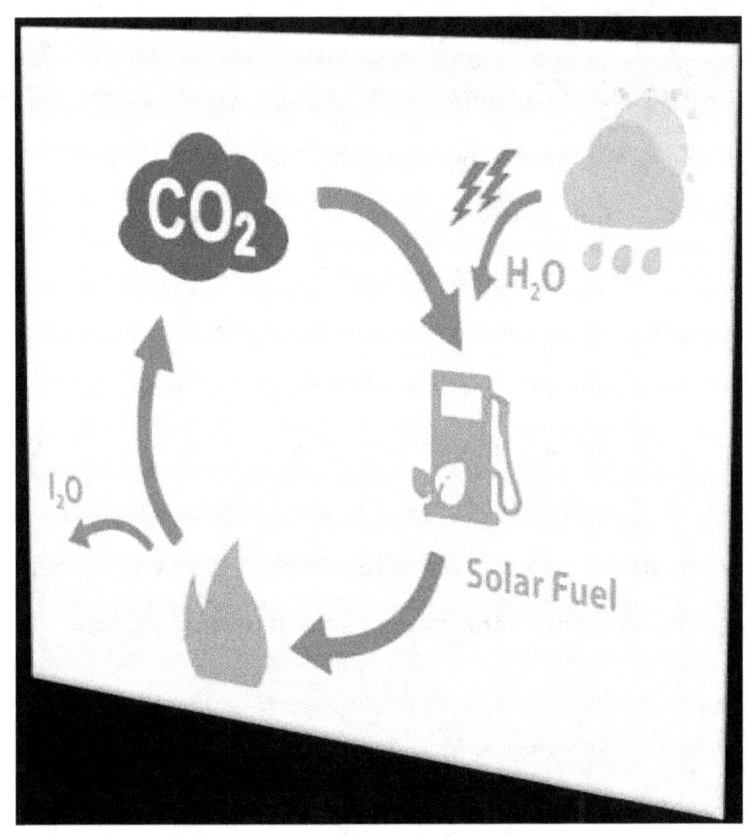

The hydrogen atom contains one proton-attracted electron whose charge is equal to and opposite to that of the electron, so two protons and two electrons are made of a hydrogen molecule. In Chapter 2, we demonstrated how the electron's wave properties result in the hydrogen atom's energy being quantified such that its value is equal to one of a number of unique energy levels; the atom is in the lowest of these energy states, known as the 'earth state' in the absence of excitation.

If we bring two hydrogen atoms into each other, now imagine how the total energy of the system would be affected. The potential energy that changes in three ways is considered first. First, it increases because of the electrostatic repulsion between the two protons that are positively charged; second, it decreases because both protons are now subject to attraction by each electron; third, it increases because of the repulsion between the two electrons that are negatively charged. Also, since the electrons will pass around and between the two nuclei, the kinetic energy of the electrons decreases, so the size of the effective box confining them is increased.

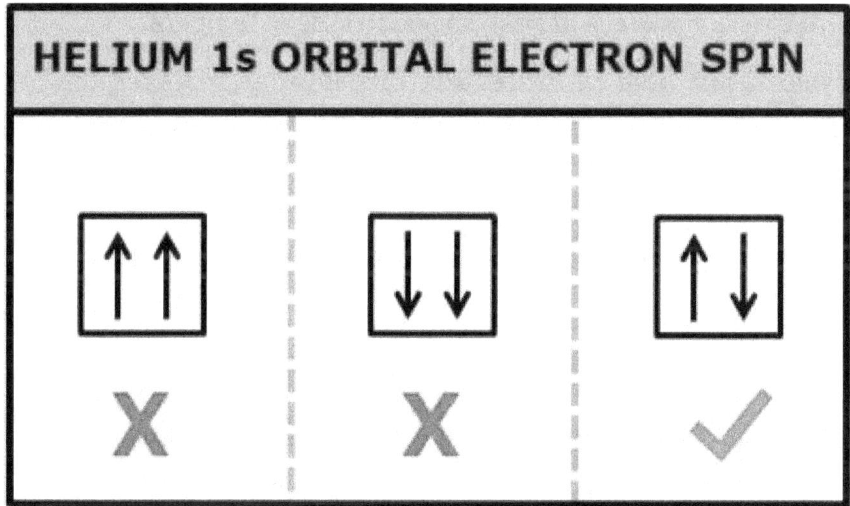

We note that Pauli's exclusion theory allows all electrons to occupy the ground state if they have the opposite spin. The net result of all these changes depends on how far the atoms are apart: there is no difference in total energy when they are wide apart, and electrostatic repulsion between the nuclei dominates when they are very similar. However, there is an overall decrease in the total energy at intermediate distances, and this decrease is at its highest when the protons are around 7. 4 Roughly 10-10 m apart.

At this point, approximately one-third of the hydrogen atom's ground-state energy is equal to the difference between the molecule's energy and that of the widely separated hydrogen atoms. Where does it end up with this surplus energy? The response is that some of it go into the moving molecule's kinetic energy, while the rest is given off in the form of photons. Both are efficient sources of heat, so an increase in temperature, which is just what we expect from fuel, is the ultimate result.

As we shall see later, both useful chemical fuels and indeed nuclear energy underlie the concepts involved in this case. A hydrocarbon fuel, such as oil or gas, comprises molecules that have remained stable for a long time, perhaps millions of years, consisting primarily of carbon and hydrogen. Even when the substances are exposed to air at room temperature, this equilibrium is retained, but if energy is supplied to separate the molecules, the atoms rearrange themselves with the release of energy into a mixture of water and carbon dioxide.

The concepts involved are those of quantum physics: the total energy of the water and carbon dioxide molecules' quantum ground states is smaller than that of the original hydrocarbon molecules. However, to induce this transition, energy must be supplied; once the mixture has been heated to a sufficiently high temperature, the process becomes self-sustaining, and energy continues to be released until the fuel is depleted (unless the process is extinguished).

Nuclear Fuels

Nuclear power concepts are remarkably similar to those underlying the combustion of chemical fuels, but the amount of energy involved in nuclear processes is much larger. As we saw in Chapter 1, the nucleus of an atom is made up of many protons and neutrons bound together by a strong nuclear force.
Even though the specifics are much more complicated than the atomic case mentioned in Chapter 2, the structure of the nucleus is still subject to the laws of quantum physics.

This is because the latter is regulated by the electrons' attraction to the heavier nucleus, while the interactions inside the nucleus between the protons and neutrons are all of a similar mass. In both cases, however, the results are very similar: the energy of the nucleus is quantized into a number of energy levels, like the atom, the lowest of which is known as the 'ground state.'

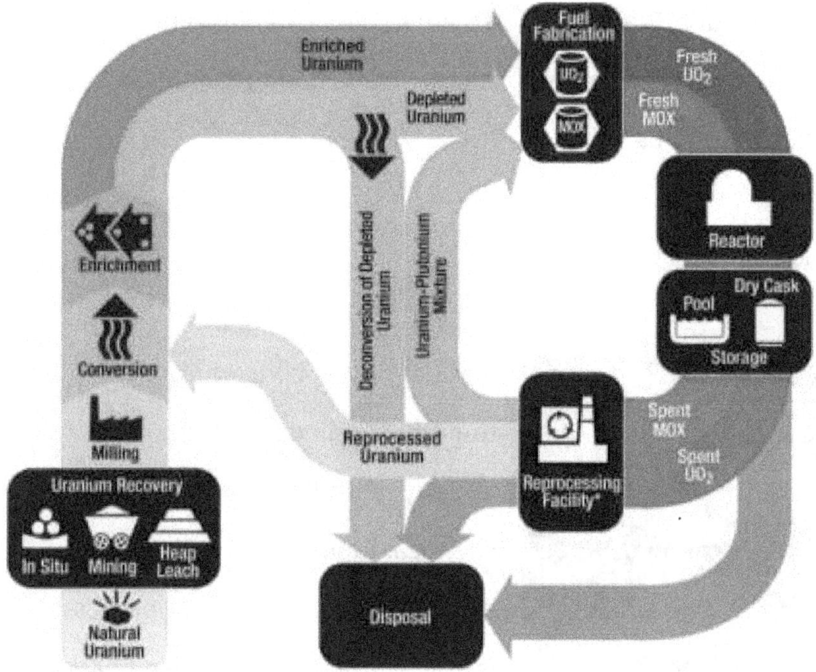

The 'fusion' of two hydrogen nuclei into a single nucleus is closely similar to the earlier example of the merger of two hydrogen atoms into a hydrogen molecule. The nuclei of hydrogen are protons, and 'deuterium' is known as the resulting nucleus.

Deuterium is, as discussed in Chapter 1, a hydrogen isotope whose nucleus is composed of a proton and a neutron and which makes up approximately 0.02% of natural hydrogen gas. The extra positive charge must go somewhere because the neutron holds no charge, and it is carried off by the emission of a positron (which is the same as an electron but with a positive charge) and a neutrino (a very small neutral particle). The ground state energy of the deuterium nucleus is slightly lower than that of the two protons, so we would have predicted that many years earlier, all the protons in the universe would have been fused into deuterium nuclei in the same way that nearly all hydrogen atoms form hydrogen molecules. The reason that this has not occurred is because of the electrostatic repulsion between the two protons that are positively charged.

One location where temperatures as high as a million degrees occur naturally is the sun, and the mechanism that keeps the sun shining is actually nuclear fusion. In addition to the two protons that form deuterium, several other fusion processes occur, and the endpoint is the most stable nucleus of all, that of iron. Fusion is also one of the concepts behind nuclear weapons, such as the 'hydrogen bomb.' In this case, the ignition from a nuclear explosion produced using atomic fission is achieved, which will be addressed shortly.

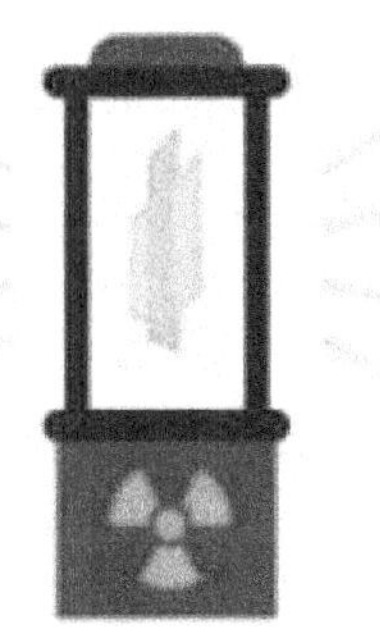

This heats the material to a temperature high enough to cause fusion, after which it is self-sustaining and results in a massive explosion. For over fifty years, nuclear engineers have been aiming to generate controlled fusion power that could be used for peaceful purposes.1 The technical challenges are enormous, and the machines needed to produce and sustain the necessary temperatures are enormous and amount to an investment of several billions of pounds. International partnerships such as the JET2 project have been developed, and it is now assumed that within the first half of the twenty-first century, a computer capable of generating substantial quantities of fusion power would be installed. Towards the end of the twentieth century, rumors of 'cold fusion' created some interest, suggesting fusion energy was released without first providing heat. This work has been widely debunked, but some attempts in this direction continue.

Green Power

Over the last twenty or so years of the twentieth century, and since then, we have become increasingly aware of the fact that our exploitation of the Earth's energy supplies has given rise to major pollution-related problems and the like. Any of the initial concerns centered on nuclear technology, where the inevitable radiation that follows nuclear operations and the handling of radioactive waste products represent risks that some believed could not be handled. This was compounded by a small number of very large nuclear accidents, notably that in Chernobyl in Ukraine, which released a substantial amount of radioactive material across Europe and beyond.

However, more recently, the long-term implications of more conventional energy production approaches have become apparent. The threat of climate change correlated with 'global warming' is chief among these: there are clear signs that the combustion of fossil fuels contributes to a rapid increase in the temperature of the Planet, which in turn could contribute to the melting of the polar ice caps, a consequent rise in sea levels and the flooding of important parts of the populated areas of the Earth. There is also the possibility of a runaway mechanism in which, before the Planet was fully uninhabitable; heating would result in further heating.

There have been a rapid increase in interest in alternative,' renewable' forms of energy production in the face of such expected disasters. In this segment, we will first address how quantum physics plays a role through the 'green-house effect' in triggering global warming and how it can also lead to some of the sustainable alternatives.

The greenhouse effect is so-called because it mimics the processes found in many gardens that regulate a type of glass greenhouse activity. Sunlight passes without being absorbed through the translucent glass and hits the earth and other greenhouse contents, warming them up. By emitting heat radiation, the warmed objects then begin to cool off, but this has a much longer wavelength than that of light and does not move easily through the glass, which reflects most of the heat into the greenhouse.

This process continues until the glass has warmed up to the point that it radiates outward as much strength as the sunlight that comes through it. Convection supports the above process: air is heated at the bottom of the greenhouse, becomes less dense, and rises to the top of the greenhouse, where it helps to steam the glass as it cools and then falls back downwards.

CHAPTER 4: METALS AND INSULATORS

Those of us lucky enough to know how important electricity to modern life is to experience it. It gives us the power we use to illuminate our homes and our streets, cook our food, and drive the computers that process our data. The purpose of this chapter is to illustrate how all of this is a manifestation of quantum physics principles and, in particular, how quantum physics enables us to understand why the electrical properties of different solids can vary from metals that conduct electricity readily to insulators that do not.

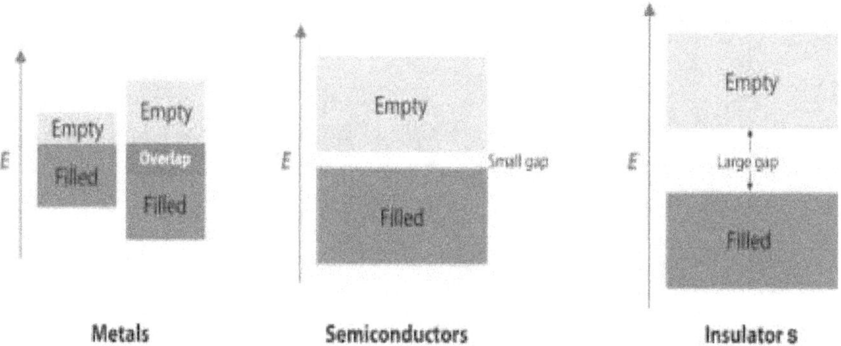

Chapter 5 expands this topic to 'semiconductors'-materials with the necessary properties to allow us to develop the computer chips at the center of our information technology. First of all, I must stress that electricity is not in itself a source of energy, but rather a means of transferring energy from one location to another. In a power station, electricity is produced, which in turn gets its energy from some sort of fuel (e.g., oil, gas, or nuclear material) or from wind, waves, or sunlight. Quantum physics plays a part in some of these processes, too, as we saw in Chapter 3. Electricity comes to us in the form of an electric current that flows through a network of metal wires extending from the power station to the machine I use to write this portion through the plugin the wall.

An electric circuit consists of a battery that moves an electric current around a resistor-containing circuit. We need to have some knowledge of how this works and what these words mean. Next, the battery consists of several 'electrochemical cells' that use a chemical process on opposite ends of each cell to produce positive and negative electrical charges. This can then exert a force on any mobile charges connected to them, and the 'voltage' produced by the battery is called their capacity for doing so. First, the connecting wires are made of metal, and metals are materials that contain electrons that can travel freely inside the material (as I will explain in some detail shortly). When a wire is attached to a battery, electrons near the battery's negative terminal undergo a repulsive force that pushes them through the wire; they move around the circuit until they enter the positive terminal to which they are drawn; then, they travel through the battery and emerge at the negative terminal where the process is repeated.

As a consequence, a current flows through the circuit, and we should note that the traditional direction of current flow is opposite to that of the electrons since the electrons bear a negative charge. The reasoning for this is simply because the principle of electric current was developed, and before electrons were discovered, the traditional concept of positive and negative charge was established. The current passing through a resistor, as its name suggests, is a device that resists the current flow; its ability to do so is determined by a property known as its 'resistance.'

The voltage required to move a given current through a given resistor is proportional to the current and resistance size; this relationship is known as the 'law of Ohm,' which we will address in more detail towards the end of this chapter. All materials exhibit some resistance to electric current, apart from

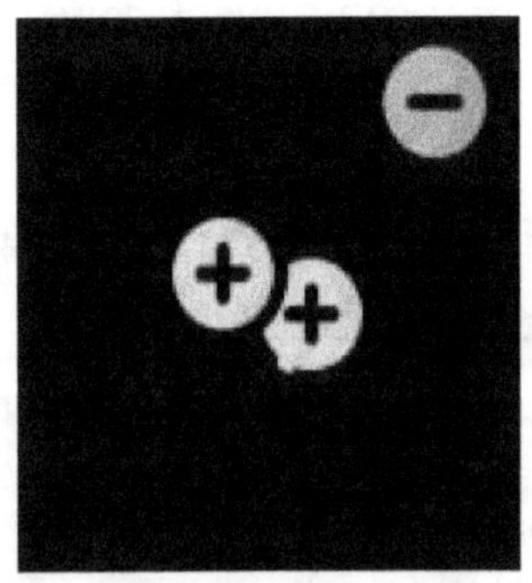

superconductors (to be discussed in Chapter 5), although the resistance of a standard copper wire is very weak. Resistors are often made from special metal alloys, built to have considerable resistance to current flow; some of their energy, which is transformed into heat, is lost by the current that flows through them. This is the mechanism that underlies the operation of any electric heater, such as that contained in or used to heat a room in a kettle or a washing machine.

What about the Ions?

We have so far assumed that electrons are free to travel unhindered everywhere in the metal, but we realize that atoms are made of all solids. We might fairly assume that one or more electrons would be able to travel easily from one atom to the other in the highest energy shell, and we have ignored any interaction between them and the ions as a first approximation. However, because the latter carries a net positive charge, which should interact strongly with the negatively charged electrons, it is difficult to see how we can justify ignoring the ions entirely. Therefore, we might expect an electron seeking to pass through the metal to undergo a series of collisions with the ions, which would significantly hinder its motion, preventing the substantial flow of current.

Consider attempting to walk directly through a dense forest as an analogy: bumping into trees will continuously hamper your progress, slowing you down or even stopping your progress entirely. Why isn't anything similar happening with electrons? There are two explanations for this: the first is due to quantum mechanics and the fact that electrons have wave properties; the second is that their ions are arranged in a regular, periodic pattern since they are made up of crystals as a main characteristic of solids. In order to determine the electrical properties of solids, we can now see how these characteristics interact.

Although we may think of them as very exotic objects, such as expensive gemstones or crystals that have developed carefully in a science lesson in school, we are all familiar with crystals. It can come as a surprise to learn that many solids are crystalline, including metals. We will soon return to this stage, but first, we will look at some of the crystals' key properties and how they are expressed in their atomic structure. For their flat faces, sharp edges, and periodic forms, crystals are noted. In addition, these properties, particularly the normal form, are retained if a crystal is split into one or more pieces. This led to the discovery that crystal forms were a result of regularities in their atomic structure when the atomic composition of matter was discovered in the nineteenth century. In other words, a vast number of similar building blocks with atomic dimensions are made of crystals.

While many materials have a crystalline structure, this is not always immediately evident since a sample often does not consist of a single crystal but consists of a large number of crystalline 'grains' that are randomly oriented. These grains, usually one micrometer (106 m) in size, are small on a daily scale but are around a thousand times the size of a normal atom. We can presume that a solid consists of a single crystal and that it is rational to assume that current will flow from one grain to another in a typical wire if we can understand how a metal crystal can conduct electricity; this hypothesis is well confirmed experimentally.

A bit more about Metals

The fact that an electron's energy in a half-filled band is autonomous of the wavelength of the wave means that, without interfering with it, the wave function of an electron in the metal may have the form of a traveling wave that can pass through a crystal lattice. Metals would be ideal conductors of electricity if this were the whole story. However, although metals conduct electricity very well in practice, they still exhibit some resistance to current flow.

The explanation for this is that the periodic atomic structure of a crystal is never entirely flawless, and the imperfections impede the flow of the current.

There are two major types of imperfection commonly encountered. Impurities are the first to be discussed, i.e., atoms of a different form from the main material component. These would usually be dispersed through the crystal more or less randomly, disrupting its periodicity at these points. The second imperfection happens because the ions are continually shifting because of the effects of temperature: some of them can be a large distance away from their normal positions at any moment so that the periodicity of the crystal is disrupted again. The net effect of all this is that, for the reasons discussed above, while electrons in metals move very freely through the crystal, they are distributed from time to time by impurities and thermal defects.

Usually, before encountering an impurity or thermally displaced ion, an electron travels a distance of several hundred ion spacings, but when it interacts with such a defect, it loses its forward momentum and moves in a random direction. The electric force acts on the electron at the same time to drive it forward again in the direction of the movement of the current. There is also tension between the electrical force driving forward the electrons and an efficient force associated with the scattering of the defect that attempts to resist this. As a consequence, in relation to the electric field and thus, the voltage applied, the size of the current flowing through a given sample increases. This effect is a familiar electrical conduction property known as 'Ohm's law.' The magnitude of the resistance to the current is also determined by the number and size of the defects that provide the dispersion.

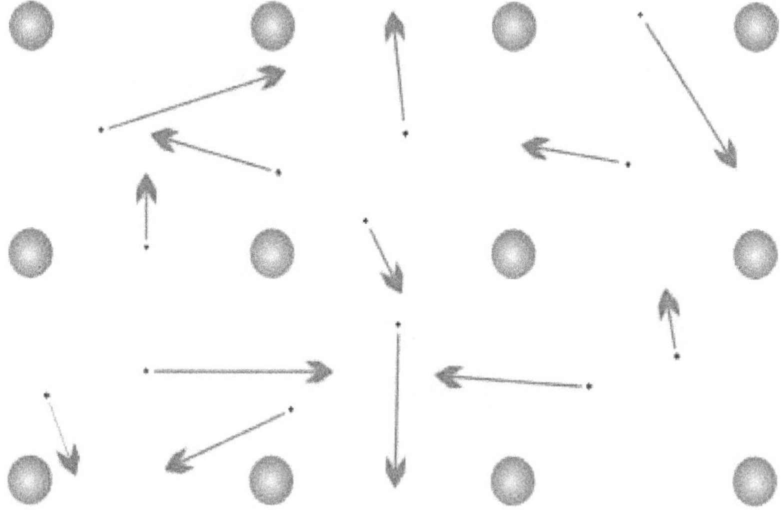

Those associated with thermal motion are typically the most important for relatively pure samples at room temperature. We want to engineer materials that resist current flow very strongly for some applications, such as electric heaters. This can be achieved by alloying two metals into a periodic crystal lattice of another, which can be considered adding a large proportion of impurity atoms of one kind.

This high impurity density then very strongly disperses the electrons and creates a completely independent resistance of temperature. In this chapter, we have seen how quantum physics is important for understanding the properties of metals and insulators and why they vary so significantly. In the next chapter, we will address semi-conductors to see how quantum physics plays a role in deciding semiconductors' properties, which are important for information technology that plays such a large role in modern life.

CHAPTER 5: SEMICONDUCTORS AND COMPUTER CHIPS

We saw in the last chapter how the dramatic contrast between metals and insulators was a function of the interaction between the electron-associated waves and the crystal's periodic array of atoms. As a consequence, the permitted energies of the electrons form a collection of bands separated by gaps. If there are enough electrons in the solid to only fill one or more bands, they do not respond to an electrical field, and the substance is typically an insulator. In comparison, in a typical metal, the highest occupied energy band is only half full, and the electrons react readily to an applied field, creating a current flow.

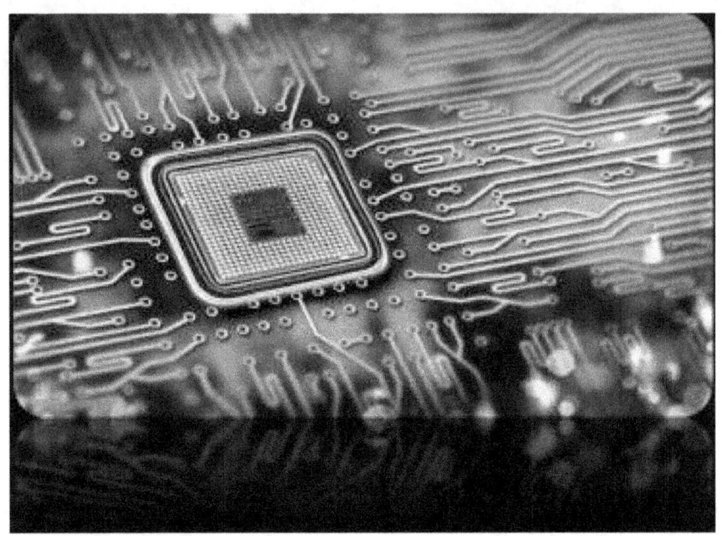

This chapter explains the properties of a class of materials that are known as 'semiconductors' that lie between metals and insulators. Semiconductors have an even number of electrons per atom, like insulators, and are thus only sufficient to fill many bands. The distinction is that the size of the distance between the top of the maximum complete band and the foot of the next empty band is fairly small in semiconductors, meaning not much greater than the energy at room temperature associated with an electron's thermal motion. There is then a large likelihood of thermal excitation of certain electrons from the complete band into the empty band. This has two electrical conduction effects. Next, the electrons excited in the upper band (known as the 'conduction band') will pass freely through the metal, bringing an electrical current, as there are plenty of empty states available to move in.

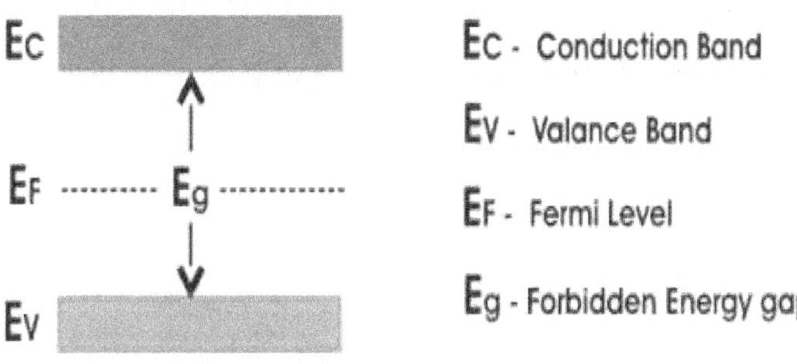

Second, the empty states left behind in the lower band (known as the 'valence band') are accessible in this band to the electrons, so they can pass freely and bring current as well. Thus, both bands contribute to the current flow, and a perfect insulator is no longer the material. We are now considering in a little more detail the behavior of the nearly full lower band. We will discover that its properties are not negative electrons but only charged particles. First, to see how this works, we remember that an equivalent number of electrons pass in opposite directions in a complete band.

We see that an imbalance occurs if one of these electrons is removed, and the net effect is a current similar to but opposite to that associated with the missing electron, but this is just the current that would result from a single positive charge traveling at the same velocity as the missing electron. The effect of applying an electric field to the device exerts the same force on all electrons, causing their velocities to change by the same amount, so the net change is again equal and opposite to what the missing electron would have experienced. The behavior of a collection of electrons with one removed is, therefore, the same as that expected from a particle that has all the properties of a single electron, except that its electrical charge is positive.

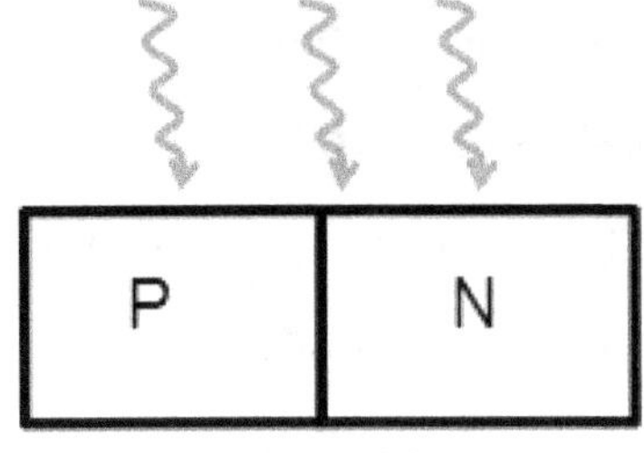

The p–n Junction

By joining a piece of p-type semiconductor to one of n-type to form a 'p-n junction,' one of the simplest devices to exploit the above characteristics is made. Such a junction is found to operate as a current rectifier, which means that if the current flows in one direction (from n to p), it is a strong electrical conductor but provides a large resistance to current flow in the opposite direction. We first consider the junction area where the n-type and p-type meet to understand how this comes about. An electron entering this region will make a transition in the lower band into a vacant level, thus removing the electron along with a hole; as discussed above, we say that the electron and hole have been annihilated.

As a consequence, in the junction area, there is a deficiency of both electrons and holes, and the charges on the ions are not fully canceled, leaving narrow bands of positive and negative charges on the junction's n-type and p-type sides, respectively; these charges are referred to as 'space charges.' Consider applying a voltage that would push a current from p to n: the holes move in the direction of that current in the p-type material, while the electrons move in the reverse direction in the n-type.

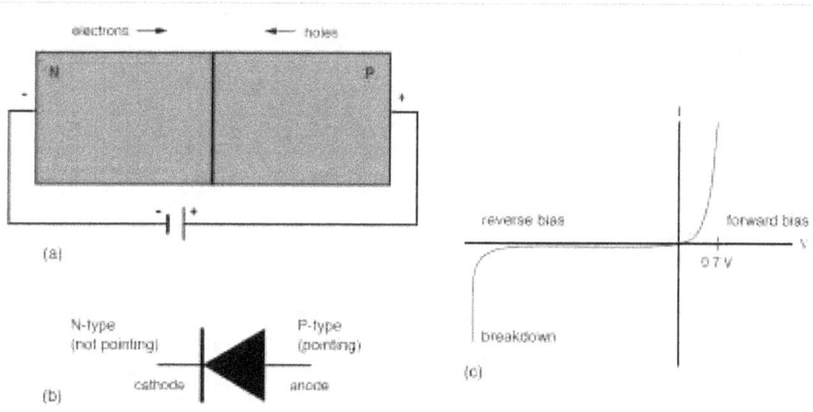

This leads to a rise in the number of charging carriers in the junction area as well as a consequent decrease in the size of the space charges. They annihilate some of the holes as the electrons reach the middle of the junction onto the p-type material, and as holes pass through the n-type material, electrons are equally annihilated. They are replaced by those drawn in from the external circuit, and a current flows as the electrons and holes disappear from the n-type and p-type material, respectively. The junction is defined as being 'forward-biased' when a voltage is applied to drive a current in this direction. On the other hand, if a voltage is applied in a direction that appears to push a current from N to P, the electrons and holes are drawn away from the central region; as a result, the space charges are increased, and it becomes more difficult to cross the junction for charge carriers.

The current will then not continue to flow, and the junction is said to be 'reverse-biased' in this configuration. Thus, when a voltage is applied in one direction but not when it is applied in the other, a current flows, which means that a p-n junction has only the above-mentioned rectifying properties. In the domestic and industrial applications of electricity, rectifiers like those made from p-n junctions have many applications. In a power station, electricity is generated by a generator powered by a spinning motor. One effect of this is that the electricity produced is 'AC,' which means that any time the motor rotates, the voltage generated alternates from positive to negative and back, usually fifty times a second. For certain applications, such alternating currents are perfectly satisfactory, such as room heaters and electrical engines used in washing machines, etc.

However, some systems need a power source where the current always flows in the same direction; this is important, for example, when we charge a battery in a car or use a charger supplied with a cell phone. Rectifiers can be used to convert AC to DC (direct current) based on p-n junctions, where we see that current flows during only half of the cycle when an alternating voltage is applied to a p-n junction, so the resulting output would have only one sign, while half of the AC cycle is zero. If we use four connected rectifiers at all times, the output voltage again has the same sign but is now on during the loop. In

comparison to the 'half-wave rectification' accomplished by a single rectifier, this is known as 'full-wave rectification.' Rectifiers are part of all battery chargers based on p–n junction units. A steady DC source is often required: this can be supplied by a charged battery or can be generated by smoothing the output using an electrical part known as a 'capacitor' from a rectifier.

The Transistor

Essentially, the semiconducting properties of silicon are the foundation of all modern information and communication technologies. Its use as 'a a transistor' is especially important. A transistor is a device that can be used to convert a small signal into one of a similar shape but strong enough to control a loudspeaker or similar device, such as that detected by a radio receiver. As a controlled switch, a transistor may also be used and, as such, plays an important role in the operation of computers and other digital devices. We shall define the construction of a transistor in this section and illustrate how it can be used in each of these ways.

We apply a positive voltage between the emitter and collector to operate a transistor. We see that holes can easily flow across the emitter-base junction from the earlier discussion of p-n junctions because it is forward biased, but we expect no current to flow between the base and the collector because it is reverse biased. A significant aspect of a transistor design, however, is that the base region is purposely made very thin and is lightly doped with impurities so that at least some of the holes can pass through the base from the emitter to the collector without meeting any electrons to be recombined with.

A current will flow around the circuit as a result. Now, consider the result of injecting electrons into the base, which corresponds to drawing a current from it. Some of the electrons will cross the base and pass between the base and the emitter through the forward-biased junction, while others will be annihilated by combining holes that flow from the emitter to the collector through the base.

The resultant current going through the collector would be very much greater (typically one hundred times) than the base current if the system is properly constructed. Tiny changes in the base current cause correspondingly large changes in the collector current, so we have a 'current gain.' This gain depends on the densities of holes in the p-type regions and of electrons in the base region and the dimensions of the base; if the voltage of the base-emitter is not too large, the gain for a given transistor is constant. The collector current reaches a 'saturation' value as greater voltages are added to the base and stay at this level even if the base voltage is further elevated.

By constructing the circuit, the current gain can be converted to a voltage gain. An input voltage drives a current into the base of a transistor through a resistor and then enables the supply voltage (i.e., a battery or other power source) to push a current from the emitter to the collector through the transistor and then through a second resistor. Therefore, through it, an output voltage equal to the current through this resistor occurs.

As a consequence, the output voltage is equal to the voltage of the input, and we have a gain in voltage. Now we are turning to the topic of how to use a transistor as a controlled switch. The theory is that we add either a zero voltage or a significant voltage to the input resulting in either a very small current or a relatively large (i.e., saturation) current flowing through the emitter. Depending on the base voltage's size, the emitter current, and hence the output voltage, is thus turned on or off. For the design of basic operating units in a digital machine, this theory can be extended. First, we notice that a series of 'binary bits' can represent any number, each of which can have a value of 1 or 0.

'10' represents 1 2 + 0 1 (i.e. 2) following this convention, while '100' represents 1 2 2 + 0 2 + 0 1 (4) and so on. Therefore, for instance, 101101 = 1 32 + 0 16 + 1 8 + 1 4 + 0 2 + 1 1 = 45

A binary bit can be used to represent any physical system that can occur in any of the two states. In applying this concept in the sense of transistors, we embrace the convention that a voltage greater than a certain threshold represents 1, whereas a voltage greater than a certain threshold represents 0. The numerical value of the binary bit expressed by the output voltage in Figure 5.7(b) will therefore be 0 if the input voltage is 0 and 1 if the output voltage is 1.

Let us consider one of the basic computer operations as a further example: the 'AND' gate, which is a system in which an output bit equals one if and only if there are two input bits each.

Such a unit can be built using two transistors. Only if both base currents are high enough will a current flow through both transistors. Both input voltages must be high for this to happen, meaning that the digits represented by them are both 1. The digit defined by the output voltage, in this case, will also be 1, but otherwise, it will be 0. This is just the property that an AND gate needs. The other simple operations such as 'OR' can be configured to perform similar circuits, where the output is one supplied, either input is 1, and 0 otherwise.

All computer operations are made up of combinations of these and other related basic components, including those used in arithmetic. Computers designed shortly after the transistor was created in the 1950s and 1960s were actually constructed along the lines mentioned above from individual transistors.

However, large numbers of transistors were required to meet their requirements as their operation became more sophisticated. The invention of the 'integrated circuit' was a significant development in the mid-1960s, in which many circuit components such as transistors and resistors, as well as the equivalents of the wires connecting them, were contained on a single semiconductor piece, known as a 'silicon chip.' It became possible to reduce the size of the individual components as the technology advanced and thus have more of them on each chip. This had the added benefit that it was also possible to reduce the switching times, so machines have become increasingly more efficient and faster over the years.

The Pentium 4 processor in the machine on which I write this text consists of a silicon chip in the region of about one square centimeter; it has around 7.5 million circuit components, many smaller than 10-7 m in size, and the basic switching time or clock speed is about 3 GHz (i.e., 3 109 operations per second). However, 10-7 m is several hundred times the atomic separation, so it is still possible to view each part as a crystal, and the transistors in a silicon chip work according to the same principles of quantum physics as we have mentioned in this chapter.

The Photovoltaic Cell

A photovoltaic cell is a semiconductor-based system that converts the energy from sunlight into electricity. Because all the energy comes from the sunlight that will, in any event, hit the Earth, it does not contribute to the greenhouse effect and does not absorb any of the fossil or nuclear fuel reserves on Earth. Over the years, numerous such devices have been developed, and the research is motivated by the desire to improve this non-polluting type of energy to the point that a significant portion of human energy consumption can be fulfilled. The semiconductors are all made of photovoltaic cells.

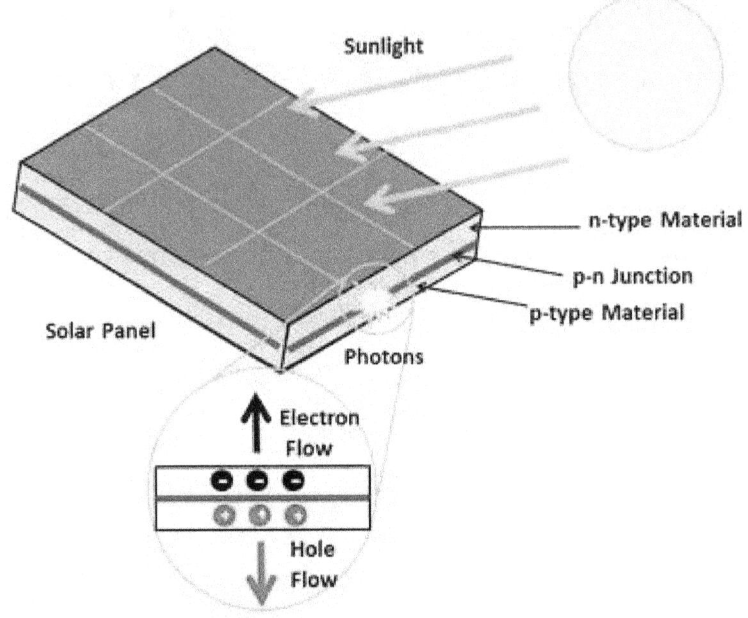

If a photon of the correct energy reaches a semiconductor, it may cause the upper band to be excited by an electron, leaving a positive hole in the lower band. We need the electron and the hole to shift away from each other and drive a current into an external circuit in order to generate a voltage. Using a p-n junction is one method of doing this. As mentioned above, there are very few charge carriers in the junction region where the p-type and n-type materials meet since the electrons and holes cancel each other out; and on the n-type and p-type sides of the interface, respectively, there are excess positive and negative charges.

The photons can be absorbed if we shine a light on this junction field, exciting electrons from the valence to the conduction band

and producing an electron-hole pair. These can easily recombine, but there is a large likelihood that the electrons will instead be accelerated by the electrostatic forces acting on them into the n-type region, while the holes are similarly accelerated into the p-type material. Consequently, to charge a battery, the unit will push a current through an external circuit.

CHAPTER 6: SUPERCONDUCTIVITY

We saw in Chapter 4 how the fact that electrons can behave as waves makes it possible for them to travel through a perfect crystal without bumping on the way through the atoms. Provided empty states are open, as in a normal metal, the electrons will react to an applied field, and a current will flow, whereas the presence of an energy gap in an insulator implies that there are no such empty states and thus no flow of current. In practice, we also saw that the current flow through a metal encounters some resistance because all actual crystals involve imperfections related to the thermal displacement of atoms from their regular crystal positions and the substitution by impurities of some of the atoms. We will address another class of substances in this chapter, known as 'superconductors,' in which resistance to current flow fully disappears, and electric currents will flow once they have begun. Ironically, we can find that this behavior often results from the existence of an energy gap that has certain parallels to the energy gap that prevents current flow in an insulator, as well as major variations.

A Dutch physicist, Kamerlingh Onnes, discovered superconductivity, more or less by mistake, in 1911. He was performing a program of calculation of the electrical resistance of metals at temperatures reaching absolute zero, which had recently become accessible thanks to technical advances in the liquefaction of gases. In fact, helium liquefies at normal pressure at just a few degrees above absolute zero and can be cooled much more by reducing its pressure using vacuum pumps. Onnes finds that as the temperature is decreased, the resistance of all metals decreases, although, in most situations, there is still some resistance to current flow at the lowest possible temperatures and, by inference, at absolute zero. In terms of the model that we built in Chapter 4, we can understand this behavior.

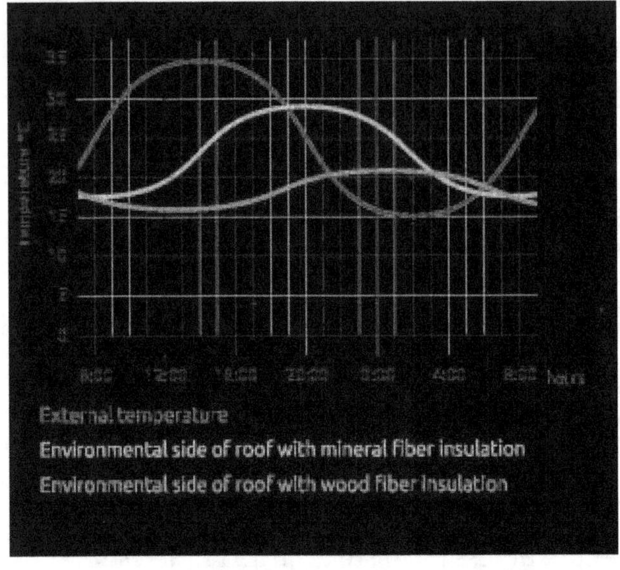

The thermal displacement of the atoms from their average locations as the temperature decreases, and there is less possibility of these interfering with the electrons; however, the resistance due to impurities is temperature-free and is still present at absolute zero. It was when Onnes concentrated his attention on the lead of the metal that unexpected results arose. This does not suggest that it actually becomes much smaller than it is zero for copper. In research, this is quite rare. Normally, "zero" means much less than any comparable quantity in the same way as "infinite" means something much greater than other comparable quantities, but "zero resistance" really means what the word implies in this case. This is another result, as we can see, of quantum mechanics influencing the everyday world.

'High-Temperature' Superconductivity

We stated above that when Kamerlingh Onnes used liquid helium to cool the material down to below 4 K; superconductivity was first observed in the lead. Superconductivity was observed in some metals and alloys in the seventy-five years that followed this discovery, but the highest critical temperature was less than 23 K, and the use of liquid helium was still needed to achieve this temperature. Helium is, still now, a gas that is difficult and costly to liquefy. It must be surrounded by two vacuum flasks with the space between them filled with liquid nitrogen to keep the liquid from boiling. Thus, superconductivity was considered a pure-science subject with only the most specialist applications until the 1980s.

Later, in 1986, superconductivity for 'high-temperature' came along. J. Two scientists who worked for IBM in Zurich were Georg Bednorz and Karl Alex Müller. They realized the promise of a superconductor that would work at temperatures higher than that of liquid helium and started a program of testing various materials almost as a spare-time task to see if any would live up to this dream.

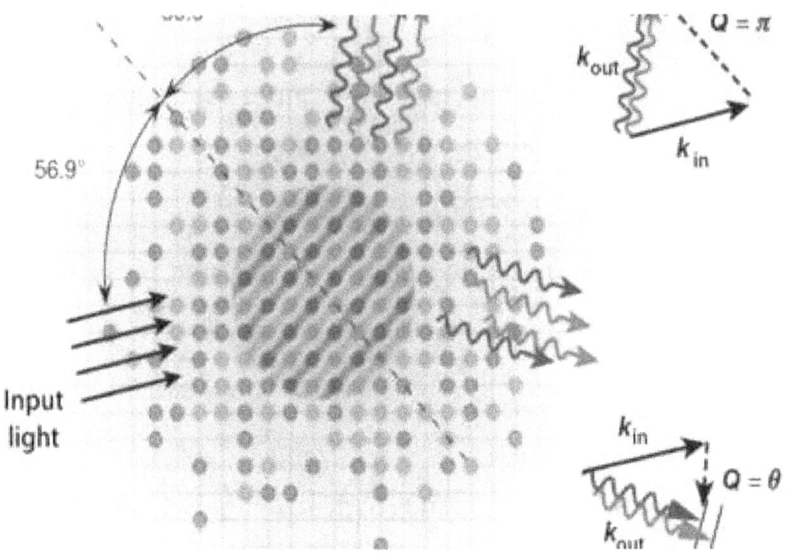

When they turned their attention to a particular compound of lanthanum, bismuth, copper, and oxygen, they were probably as shocked as anyone else, and they discovered that its electrical conductivity fell dramatically to zero when it was cooled below 35 K-which, while still a very low temperature, is more than one and a half times the previous record. In January 1987, a research team at the University of Alabama, Huntsville, substituted yttrium for lanthanum in a compound close to that found by Bednorz and Müller and discovered that the compound superconducts up to 92 K.

Not only was this another major development on the temperature scale, but the nitrogen boiling point, which is 77 K, has also passed a significant milestone. This meant that it was now possible to demonstrate superconductivity without the use of liquid helium. It is much simpler to manufacture liquid nitrogen than liquid helium, more than ten times cheaper and can be stored and used in a simple vacuum flask. Superconductivity could be examined for the first time without costly, specialist equipment; on the laboratory bench, superconducting phenomena such as magnetic levitation that had previously been seen only through many layers of glass, liquid nitrogen, and liquid helium could be seen.

Progress has been less dramatic since 1987. For a composite of the elements mercury, thallium, barium, calcium, copper, and oxygen, the highest known transition to the superconducting state occurs at normal pressures at 138 K; under intense pressure, its transition temperature can be further increased to over 160 K at a pressure of 300,000 atmospheres. They have been named 'high-temperature superconductors' due to the fact that the transition temperatures of these compounds are so much higher than those previously found.

This title is potentially misleading since it seems to suggest that at room temperature or even higher, superconductivity can exist, which is definitely not the case. The maximum superconducting temperature, however, was increased between 1986 and 1987 from 23 K to 92 K, i.e., four times; if another factor of three could be achieved, the dream of a superconductor at room temperature would have been achieved. We may have predicted that the advance to liquid nitrogen temperatures would have significantly improved the potential for practical superconductivity applications, but these were less drastic than originally planned.

For this, there are two main explanations. Next, what is known as 'ceramics' are the materials that constitute high-temperature superconductors. This ensures that they are physically identical to other ceramics (such as those used in kitchens) because they are hard and brittle, making them very hard to produce in a shape that is ideal for replacing metal wires.

The second issue is that the overall current that can be sustained by a high-temperature superconductor is rather too small to be practical for electricity transport or the development of strong magnetic fields. This is still, however, a field of active research and development. For example, in the early years of the 21st century, the design of motors based on high-temperature superconductors entered the prototype stage. Their greatest ability is where high power is required, combined with low weight: an electric motor to power a boat, for example.

Flux Quantization and the Josephson Effect

We have shown that there are Cooper pairs in superconductors in which the electrons are bound together. As a consequence, it is possible to conveniently characterize the quantum mechanics of superconductors as the motion of such pairs rather than the individual electrons. In fact, such a pair can be thought of as a particle with a mass equal to twice the mass of the electron and a charge equal to twice the charge of the electron, traveling at speed equal to the pair's net velocity. From the pair's velocity and mass, the wavelength of the matter-wave associated with such a particle can be determined using the de Broglie relation. This places constraints on the value possessed by the magnetic field through the loop for very subtle reasons: its flux always equals a whole number of times the 'flux quantum,' which is defined as Planck's constant divided on a Cooper pair by the charge. This works out as equal to a field of magnitude around two-millionths of the Earth's magnetic field passing across an area of one square centimeter.

CHAPTER 7: Spin Doctoring

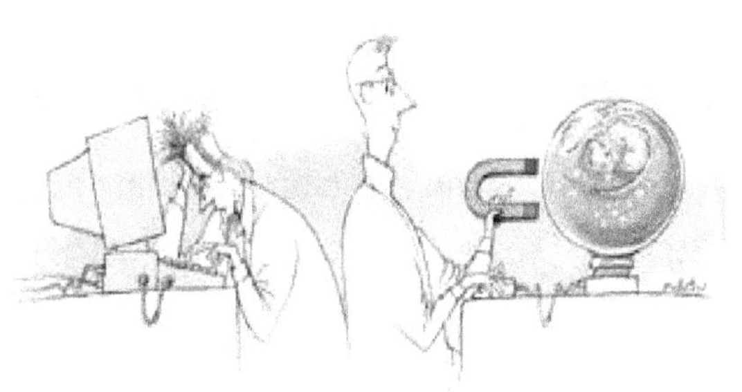

There has been a growing interest in the application of quantum physics to the processing of knowledge in computers, for example, over the last decade of the twentieth century and ever since. Chapter 5 reveals that modern computers are built on semiconductors, which are, in turn, governed by the laws of quantum physics. Despite this, these computers are still widely referred to as 'classical' since the calculations are done in a completely classical way, whereas quantum physics underlies their operation. In order to better understand this, we must first note that all data on a standard machine is represented by a set of binary 'bits' that can equal either 1 or 0.

How these are interpreted is unrelated to the manner in which equations are manipulated to perform. However, quantum mechanics is central to the actual operations of computation in quantum information processing: information is expressed by quantum objects known as 'qubits' where behavior is governed by quantum rules. A qubit is a quantum system that can be in one of two states (like a classical bit) and can represent 1 and 0, but a qubit can also be in what is referred to as a 'quantum superposition' of these states, in which both 1 and 0 are concurrently in some way.

What this implies should soon become clearer as we consider some particular instances where we can see that some items that are classically impossible can be achieved by the quantum processing of information. While several different quantum systems could be used as qubits, we will restrict our discussion to the electron spin example. We found that electrons, and indeed other fundamental particles, have a quantum property that we referred to as 'spin' in earlier chapters.

By this, we say that a particle behaves as though it were rotating around an axis in a manner reminiscent of the Earth's rotation or that of a spinning top. Like too often occurs in quantum mechanics, if we try to take it too literally, this classical model is best thought of as an example, and difficulties arise. For our purposes, the main thing to remember is that spin determines a direction in space, which is the axis around which the particle 'spins,' and that when we calculate the spin of a fundamental particle, such as an electron, we find that it often has the same magnitude, while its direction is either parallel or anti-parallel to the rotation axis.

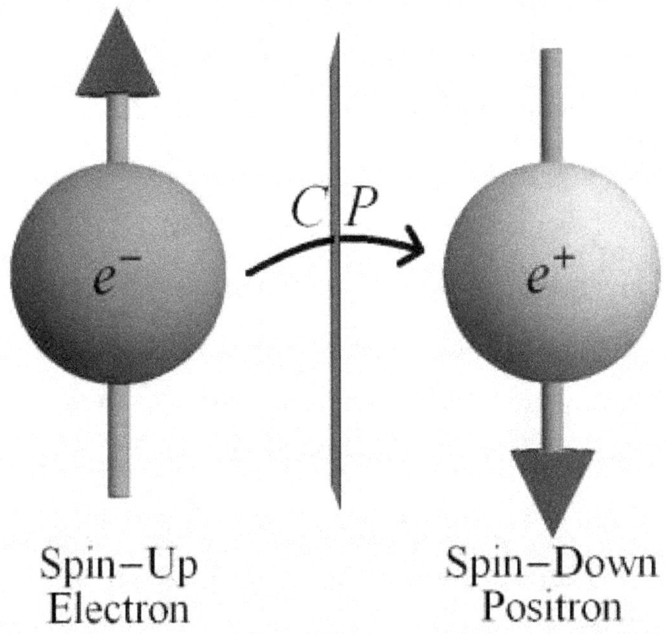

As a shorthand, we can assume that either 'up' or 'down' the spin is pointing;1 and we saw in Chapter 2 that these two possibilities play an important role in deciding the number of particles permitted to inhabit any given energy state by the exclusion principle. Therefore, we see that spin has at least one of the necessary properties of a qubit: it can exist in one of two states that can be used to describe the binary digits 1 and 0. Now we are going to try to explain how it can also be placed in a state of superposition and what this means. What do we, we may wonder, mean by 'up' and 'down'? The electron can certainly not be influenced by such a concept, which relies on our experience of living on the surface of the Earth and, in any case, the directions that we think of as 'up' and 'down' change as the Earth rotates.

Why shouldn't we be able to calculate spin relative to a horizontal axis, for example, so that it is either 'left' or 'right'? The answer to this question is that we can measure spin relative to any direction we like, but we always find that the spin is either parallel or antiparallel to it once we choose such a direction. The act of doing such a measurement, however, destroys any data we may have previously had about its spin relative to some other direction. That is, the measurement appears to force the particle to reorient its spin so that either parallel or anti-parallel to the new axis is oriented.

How do we, in fact, calculate spin? The most straightforward approach is to use the assumption that there is also a related magnetic moment with every particle that possesses spin. By this, we say that an electron-like fundamental particle acts like a tiny magnet pointing along the spin axis. Thus, if we can calculate this magnetic moment's direction, the effect also informs us of the direction of the spin. One way to calculate this magnetic moment is to position the particle in a laboratory-generated magnetic field; if this field is greater when we move in, say, an upward direction, then a magnet pointing in that direction will move upward, while one pointing down will move downward.

Moreover, the size of the force causing this motion is proportional to the magnitude of the magnetic moment and hence of the spin, which can therefore be deduced from the amount the particle is deflected. Otto Stern and Walther Gerlach, two physicists, based in Frankfurt, Germany, first performed this technique in 1922. Via a specially built magnet that divided the particles into two beams, one corresponding to spin up and one to spin down, they passed a beam of particles 2.

Quantum Cryptography

Cryptography is the science of coding messages using a key or cipher so that they can be transmitted to another ('the recipient,' named 'Bob') from one person ('the sender,' historically called 'Alice') while remaining incomprehensible to an 'eavesdropper' ('Eve').

There are several ways to do this, but we will focus on one or two basic examples that explain the values involved and the contribution that can be provided by quantum physics. Suppose the message is the word 'QUANTUM' that we want to give. A simple code is simply to substitute each letter in the alphabet with the one that follows it unless it is Z that is 'wrapped around' to become A.

More generally, by substituting each letter with n letters later in the alphabet and wrapping around the last n letters of the alphabet to be replaced by the first n, we can encode any message. We would, therefore, have

Plain Q U A N T U M message

Coded using n = 1 R V B O U V N

Coded using n = 7 X B H U A B T

Coded using n = 15 F J P C I J B

This code is really easy to crack, of course. There are only twenty-six different possible values of n, and it would take only a few minutes to try them all with a pencil and paper; in a tiny fraction of a second, a machine could do this. The correct value of n will be defined as the only one that produces a sensible message; if the original message is relatively long, the chances of there being more than one of these are very small.

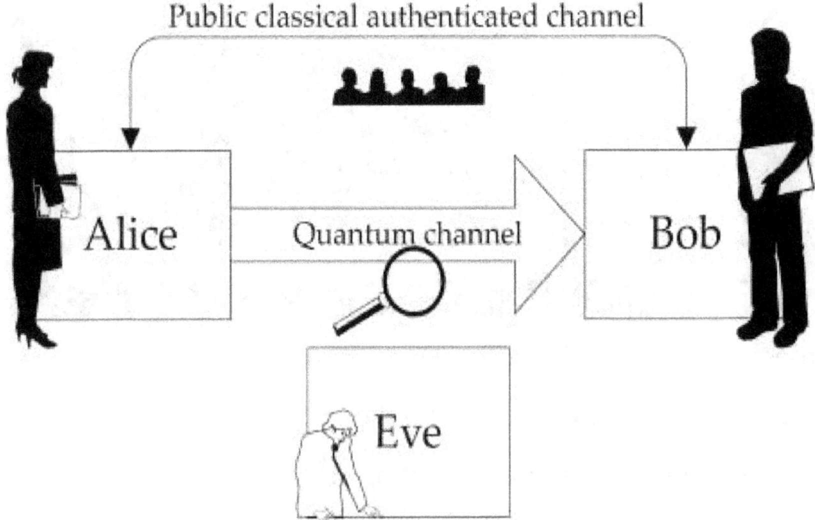

The use of arithmetic relies on a basic yet slightly more sophisticated method. First, we substitute a number for every letter in the post so that A becomes 01, B becomes 02, and so on, so that Z is defined by 26. We then add a known 'code number' to the message, which can be created as many times as possible to generate a number as long as the message by repeating a shorter number (known as the 'key' to the code).

Underneath the note, this number is written, and the two rows of digits are applied to create the coded message.

In the instance below, where we choose the key to be 537, this procedure is illustrated.

Plain Q U A N T U M message

Numbers 1 7 2 1 0 1 1 4 2 0 2 1 1 3 3

Code number 5 3 7 5 3 7 5 3 7 5 3 7 5 3

7 0 9 6 3 8 6 7 9 5 5 8 6 6 6 Coded message

Alice gives Bob the last line, and he can retrieve the message by regenerating the code number and subtracting it from the coded message, given he knows the method and the values of the three digits. If Eve intercepts the message and attempts to decipher it, once she sees a meaningful message, she will have to try all the one thousand possible values of the key. A machine can still do this quite easily, of course. Such instances have a major characteristic in common, which is that the code key is much shorter than the message itself. Mathematical methods that can be used are far more complicated.

A message can be encoded in such a way that a present-day classical machine will have to operate for several years to be sure of cracking the code, using a key that consists of around forty decimal digits. Therefore, if in full secrecy, Alice and Bob could exchange a short message, they could use this to determine which key to use before sending the message, and then freely exchange coded messages, sure that Eve won't understand them. This does depend, however, on Alice and Bob knowing the key and Eve not having access to it. It is this protected key exchange that, as we shall now see, is enabled by the use of quantum techniques.

Quantum Computers

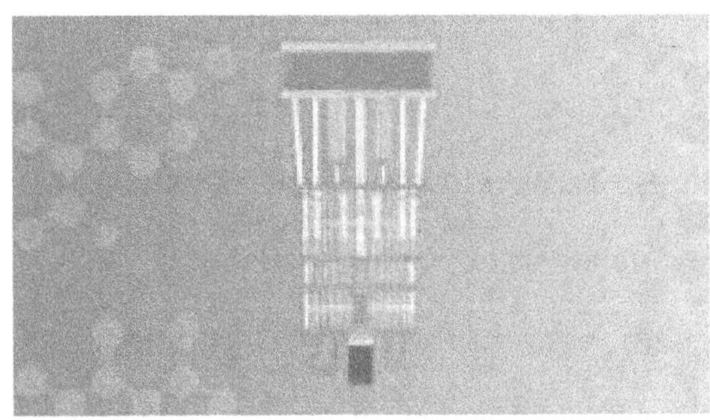

The quantum computer is another instance of quantum information processing. In the present tense, we should note that it is incorrect to speak about quantum computers because the only machines that have been designed to date are capable of only the most trivial calculations that can be carried out more easily on a pocket calculator or even by mental arithmetic. Nonetheless, if the technical challenges could be solved, quantum computers would have the capacity to conduct certain calculations much faster than any traditional machine imaginable.

For this reason, in recent years, the promise of quantum computing has become something of a holy grail, and a great deal of scientific and industrial investment is being devoted to its growth. It remains to be seen if this will pay off or not. So how is it possible to manipulate the principles of quantum physics to this end, except in principle? A comprehensive discussion of this is well beyond the boundaries of this book, but we may expect to grasp some of the fundamental concepts involved. The first important argument is that a binary bit is not represented in a quantum computer by an electric current flowing through a transistor but by a single quantum entity such as a spinning particle. In the previous section, we saw an example of this when we discussed quantum cryptography.

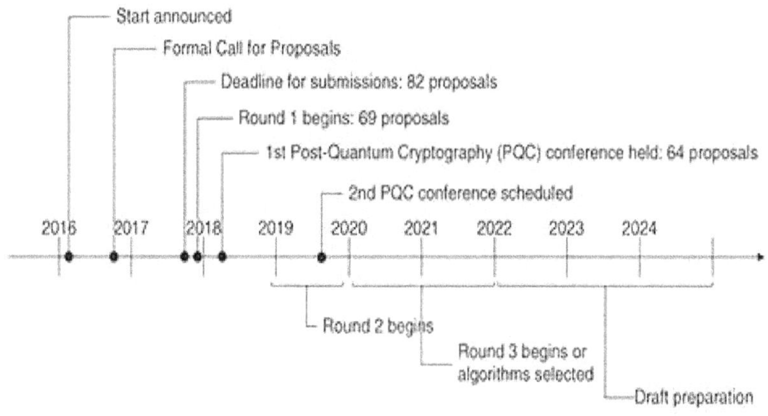

As before, we will assume that a particle with a positive spin in the vertical direction (spin-up) represents 0, while a negative spin component represents 1 (spin down). It is generally referred to as a 'qubit' when a quantum entity is used to represent a binary bit in this way. We consider how we can perform the 'NOT' operation as a first example, which is one of the simple Boolean operations that make up the computation and consists of replacing 1 with 0 and 0 with 1. Note that a particle that spins behaves like a small magnet.

This implies that it would want to turn like a compass needle to match up with the direction of the field if it is put in a magnetic field. The inertia of the spin would resist this motion, three but by applying a carefully regulated magnetic field to a spinning particle, the spin can be rotated at any known angle. If this angle is 180 °, for example, an up spin will be rotated to point down, and a down spin will be rotated to the up position, which is just what we do NOT need to reflect the process.

It can also be seen that by subjecting spinning particles to properly engineered magnetic fields, all the operations that a traditional computer performs on bits can be performed on qubits. Some of these include interactions between qubits, which is one of the obstacles to a quantum computer's practical realization.

What does it all Mean?

With wave-particle duality, we started our discussion of quantum physics. Light historically thought of as a type of wave motion often acts as if it were a stream of particles, while it was found that artifacts, such as electrons, which were once thought of as particles, had wave properties. We avoided any thorough explanation of these principles in the earlier chapters and instead focused on explaining how they are applied to model the action of atoms, nuclei, solids, etc.

We shall return to questions of theory and the philosophical problems of the subject in this chapter. A word of warning: this is a field of significant controversy, where many alternative approaches exist, which means that our debate is more about philosophy than physics. By considering the 'Copenhagen interpretation,' which is the traditional view among physicists, we will begin our discussion. Towards the end of the section, some alternative methods are briefly discussed.

A mineral calcite crystal is a less familiar type of polarizer: it is split into two beams as unpolarized light passes through this system, one of which is polarized parallel to a particular direction specified by the crystal, while the other is perpendicular to it. In one or other of these lights, unlike Polaroid, where half the light is lost, all the light emerges. It is important to remember that a calcite crystal is not like a filter that only makes a limited amount of light that has already been polarized in the right direction. Instead, with perpendicular polarization, it splits or 'resolves' the light into two components, and the sum of their strength is equal to that of the incident beam; regardless of its initial polarization, no light is lost. We will describe a polarizer such as a calcite crystal as a box where a beam of light enters from one side and emerges as two beams of perpendicular polarization from the other—the specifics of how all these works are not important to our intent.

Polarization is an electromagnetic wave property, but does it have any relation to light's particle model? By passing very weak light through a polarizer set up, we might test this: we will find photons (the light particles first described in Chapter 2) arising at random through the two output channels, corresponding to horizontal polarization (H) and vertical polarization (V). To confirm that the photons really can be regarded as having the property of polarization, we could pass each beam separately through other polarizers also oriented to calculate HV polarization.

We can find that all photons emanating from the first polarizer's H channel would emerge from the second one's H channel, and similarly, for V. This gives us an operational concept of photon polarization: we may assume that horizontally and vertically polarized photons are those that emerge from a polarizer's H and V channels, respectively, whatever this property might be. Thus, the properties of polarized photons are identical to those of spinning electrons described in Chapter 7 in certain respects, and another example of a qubit is a polarized photon.

The Measurement Problem
The above may be difficult to embrace, but it works, and if we apply the rules and use the map book properly, we can correctly determine predictable outcomes of measurement: the energy levels of the hydrogen atom, the electrical properties of a semiconductor, the product of a calculation carried out by a quantum computer and so on. However, this implies that we understand what 'measurement' means, and this turns out to be the most challenging and contentious topic in quantum physics interpretation.

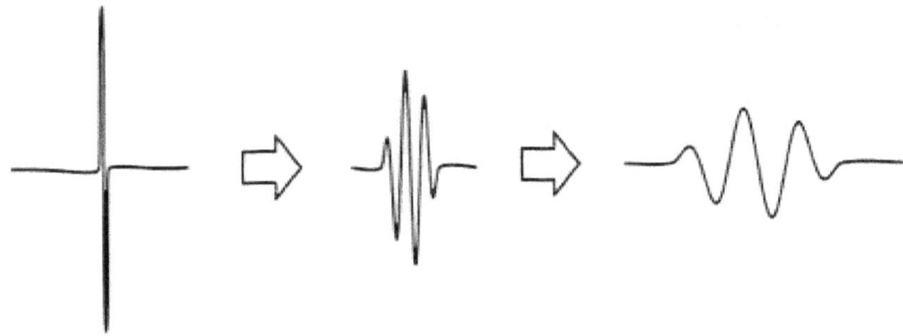

This is consistent with the positivist approach discussed earlier since we do not know that the photon has polarization in the absence of detection, so we can not conclude that it does. Therefore, by the presence or absence of a detector in the experimental arrangement, we seem to be able to divide the quantum universe from the classical world.

Alternative Interpretations

Subjectivism

To escape into 'subjective idealism' is one response to the issue of quantum measurement. In doing this, we simply agree that

quantum physics means that an objective account of physical reality can not be given. Our personal subjective experience is the only thing we know that must be real: the counter may fire and not fire, the cat may be both alive and dead, but I definitely know what has happened when the knowledge enters my mind through my brain

.

For photons, counters, and cats, quantum physics may apply, but it does not apply to you or me! I don't know, of course, that the states of your mind are real either, so I'm in danger of relapsing into 'solipsism' in which only I and my mind have any truth. Philosophers have long proposed that they could prove the existence of an actual physical universe, but science's aim is not to address this question but to provide a clear account of the current objective world. If quantum physics were to eventually ruin this mission, it would be ironic. Most of us would much prefer to explore an alternative path forward.

Hidden Variables

An understanding that rejects Bohr's positivism in favor of realism is based on what is known as 'hidden variables' (or 'naïve realism' as some of its critics prefer), implying that a quantum object has properties, even though they can not be observed. After Louis de Broglie, the first person to postulate matter waves, and David Bohm, who developed and extended these ideas in the 1950s and 1960s, the leading theory of this kind is known as the 'de-Broglie-Bohm model' (DBB). Both the particle position and the wave are believed to be actual properties of a particle at all times in DBB theory.

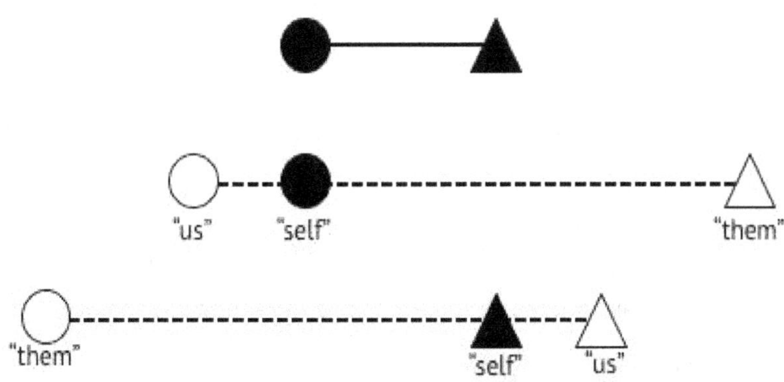

The wave forms according to the laws of quantum mechanics, and both the wave and the classical forces acting on it direct the particles. The direction taken by any particular particle is then fully decided and at this stage there is no ambiguity. However, various particles arrive at different locations depending on where they originate from, and the theory ensures that the numbers arriving at different points are compatible with the probabilities predicted by quantum physics. Consider the two-slit experiment as an example: the form of the wave is determined by the shape, size, and location of the slits, according to DBB theory, and the particles are directed by the wave so that most of them end up in positions where the pattern of interference has high intensity, while none reaches the points where the wave is zero. As we have mentioned before, in a classical sense, the appearance of seemingly random, statistical effects from the action of deterministic systems is very familiar.

If we toss a large number of coins, for example, we can find that approximately half of them come down heads while the rest display tails, even though the action of any individual coin is controlled by the forces acting on it and when it is tossed, the initial spin imparted. Similarly, it is possible to statistically analyze the behavior of the atoms in a gas, even though the motion of its atoms and the collisions between them are governed by classical mechanical laws.

Many Worlds

We discussed earlier how the issue of measurement occurs because a literal implementation of quantum physics results in the superposition condition of not only the photon but also the measuring apparatus, such that we have a cat that is both alive and dead in the case of Schrödinger's cat. It turns out that avoiding it is one way to avoid this problem. Suspending disbelief, let us see what happens if we take the above scenario seriously and ask how we could say the cat was in such a state.

The reason we know that a particle is in a superposition of being in one slit and being in the other, going through a two-slit apparatus, is that we can establish and observe an interference pattern. However, to do the same thing with the cat, we will have to put together the wave function representing all the electrons and atoms in both live and dead cats to form an incredibly complicated pattern of interference. This is a totally unrealistic assignment, in fact.

CHAPTER 8: CONCLUSIONS

The twentieth century may well be referred to as the quantum age. One hundred years after Einstein discovered that light consists of fixed energy quantities, how far have we come, and where will we go? This chapter aims to collect some of the earlier chapters' threads, to put them in historical context, and to make some guesses about what could be in store for the 21st century.

Early Years

 For the first twenty years or so, after Einstein demonstrated the photoelectric effect in 1905, progress was very slow. However, once the wave-particle duality theory and its mathematical development were developed in the Schrödinger equation, they were easily applied to elucidate the atom's structure and its energy levels.

Within another twenty years, quantum mechanics had been successfully extended to a wide variety of physical phenomena, including the electrical properties of solids (Chapter 4) and the atomic nucleus's fundamental properties. In the late 1930s, the probability of nuclear fission (Chapter 3) was recognized, and this led to the first nuclear explosion in 1945, less than 20 years after his equation was first published by Schrödinger.

Since 1950

In the growth of our understanding of quantum physics concepts and applications, the discovery of quarks, which are now part of the modern particle physics model, was one instance of this. This resulted from the results of experiments involving very high-energy collisions between fundamental particles, such as electrons and protons; to answer the issue of the internal structure of the proton and neutron, it applied the principles of both quantum physics and relativity.

Much as an atom or a nucleus may be excited into higher energy states when fundamental particles collide at extremely high speeds with each other, similar excitations occur. It is possible to think of the results of these collisions as excited states of the original particles and the fields associated with them, but the changes in energy are so large that the related relativistic mass shift may be many times the mass of the original article.

As a consequence, excitations to such states are often thought of as producing new short-lived particles, which in a very short time, usually 10-12 s, regain their original form. The design of the machines needed to conduct such simple experiments required effort and cost approaching that of the space program.

During the second half of the twentieth century, development in the practical application of quantum physics was also tremendous. The invention of controlled nuclear fission (Chapter 3) quickly led to the creation of the nuclear power industry, which now produces much of the nation's electricity in some countries (over seventy-five percent in the case of France). A much greater problem has turned out to be the civil application of fusion, but research has now taken us to the point that this could soon be a real possibility.

In the last quarter of the twentieth century, the information revolution arising from the production of semiconductors and the computer chip (Chapter 5) took place and has undoubtedly been as dramatic and relevant as the industrial revolution two hundred years earlier. We can compute at enormous speeds, connect around the globe and beyond, and download information from the world wide web due to the quantum properties of silicon. Moreover, applying quantum physics directly to the processing of information (Chapter 7) has recently opened up the possibility of developing techniques in this field that are even faster and more efficient.

The Future

As far as fundamental physics is concerned, the more powerful machines currently being developed would allow the study of even higher-energy particle collisions: many expect this regime to break down the standard model of particle physics and to be replaced by another one that will create new and exciting insights at this level into the nature of the physical universe. Investigations into the behavior of matter at extremes of temperature and field will proceed in the area of condensed matter and could well yield new and fundamental manifestations of quantum physics.

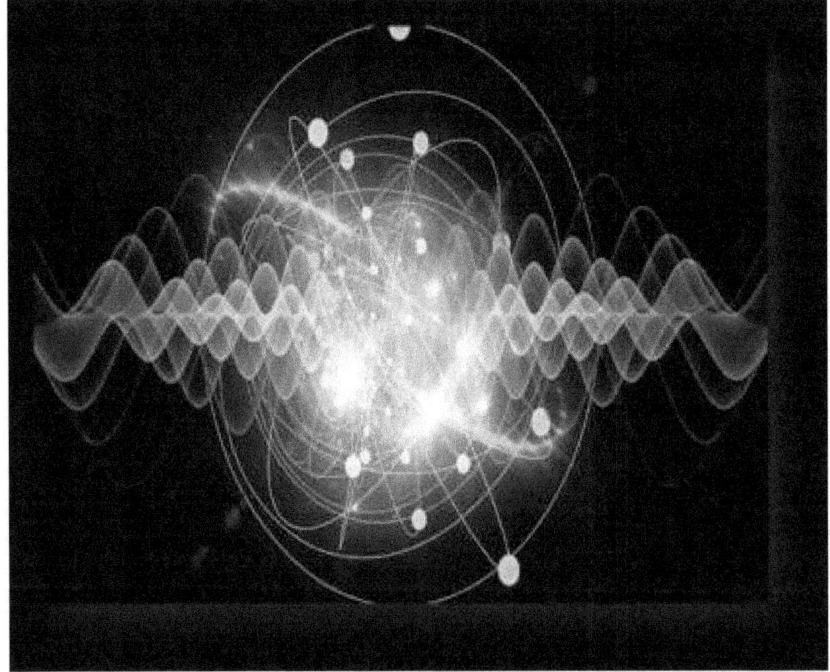

It would be perilous to forecast potential applications in quantum physics without a secure crystal ball. For several years to come, we can definitely expect traditional computers to continue to increase in power and speed: silicon's potential to surprise can never be under-rated. The superconductivity research will definitely proceed, but only very specialized applications seem possible unless and until malleable materials tend to remain superconducting up to room temperature. A major effort is currently being made to build devices for quantum computing (Chapter 7).

It is difficult to judge if this would work in the near future; it would be well advised for anyone thinking of betting on this happening to exercise considerable caution. Hopefully, very soon, the risks of continued fossil fuel burning will be better known, and the impetus to find alternatives will rise. The development of a new generation of nuclear reactors and advances in green technology, including those based on quantum physics, such as photovoltaic cells, could well result in this (Chapter 5).

The issue is so critical that we would do well to abandon debates about the advantages and drawbacks of the various alternatives: almost inevitably if we are to prevent a major disaster over the next fifty to one hundred years, all practicable methods will have to be exploited. The philosophical questions associated with quantum physics (Chapter 8) appear unlikely to be answered shortly.

Quantic physics seems to be a victim of its performance in this regard. The fact that such a large number of physical phenomena has been successfully explained and that it has not so far failed suggests that the debate is over alternate explanations rather than any need for new hypotheses. At least so far, any new way of looking at quantum phenomena that predicts outcomes other than those of normal quantum physics has proven to be incorrect.

In the future, a new theory might break this trend and, if it did, this would possibly be the most exciting fundamental breakthrough since quantum physics itself was invented. Perhaps such a development will arise from the study of the black holes' quantum properties and the big bang that our universe produced. New theories will almost certainly be required in this field, but it is by no means obvious that these will also answer fundamental questions such as the measurement issue. For a long time to come, the intellectual debate seems likely to continue.

I hope the reader who got this far enjoyed the ride. I hope you accept that quantum physics need not be rocket science and that you now understand why some of us have dedicated a large portion of our lives to trying to understand and appreciate what is undoubtedly the human race's greatest intellectual accomplishment.